MULTICULTURAL EDUCATION SERIES

James A. Banks, Series Editor

(continued)

Achieving Equity
for
Latino Students

Expanding the Pathway
to Higher Education
Through Public Policy

FRANCES CONTRERAS

Teachers College, Columbia University

New York and London

Published by Teachers College Press, 1234 Amsterdam Avenue, New York, NY 10027

Portions of Chapter 3 first appeared in Contreras, F. (2010). Accountability and high stakes testing. In Murillo et al., *Handbook of Latinos and education: Research, theory & practice*. Routledge/ Taylor & Francis Group.

Portions of Chapter 5 were first published in Contreras, F. (2009). *Sin Papeles y Rompiendo Barreras:* Latino Students and the Challenges of Pursuing College. *Harvard Educational Review*.

Library of Congress Cataloging-in-Publication Data

Contreras, Frances, 1972–
  Achieving equity for Latino students : expanding the pathway to higher education through public policy / Frances Contreras.
    p. cm.
  Includes bibliographical references and index.
  ISBN 978-0-8077-5210-4 (pbk.) — ISBN 978-0-8077-5211-1 (hardcover) 1. Hispanic Americans--Education (Higher) 2. Educational equalization—United States. I. Title.
  LC2670.6.C66 2011
  378.1'982968073—dc22   2010052937

ISBN 978-0-8077-5210-4 (paper)
ISBN 978-0-8077-5211-1 (hardcover)

Printed on acid-free paper
Manufactured in the United States of America

18 17 16 15 14 13 12 11   8 7 6 5 4 3 2 1

Contents

Series Foreword

The positive ways in which the immigrant population enriches the United States is almost completely invisible in the polarizing debate and punitive actions that are directed toward immigrants who arrive in the United States seeking the American dream and better opportunities and lives for their children. The ways in which immigrant groups and their children enrich American culture and society need to be identified, publicized, and included in the construction of transformative educational policies and practice. Recognition of the positive aspects of immigration will help educational policy makers and practitioners grapple effectively with the "Brown Paradox" that Frances Contreras describes in this needed, timely, and informative book.

Many nations in both Europe and Asia are experiencing serious population growth problems because of declines in fertility and the aging of their mainstream populations (Longman, 2010). Most demographers consider an average birthrate of 2.1 children per woman essential to replace a nation's population. European nations that have birthrates below the essential level include Ireland, France, Norway, Sweden, the United Kingdom, The Netherlands, Germany, Italy, Spain, and Greece (BBC News, 2006). A number of nations in East Asia—including Japan, South Korea, and Singapore—also have birthrates insufficient to replace the population (Skeldon, in press). Japan's population is actually declining. Low population growth has negative consequences for the economic development of a nation. Population growth is needed for a nation to remain economically viable and dynamic in a highly competitive "flat world" and global context (Darling-Hammond, 2010).

Ironically, many of the nations that are experiencing population growth problems—such as Japan, Ireland, and Germany— are unreceptive to immigrant groups and have restrictive immigration policies. At a meeting in October 2010, German Chancellor Angela Merkel epitomized her nation's historic attitudes toward non-German immigrant groups when she said, "The approach [to build] a multicultural [society] and to live side by side and to enjoy each other . . . has failed, utterly failed" (cited in Clark, 2010). An article in *The New York Times* on January 3, 2011 pointed out that Japan's population "will fall by almost a third to 90 million within 50 years."

However, despite its plummeting population, a survey indicated that 65% of the Japanese respondents are opposed to more open immigration policies (Tabuchi, 2011).

Immigrants in the United States and their children are making major contributions to keeping the U. S. population growing, vigorous, and globally competitive. In 2008, the average number of births per woman in the United States was 2.1 (The World Bank, 2010), which is a sufficient birthrate to keep the nation's population viable. According to a report issued by the Pew Research Center, Latinos will "triple in size and will account for most of the nation's population growth from 2005 through 2050. Hispanics will make up 29% of the U. S. population in 2050, compared with 14% in 2005" (Passel & Cohn, 2008). Students who speak a home language other than English are the fastest growing segment of the public school population in the United States (Suráez-Orozco & Suráez-Orozco, 2002). The National Center for Education Statistics (2008b) projects that by 2020 one in five students in the U. S. public schools will be the children of immigrants.

Immigrants and other groups of color are also enriching American society in other ways (Massey, 2008), and are facilitating its transformation from an Anglo-centric dominant nation to one that reflects myriad and diverse racial, ethnic, cultural, religious, and language groups that has the potential to become a cosmopolitan leader in an increasingly multicultural and global world. Important contributions that immigrant groups can make to the United States include a variety of languages and different ways to conceptualize and view the world, which are tremendous assets in a rapidly changing, competitive, complex, and dangerous world. However, as Contreras points out in this compassionate and engaging book, substantial changes must be made in the policies and practices in schools and in colleges and universities in order for the United States to benefit from the gifts that Latino students can give to America. These changes will be reciprocal—while enriching the nation, they will enable Latino students to acquire equal educational opportunities and to realize the American dream that they have internalized and that motivated many of their parents to seek their fortunes in a foreign and sometimes hostile land (Gándara & Hopkins, 2010).

This informative book will help practicing educators deal effectively with the growing ethnic, cultural, and linguistic diversity within U. S. society, schools, colleges, and universities. American classrooms are experiencing the largest influx of immigrant students since the beginning of the 20th century. About a million immigrants are making the United States their home each year (Martin & Midgley, 1999; Roberts, 2008). Between 1997 and 2006, 9,105,162 immigrants entered the United States (U. S. Department of Homeland Security, 2007). Only 15% came from nations in Europe. Most came from nations in Asia, from Mexico, and from nations in Latin America, Central America, and the Caribbean (U. S. Department of

Homeland Security, 2007). A large but undetermined number of undocumented immigrants also enter the United States each year. In 2007, *The New York Times* estimated that there were 12 million undocumented immigrants in the United States (Immigration sabotage, 2007). The influence of an increasingly ethnically diverse population on U. S. schools, colleges, and universities is and will continue to be enormous.

Schools in the United States are more diverse today than they have been since the early 1900s when a multitude of immigrants entered the U. S. from Southern, Central, and Eastern Europe. In the 34-year period between 1973 and 2007, the percentage of students of color in U. S. public schools increased from 22 to 44.3% (Dillon, 2006; Sable & Plotts, 2010). If current trends continue, students of color will equal or exceed the percentage of White students in U. S. public schools within one or two decades. In the 2007–08 school year, students of color exceeded the number of Whites students in 11 states: Arizona, California, Florida, Georgia, Hawaii, Louisiana, Maryland, Mississippi, New Mexico, Nevada, and Texas (National Center for Education Statistics, 2008a, b, & c).

Language and religious diversity is also increasing in the U. S. student population. In 2000, about 20% of the school-age population spoke a language at home other than English (U. S. Census Bureau, 2003). The Progressive Policy Institute (2008) estimated that 50 million Americans (out of 300 million) spoke a language at home other than English in 2008. Harvard professor Diana L. Eck (2001) calls the United States the "most religiously diverse nation on earth" (p. 4). Islam is now the fastest-growing religion in the United States as well as in several European nations such as France, the United Kingdom, and The Netherlands (Banks, 2009; Cesari, 2004). Most teachers now in the classroom and in teacher education programs are likely to have students from diverse ethnic, racial, linguistic, and religious groups in their classrooms during their careers. This is true for both inner-city and suburban teachers in the United States as well as in many other Western nations (Banks, 2009).

The major purpose of the Multicultural Education Series is to provide preservice educators, practicing educators, graduate students, scholars, and policy makers with an interrelated and comprehensive set of books that summarizes and analyzes important research, theory, and practice related to the education of ethnic, racial, cultural, and linguistic groups in the United States and the education of mainstream students about diversity. The dimensions of multicultural education, developed by Banks (2004) and described in the *Handbook of Research on Multicultural Education* (Banks & Banks, 2004), provide the conceptual framework for the development of the publications in the Series. They are content integration, the knowledge construction process, prejudice reduction, an equity pedagogy, and an empowering institutional culture and social structure.

The books in the Series provide research, theoretical, and practical knowledge about the behaviors and learning characteristics of students of color, language minority students, and low-income students. They also provide knowledge about ways to improve academic achievement and race relations in educational settings. Multicultural education is consequently as important for middle-class White suburban students as it is for students of color who live in the inner city. Multicultural education fosters the public good and the overarching goals of the commonwealth.

Contreras writes insightfully and compellingly about the "Brown Paradox" in the Latino education crisis. She describes the Brown Paradox as the contradictions created by the rapid growth of Latino students in U. S. schools, the minimum investment in their education, "the savage inequalities" in the schools in which they are concentrated (Kozol, 1992), and the ugly nativistic sentiments that are deep and intractable in U. S. society. This adept and heartfelt book is rich in research data, policy analyses, and sensible suggestions that will help policy makers and practitioners take reflective actions to resolve the Brown Paradox, which is urgently needed to enrich and transform the nation as well as to provide Latino students with the educational opportunities, recognition, and respect they deserve.

—*James A. Banks*

REFERENCES

Banks, J. A. (2004). Multicultural education: Historical development, dimensions, and practice. In J. A. Banks & C. A. M. Banks (Eds.), *Handbook of research on multicultural education* (2nd ed., pp. 3–29). San Francisco: Jossey-Bass.

Banks, J. A. (Ed.). (2009). *The Routledge international companion to multicultural education.* New York and London: Routledge.

Banks, J. A., & Banks, C. A. M. (Eds.) (2004). *Handbook of research on multicultural education* (2nd ed.). San Francisco: Jossey-Bass.

BBC News. (2006, March 27). *The EU's baby blues: Birth rates in European Union are falling fast.* Retrieved December 28, 2010, from http://news.bbc.co.uk/2/hi/europe/4768644.stm

Cesari, J. (2004). *When Islam and democracy meet: Muslims in Europe and the United States.* New York: Pelgrave Macmillan.

Clark, C. (2010, October 17). Germany's Angela Merkel: Multiculturalism has "utterly failed." *The Christian Science Monitor.* Retrieved December 11, 2010, from http://www.csmonitor.com/World/Global-News/2010/1017/Germany-s-Angela-

Darling-Hammond, L. (2010). *The flat world and education: How America's commitment to equity will determine our future.* New York: Teachers College Press.

Dillon, S. (2006, August 27). In schools across U. S., the melting pot overflows. *The New York Times,* vol. CLV [155] (no. 53,684), pp. A7 & 16.

Eck, D. L. (2001). *A new religious America: How a "Christian country" has become the world's most religiously diverse nation.* New York: HarperSanFrancisco.

Gándara, P., & Hopkins, M. (Eds.). (2010). *Forbidden language: English language learners and restrictive language policies.* New York: Teachers College Press.

Immigration sabotage [Editorial]. (2007, June 4). *The New York Times,* p. A22.

Kozol, J. (1992). *Savage inequalities: Children in America's schools.* New York: Crown.

Longman, P. (2010, November). Think again: Global aging. *Foreign Policy.* Retrieved December 28, 2010 from http://www.foreignpolicy.com/articles/2010/10/11/think_ again_global_aging

Martin, P., & Midgley, E. (1999). Immigration to the United States. *Population Bulletin, 54* (2), pp. 1–44. Washington, DC: Population Reference Bureau.

Massey, D. S. (Ed.). (2008). *New faces in new places: The changing geography of American immigration.* New York: Russell Sage Foundation.

National Center for Education Statistics. (2008a). *The condition of education 2008.* Washington, DC: U. S. Department of Education. Retrieved August 26, 2009, from http://nces.ed.gov/pubsearch/pubsinfo.asp?pubid=2008031

National Center for Education Statistics. (2008b). Public elementary/secondary school universe survey, 2007–2008. *Common Core of Data.* Retrieved January, 20, 2010, from http://nces.ed.gov/ccd

National Center for Education Statistics. (2008c). State nonfiscal survey of public elementary/secondary education, 2007–2008. *Common Core of Data.* Retrieved January, 20, 2010, from http://nces.ed.gov/ccd

Passel, J., & Cohn, D. (2008, February 11). *Immigration to play lead role in future U. S. growth.* Pew Research Center Publications. Retrieved December 28, 2010, from http://pewresearch.org/pubs/729/united-states-population-projections

Progressive Policy Institute. (2008). *50 million Americans speak languages other thanEnglish at home.* Retrieved September 2, 2008 from http://www.ppionline.org/ppi_ci.cf m?knlgAreaID=108&subsecID=900003&contentID=254619

Roberts, S. (2008, August 14). A generation away, minorities may become the majority in U. S. *The New York Times,* vol. CLVII [175] (no. 54,402), pp. A1 & A18.

Sable, J., & Plotts, C. (2010). *Documentation to the NCES common core of data public elementary/secondary school universe survey: School year 2008–09* (NCES 2010-350 rev). Washington, DC: National Center for Education Statistics. Retrieved August 6, 2010, from http://nces.ed.gov/pubsearch/pubs.info.asp?pubid=2010350

Skeldon, R. (in press). Demographic divide in Asian nations. In J. A. Banks (Ed.), *Encyclopedia of diversity in education* (4 volumes). Thousand Oaks, CA: Sage.

Suárez-Orozco, C., & Suárez-Orozco, M. M. (2002). *Children of immigration.* Cambridge, MA: Harvard University Press.

Tabuchi, H. (2011, January 3). Japan keeps a high wall for foreign labor. *The New York Times.* Retrieved January 6, 2011 from http://www.nytimes.com/2011/01/03/world/ asia/03japan.html?nl=todaysheadlines&emc=tha22

U.S. Census Bureau. (2003, October). Language use and English-speaking ability: 2000. Retrieved September 2, 2008, from http://www.census.gov/prod/2003pubs/c2k-br-29.pdf

United States Department of Homeland Security. (2007). *Yearbook of immigration statistics, 2006.* Washington, DC: Office of Immigration Statistics, Author. Retrieved August 11, 2009 from http://www.dhs.gov/files/statistics/publications/yearbook.shtm

The World Bank. (2010, December 21). *World development indicators.* Retrieved December 28, 2010, from http://data.worldbank.org/data-catalog/world-development-indicators?cid=GPD_WDI

Acknowledgments

There are several people who contributed to the culmination of this book, as well as my personal and professional development. I am thankful for these professional relationships and friendships along my educational and professional pathway that have contributed to my commitment to social justice and equity. I am grateful to Dr. Gloria Rodriguez, Dr. Melissa Contreras-McGavin, Dr. Julie Figueroa, Dr. Luis Fraga, Dr. Roberto Haro, Rosalinda Valdez, Patricia Osorio-O'Dea, Patricia Loera, Leona Smith, Jennifer Courmier, and Tuyet de Leon who always provide me with both inspiration and support.

Professionally, I thank the Washington State Commission on Hispanic Affairs for supporting my research on Latino students in Washington, especially, Uriel Iniguez, Lilian Ortiz-Self, Lourdes Portillo Salazar, and Roger Barron. I also want to acknowledge Ricardo Sanchez for his support, editorial feedback, and sharing his expertise on Washington state policy.

I have also had support from the University of Washington. I warmly thank the Institute for Ethnic Studies in the United States at UW for supporting my study of undocumented students in Washington. I humbly thank the inspirational undocumented students who participated in my study. I also thank the West Coast Poverty Center for providing me with an Emerging Scholar's grant to analyze my data from the Washington State Opportunity to Learn Study on Latinos. Finally, I thank Eric Godfrey and Phil Ballinger for access to UW admissions data.

I am also grateful to my students, including the Proyecto Acceso research team at the University of Washington. In particular, Kathryn Torres, a doctoral student in Education Leadership and Policy Studies, assisted with data cleaning and analysis of the Washington State data. Student members of the Proyecto Acceso team include: Karen O'Reilly-Diaz, Irene Sanchez, Monica Esqueda, Luis Ortega, Arthur Sepulveda, and Barbara Guzman. I also thank Tim Thomas for assisting with select graphics in Chapter 1, and Ivan Barron for helping to organize references.

I especially want to thank Dr. Patricia Gándara for her mentorship, inspiration, and friendship. Working with Patricia very early on in my doctoral experience was a pivotal turning point in my career path, and motivated me to enter academia —a testament to the power of mentorship. Ten years later, she continues to provide valuable opportunities, feedback, and *consejos*. I also want to thank Dr. James A. Banks for his ongoing support for my scholarship while I have been at the University of Washington, and for the opportunity to publish this book through Teachers College Press. To my editors, Brian Ellerbeck and Lori Tate, thank you for your invaluable feedback throughout the publishing process.

To my parents, my first educators, Gilbert and Celia Contreras, thank you for emulating what parental engagement and support looks like, and for your unwavering commitment to education. The early lessons you shared with your four children and value for education not only produced college graduates, but individuals who care about their communities. My late sister Lupe Contreras and my brothers Gil and Rick have dedicated their lives to children and promoting equity for all youth, a testament to your strict yet loving upbringing.

And to my godchild, Alyssa, thank you for allowing me to see the K–12 system through your eyes, and the inequities that still exist in the schools 20 years after I walked through the very same halls. May all of my godchildren emulate your wonderful example of hard work and dedication. You are a star in the making.

Finally, I want to thank my husband Javier for his loving support, friendship, and commitment to our family. I could not have made it through the final stretch of writing without you. I am grateful to have you as my partner on this journey.

This book is dedicated to my son, who is my greatest gift—who represents the love, joy, and hope for the future that only a baby can inspire.

CHAPTER 1

The Role of the Public Policy Arena in Educating Latino Students

Nina, I know I go to a poor school. My school does not have the buildings that other schools have . . . and some of our book chapters are copied and we can't even take them home. We do not have a lot of school supplies, and we do not have any supplies for recess—no balls, bats, or equipment to play with. And do you want to know how I really know that I go to a poor school? My school does not look like the schools on Nickelodeon.
—*8-year-old Chicana Public Elementary Student from California*

At the age of 8, my niece and goddaughter already knew inequity when she saw it. She knew that the resources within her school were unequal to those she witnessed on various television shows like those on the popular youth-centered cable channel Nickelodeon. Moreover, and perhaps more tragically, she already knew that she was attending a school that looked and felt inferior to the schools that more wealthy children experienced. And though she herself is doing well—she is a high achiever who continues to score high on state assessments, plays an instrument, and has highly educated role models around her in addition to college-educated parents—my niece questions the fairness of the educational setting she is experiencing, a public school that is over 85% Latino.

Unfortunately, the story of unequal investment in the schools that Latino students attend is far too common: highly segregated schools with limited resources such as access to music programs, highly qualified teachers, or academic supports (Gándara & Contreras, 2009). It is imperative that this story be rewritten to alter the fate of the fastest-growing segment of the school-age population and, in turn, the livelihood of future generations. By 2025, one in five U.S. residents and one in four school-age children will be Latino. And by 2050, over 30% of the total U.S. population will be of

1

Latino origin (U.S. Census Bureau, 2009). Such dramatic changes in demography represent the browning of America—a United States that has rapidly become both multicultural and multilingual. While the country has historically touted such diversity as a strength, underrepresented communities of color in this nation have not had full and equal participation in all facets of American life, and the inequality begins with education. The public education system in the United States, often characterized as a "great equalizer" in our democratic system, has fallen short of its potential to facilitate social and economic mobility among communities of color. And the situation stands to get worse in the face of the systematic rollback of civil rights evidenced through a myriad of public policies around the nation: Arizona's 2010 requirement that individuals carry documentation to prove U.S. citizenship or lawful residency (SB 1070), and its ban on ethnic studies (HB 2281) in 2010; California's Proposition 187, which targeted immigrants' rights to public services; English-only initiatives in California (Proposition 227), Arizona (203), and Massachusetts (Question 2); and a host of anti-affirmative action initiatives in California, Washington, Michigan, and Texas since 1995. Such policies ultimately thwart the movement toward greater educational equity not just for Latinos but for all children in the United States.

The public policy arena is where these debates take place, where regressive laws are proposed and enacted, and where public frustration is vented. It therefore represents the venue for making greater progress toward equity and acknowledging the multiculturalism that already exists in the United States, particularly among the youth in this country. This book addresses the central role that select educational policies and issues play in the advancement of Latinos in the United States.

The discrepancy between the dramatic increase of Latinos as a proportion of the population and the significant gap they experience in educational achievement, access, and integration into the social and economic fabric of the United States represents an interesting contradiction, which I have termed the *Brown Paradox*.The influence of Latinos is expanding in several aspects of American life, particularly their importance to the economy as consumers and workers, their presence in neighborhoods and regions across the country, and their visibility in popular culture, politics, and the media. Yet very little investment has accompanied such shifts to ensure educational success and economic sustainability among Latinos. This combination underlies a pending dilemma for the entire nation (Gándara & Contreras, 2009). A xenophobic approach to Latinos in the United States has led to several policies and proposals that attempt to deny Latinos access to human and civil services and exclude them from the very institutions that shape a democratic society, institutions that the Latino community has worked for generations to defend and support. As I write, the immigration debate is at the forefront of national discourse, following the passage of Arizona's "Papers Please" law (SB 1070), which allows the police the right to profile individuals suspected of illegal status—essentially *all* Mexican and Latino residents of Arizona. This legislation has led other states to engage in similar racist attacks on undocumented immigrants; Mississippi and South Carolina have passed similar legislation. In Utah, a group calling itself Concerned Citizens of Utah produced a list of over 1,000 suspected undocumented residents for the state, federal agencies, and media outlets to act upon. Most ominously, some elected members of Congress from the Republican Party have called for revising the Fourteenth Amendment to take away the automatic right to citizenship from children born on U.S. soil to undocumented parents.

Unless the pattern of racial profiling ends and addressing the limited investment in Latino education becomes an urgent priority, the fate of the nation is also at stake, with a large portion of the population likely to be consigned to an underclass. The nation's workforce will fall short of meeting the demands of the global marketplace rather than being a strong base of multicultural, multilingual, and highly educated workers able to elevate the economic status of the United States internationally (Gándara & Contreras, 2009). Numerous studies have shown that the private and public returns gained from enhanced educational attainment are considerable (Baum & Payea, 2004; Baum, Ma, & Payea, 2010; Day & Newburger, 2002). Over a lifetime, a person who completes a college degree can expect to earn nearly twice as much as a person with only a high school diploma (Day & Newburger, 2002). This translates into greater spending power that contributes to the economy, expands tax revenues, expands homeownership, increases civic engagement, and helps to support public expenditures such as education. The average college graduate working full time pays over 100% more in federal income taxes annually and approximately 82% more in total federal, state, and local taxes than the average high school graduate (Baum & Payea, 2005, p. 2).

The influence of the Latino community has been confined primarily to the business sector—largely because it makes economic sense to pay attention to an increasing market—but has not been able to alter the limited levels of investment in this community's human capital through education. There is much to be gained by addressing this disparity (Gándara & Contreras, 2009). The present crisis of underachievement, including a 54% high school dropout rate (Orfield, 2004), calls for a combined effort to alter this path, which has larger national implications for the greater economy and the state of civic life. The *Brown Paradox* is essentially society's paradox, because minimal investment in Latino students in the United States has larger implications for American society as a whole, potentially undermining our future viability as a nation. Doing nothing to alter the current trend toward an expanding Latino underclass in the United States is not an option the United States can afford. As Gándara and Contreras (2009) explain:

> Education is the single most effective way to integrate the burgeoning population of Latinos into the U.S. economy and society. Thus, if the high dropout rates and low educational achievement of Latino youth are not turned around, we will have created a permanent underclass without the hope of integrating into the mainstream or realizing their potential to contribute to American Society. If we find a way to educate them well their future and ours is bright. Regardless of how they got here, Latino children are America's children and America's future. (pp. 13–14)

The positive return on investing in all students, particularly the growing Latino student population, so that they can achieve higher education levels is a "payoff" for the entire nation. Medicare, Social Security, state and city services, and vital public programs rely on the workers that make up the nation's tax base. If half of the workforce is undereducated, then the tax revenues that fund public services, including schools and municipalities, will suffer tremendously. In presenting the concept of the *Brown Paradox*, this book points out the consequences at stake if we follow the current path of underinvestment in, as well as the targeted exclusion of and discrimination toward, Latino students. The book further raises an important question: What national infrastructure do we want to enjoy as a country in the next 15 years, 25 years? Will we leave a healthy and sustainable infrastructure for all children?

The chapters that follow address the key elements underlying the paradox that the Latino community faces with respect to limited educational investment, discrimination mandated through the policy sector, influence in the educational policy arena, and access to higher education, despite the dramatic shifts in student and residential composition across the United States. Specific attention is given to the role that select educational policies play in failing Latino students and to the opportunities that exist for maximizing full investment in the human capital of a community that remains largely ignored in the education policy arena. These policies encompass those at the K–12 level and beyond, including the issue of dropouts and access to resources for attending college; testing and accountability; financial aid; the DREAM Act; and affirmative action.

While language is a highly significant policy issue for Latino students, this book does not dedicate a chapter to the issue, but does address the plight of English Learner (EL) students in the first three chapters, specifically related to the issues of demographic growth, testing, and accountability and their transition to college. In addition, Chapter 4 of *The Latino Education Crisis* (Gándara & Contreras, 2009) addresses the multitude of issues surrounding the needs and shortcomings of approaches to educating English learner (EL) students. The authors describe the policy context related to educating immigrant or EL children and provide examples throughout their text that show how the issue of language is closely intertwined with targeted efforts to exclude immigrant students from receiving educational or linguistic services in schools as well as policies around testing, immigration, and the DREAM Act.[1] For example, the proposed Comprehensive Immigration Reform Act of 2006 (S. 2611 and H.R. 4437) contained an English-only clause, the Inhofe Amendment, which called for establishing English as the official national language (Sec. 767 and Chapter 6) and would have prohibited the federal government from providing multilingual services. Chapter 6, Sec. 162 of the proposed bill (S. 2611), "Preserving and enhancing the role of the national language," called for the following:

> The Government of the United States shall preserve and enhance the role of English as the national language of the United States of America. Unless otherwise authorized or provided by law, no person has a right, entitlement, or claim to have the Government of the United States or any of its officials or representatives act, communicate, perform or provide services, or provide materials in any language other than English. If exceptions are made, that does not create a legal entitlement to additional services in that language or any language other than English. If any forms are issued by the Federal Government in a language other than English (or such forms are completed in a language other than English), the English language version of the form is the sole authority for all legal purposes.

Since the majority of individuals in the United States who speak a language other than English speak Spanish (35 million according to the Census Bureau), it is difficult not to see such legislative proposals as directly targeted toward the Latino immigrant population. While this act and subsequent immigration reform bills died in committee, they provide an important context for the policy environment that exists for Latinos, immigrants, and the 78% of Latinos age 5 and older who speak Spanish in this country (U.S. Census Bureau, 2009).

While the policy arena is not the only venue where educational change or reform efforts occur, it is the arena where the values of the nation play out historically, and it has been used successfully to alter the discriminatory practices of public institutions, as seen in the case of the civil rights movement. The book therefore ends with a discussion of the potential that exists for individuals to influence the education policy arena at various levels in order to shift the conversation from a punitive/deficit model to one that invests in the human capital of Latino students and seeks to minimize gaps in achievement.

THE CRITICAL IMPORTANCE OF PUBLIC POLICY IN INVESTING IN HUMAN CAPITAL

Public policy plays a critical role in the education sector, given its ability to develop national and statewide initiatives to influence the financing, content, and direction of educational systems and institutions. Unfortunately, unlike prior public policy responses to demographic shifts, changes in the makeup of the nation's public school population have not resulted in parallel changes in public policy regarding the education of Latinos and underrepresented students. Compare this to the initiatives undertaken during World War II, where President Roosevelt invested in veterans through the Servicemen's Readjustment Act of 1944, also called the GI Bill of Rights (Bennett, 1996). The GI Bill of 1944 made it possible for approximately 7.8 million veterans to enroll in postsecondary education. In 1947, veterans accounted for almost half of college admissions in the United States (U.S. Department of Veterans Affairs, 2010). By the end of the first GI Bill period in 1956, close to half of all World War II veterans had taken advantage of this benefit, which made it possible for more and more workers to transition from blue-collar to white-collar jobs. While White males represented the majority of veterans who took advantage of the GI Bill after World War II, the number of African Americans in college more than quadrupled from approximately 27,000 in 1930 to more than 113,000 students enrolled in college in 1950 (Bennett, 1996). This change enabled African Americans to engage in skilled, white-collar work and led to the creation of a Black middle class. Finally, home ownership increased for both Whites and Blacks during this same period. The home ownership rate for Whites went from 44% in 1940 to 55% in 1950. For African Americans, the home ownership rate rose 5% (Bennett, 1996). The investment in higher education made possible through the GI Bill was largely responsible for the growth of the middle class and the emergence of suburban neighborhoods.

During the the baby boomer era, this generation witnessed unprecedented investment in students through the construction of schools, and the development and expansion of higher education systems across the United States. Local, federal, and state policy responses to the baby boomer generation prioritized education, economic integration, and building a skilled workforce. In California, the baby boomer generation served as motivation for The California Master Plan, a strategic blueprint that established the three-tiered system for public higher education in the state (Kerr et al., 2003). In his testimony to the Joint Committee to Establish a Master Plan from Kindergarten through the University, Clark Kerr, the primary author of the plan, describes the motivation behind the creation of a plan for providing higher education opportunities to this generation:

> These were the children of the World War II GIs, and at that time, there was a tremendous sense of responsibility to the GIs who had given their time and sometimes their lives to the defense of the United States. We had some obligation to look after their children. I never met a single word of regret that the State of California should spend whatever was necessary in terms of financial support, to take care of the children of the GIs. There was a tremendous sense of patriotism and responsibility which affected what we did. We concentrated solely on the tidal wave [of students]. (Kerr, 1999)

This document, adopted through the Donahoe Higher Education Act of 1960 represented the state's attempt to ensure a level of access to higher education for all students:

> We started out in our Master Plan asking the state to commit itself, despite the size of this enormous tidal wave, to create a place in higher education for every single young person who had a high school degree or was otherwise qualified so that they could be sure if they got a high school degree or became otherwise qualified that they would have a place waiting for them. That was our first and basic commitment. It was the first time in the history of any state in the United States, or any nation in the world, where such a commitment was made. (Kerr, 1999)

The California Master Plan is but one example of direct investment in education made by a state to address the educational needs of the baby boomer generation. Other investments during the 1960s can be seen through federal approaches to investing in youth, specifically underserved minority youth.

During the civil rights era, under the Economic Opportunity Act of 1964 and the Higher Education Act of 1965, Upward Bound and the Trio programs were implemented. These federal intervention programs made it possible for underrepresented students to gain academic and social support that would assist them in raising achievement and gaining exposure to higher education. Several of the Chicano/Latino scholars who were supported through the efforts and programs established under these legislative initiatives contibuted to the formation of an expanded middle class of Latino intellectuals and scholars (Camarillo, 1979; Gándara, 1995).

Unlike the investment made in the baby boomer and subsequent generations, there are very different national and state approaches to and priorities for educating youth today. Headlines across the nation highlight teacher layoffs, the return to large class sizes, and reductions to federal and state intervention programs. California, the state with the largest concentration of Latino students in the nation, is witnessing unprecedented cuts to education at all levels, and many states attempt to use Recovery Act funds to buffer staff cuts in education sectors. While many elected officials support investing in education, spending on education has been curtailed by budgetary constraints and has not kept pace with the changing demands of this sector, which is in constant need of investment, innovation, and continued leadership that focuses on a functional pipeline for students. If the pre-K system remains inequitable in terms of access to quality preschool programs, the gaps in student performance are highly likely to persist as children progress through the educational sectors (Crosnoe, 2006; Gándara & Contreras, 2009; Garcia & Gonzales, 2006). This early uneven footing is therefore a logical place for greater attention in the education policy sector for Latino students.

According to Pre[k]now, a national think tank on early childhood education, a total of 38 states support some form of pre-K, and from 2003–2006 states have increased pre-K funding by 66%. However, the majority of 4-year-old students eligible for preschool (78%) are not served by a state-funded program.[2] In fact, Latino students represent the largest group that is less likely to enroll in pre-K programs compared to their White and African American peers (Garcia & Gonzales, 2006): Only 40% of 3- to 5-year-old Latinos enroll in pre-K programs, compared to approximately 60% of White and African American children. Garcia and Gonzales (2006) assert that high-quality publicly funded programs are often limited in Latino communities, which results in reduced access and enrollment. They further discuss how Latinos are often priced out of costly private preschool programs. And when they do attend pre-K programs, Latino children are more likely than their non-Latino peers to attend low-quality pre-K programs, which Garcia and Gonzales (2006) characterize as having "less prepared teachers, less student diversity, fewer resources, and larger class sizes" (p. 10). In addition, of the 38 states that Pre[k]now identifies as offering a form of pre-K services, only two meet all 10 benchmarks of quality as determined by the National Institute for Early Education Research.

At the K–12 and higher education levels, we are witnessing reductions in spending on teachers, supplies, and infrastructure, with overall state expenditures threatened by state legislatures and governors in order to address budget shortfalls. At the same time, in higher education, we see both tuition increases and a greater reliance on loans to finance higher education costs. Students are bearing the burden of state and institutional budgetary constraints. Belfield, Levin, and colleagues (2007a) in *The Price We Pay* explore the costs of not making the investment in education, with respect to the financial returns on such investments to society. In setting the tone of the book, Belfield and Levin (2007a) argue that attaining a society that "provides fairer access to opportunities, is more productive and has higher employment, better health, and less crime is a better society in itself" and is "profoundly good economics." (Belfield & Levin, 2007a, p. 16). This collection of research sets up the case for investing in individual human capital if the United States is to attain higher standards in realms such as education, health, and public safety.

The concept of investing in human capital is not new in the field of education. Theodore Shultz in 1961 introduced a theoretical approach for seeing investment differently—namely, by characterizing the individual as a producer of goods and services with the potential to give back to the larger society. In his work, Shultz describes human capital as an important aspect of thriving economies, where the individual is able to produce at higher levels in terms of quantity and quality, as a result of initial educational investment and training.

Several studies have applied this concept to students who remain grossly underserved in the public education system, and their results illustrate the critical importance of education in raising the social capital and standard of living among students who are born into modest family circumstances. For example, in a study that examined the pathway of 50 high-achieving Latinos, Gándara (1995) found that the educational investments made by their families, institutions, teachers, mentors, and public programs (financial aid, scholarships) resulted in significant gains in social and economic mobility. Many members of her sample were also actively engaged in civic life—participating in community organizations, mentoring students, or choosing fields through which they could "give back" to their communities.

As many scholars have shown through their research findings, individual and collective investment on the front end makes powerful sense (see for example, Belfield & Levin, 2007b; Crosnoe, 2006; Gándara & Contreras, 2009; Orfield, 2004). The American Recovery and Reinvestment Act of 2009 is one policy lever that represents an opportunity to invest in states and address budget shortfalls for public education across sectors. But with its limited one-time funding stream, this act cannot take the place of critically important efforts to make education a national, state, and local priority. This book explores policy approaches that impact Latino student progress and provides a wake-up call for multiple actors to engage in the political processes that are shaping the future of our children.

DEMOGRAPHY AND THE GROWING LATINO PRESENCE
IN THE UNITED STATES

In 2003, Latinos became the largest ethnic group in the United States. And by 2009, as a result of their having the highest immigration and fertility rates, Latinos represented 15% of the U.S. population, or 46.9 million residents. In fact, between 2007 and 2008, one out of every two people (1.5 million) added to the U.S. population were Latino (U.S. Census Bureau, 2009). The social, economic, and political influence of Latinos in the United States is now apparent. In the 1980s and 1990s Latinos were referred to as the "sleeping giant," a group that had yet to mobilize, be recognized politically, and fully participate in American society (Durand, Telles, & Flashman, 2006). Twenty years later, given the Latino population boom beyond the Southwest and its growing influence in the national political sector, it is safe to say that the sleeping giant has arisen.

One clear example is in the political arena: Latinos now account for over 9% of voters nationwide (Lopez, 2008), and Latino voters made up a significant share of the voting base in the 2008 presidential election in states like New Mexico (41%), Texas (20%), California (18%), and Arizona (16%) (Lopez, 2008).

Ninety percent of the Latino population live in 16 states across the country, as seen in Figure 1.1, with the largest concentrations residing in California, Texas, New York, Florida, and Illinois.

Figure 1.2 illustrates the growth in the number of limited English proficient (LEP)/EL students throughout the United States, the majority of whom speak Spanish. Combining these two maps shows that a Latino presence is prevalent throughout the country. The growing pains that California and Texas have encountered with a rapidly changing, multi-generational, largely bilingual Latino population are the very same educational issues and concerns that midwestern and southern states are experiencing and will continue to encounter in the coming decades. Figures 1.1 and 1.2 illustrate a story of demographic transformation and a call to address the needs of a population that will continue to grow in size and influence.

POLICY CONTEXT FOR ANTI-IMMIGRANT SENTIMENT
AND ITS IMPACT ON EDUCATION

As noted earlier in this chapter, anti-immigrant policies have specifically targeted the Latino population. This context sets up a climate for unequal access to resources within schools, particularly for EL students. A myriad of public policies and legal cases over the past 45 years have influenced how bi-

FIGURE 1.1. Concentration of Latinos in the United States

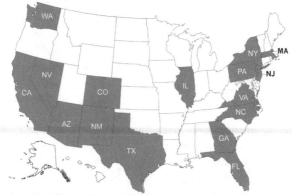

Source: U.S. Census Bureau, 2008.

FIGURE 1.2. Growth of LEP Students in the United States

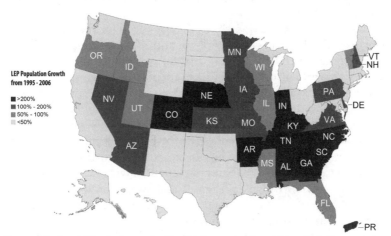

Source: National Clearinghouse for English Language Acquisition, U.S. Department of Education, 2006.

lingual education has been administered in public schools. The Elementary and Secondary Education Act of 1965 and the Bilingual Education Act of 1968 were largely fueled by the Civil Rights Act of 1964, and were adopted to ensure educational opportunities for disadvantaged and bilingual children in the United States. Title VI of the Civil Rights Act, which prohibits discrimination based on race, color, or national origin, had served in part, as the basis for addressing educational inequality in the courts.

In *Lau v. Nichols* (1974), the U.S. Supreme Court affirmed that states and districts could not deny linguistically appropriate accommodations (e.g., educational services in Chinese) or violate the requirement to provide equal educational opportunities on the basis of a student's ethnicity. *Lau* expanded the rights of EL students nationally through federal recognition (via the Supreme Court) that students' language is closely intertwined with their ethnicity. Following *Lau*, a major effort ensued to educate students in both English and their native language. The *Lau* Remedies were proposed to provide guidance for states and school districts to comply with federal regulations that mandate EL student access to the mainstream curriculum and for academic support to develop literacy and fluency in English.

One of the current challenges facing educators and policy makers alike is the anti-immigrant sentiment that is pervasive throughout the public policy arena and media outlets, which has fueld bias against investing in and addressing the needs of English Learners. In 2006, for example, H.R. 6061, which was signed into law by President George W. Bush, mandated the construction of a 700-mile fence across the southern border of the United States as part of the "keep America safe" approach and response to Mexican and Latino immigration.

With anti-immigrant sentiment as the backdrop for the current political climate, Ron Unz has launched a series of anti-bilingual education initiatives in over six states since 1998. Unz started his campaign to ban bilingual education in California successfully in 1998 and has also been successful in Arizona (2000) and Massachusetts (2002). He was unsuccessful with Amendment 31 in Colorado, and two additional initiatives in 2008, in Oregon and Nashville, Tennessee, were both defeated. These initiatives not only suggest the unpopularity of bilingual education or bilingualism; they also pose a real challenge to educational equity in states with growing Latino student populations (see Gándara & Hopkins, 2010). Figure 1.3 presents a legal history and overview of key legal cases and legislation that have involved students who speak different languages or have influenced legislation for English Learners in the United States since 1882.

English Learners have not only been targeted in the policy arena, they remain a grossly underserved segment of the student population. The greatest portion of English learners can be seen at the elementary school level, with steady increases of U.S.-born EL students who enter school speaking a second language (Aud, Fox, & KewalRamani, 2010). In 2008, English Learners constituted 11.3% of all K–12 students (U.S. Department of Education, NCES, 2008). Latino students, who make up the bulk of the EL population in the United States (over 66% in 2008), are largely concentrated in the western region of the United States, where they constitute 39% of children enrolled in public schools, compared to Whites who now comprise 43% (Aud, Fox, & KewalRamani, 2010). It is also important to note that Latinos

FIGURE 1.3. The Legal Backdrop for Immigrant Student Services (ELLs) in the U.S.: Bilingual Education, Linguistic Discrimination, and Select Legislative Milestones, 1882–2010

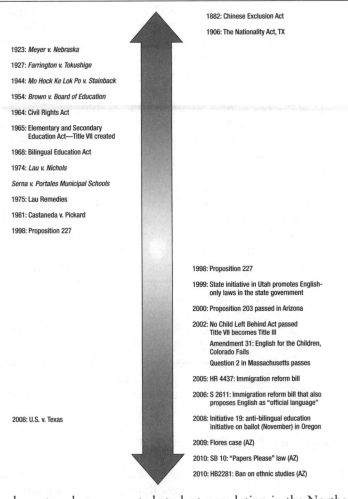

1882: Chinese Exclusion Act

1906: The Nationality Act, TX

1923: *Meyer v. Nebraska*

1927: *Farrington v. Tokushige*

1944: *Mo Hock Ke Lok Po v. Stainback*

1954: *Brown v. Board of Education*

1964: Civil Rights Act

1965: Elementary and Secondary Education Act—Title VII created

1968: Bilingual Education Act

1974: *Lau v. Nichols*

Serna v. Portales Municipal Schools

1975: Lau Remedies

1981: Castaneda v. Pickard

1998: Proposition 227

1998: Proposition 227

1999: State initiative in Utah promotes English-only laws in the state government

2000: Proposition 203 passed in Arizona

2002: No Child Left Behind Act passed
Title VII becomes Title III
Amendment 31: English for the Children, Colorado Fails
Question 2 in Massachusetts passes

2005: HR 4437: Immigration reform bill

2006: S 2611: Immigration reform bill that also proposes English as "official language"

2008: U.S. v. Texas

2008: Initiative 19: anti-bilingual education initiative on ballot (November) in Oregon

2009: Flores case (AZ)

2010: SB 10: "Papers Please" law (AZ)

2010: HB2281: Ban on ethnic studies (AZ)

are also the largest underrepreseneted student population in the Northeast (17%) and the fastest growing student population in the Midwest and South (Aud, Fox, & KewalRamani, 2010).

The issue of language is a politically charged byproduct of historical and current debates over the issue of immigration, particularly when it comes to the Latino community. However, it is important to note that the Latino community is very diverse with respect to generational status in the United States. The constant wave of immigration among Latinos makes this community complex in its history of discrimination and educational exclusion (Donato, 1997; Menchaca, 1995). The contemporary climate that targets Latinos, however, reflects yet another familiar cycle of discrimination. While 89% of Latino students in the K–12 system are American-born, approximately 56% of Latino students in schools have at least one parent who immigrated to the United States (NCES, 2010). Latino students therefore have complex lives marked by economic struggle, coupled with residential segregation and language isolation that contributes to limited generational progress in education.

Telles and Ortiz (2008), in a longitudinal study of Mexican Americans largely from California and Texas, examined the generational progress among 684 respondents to a study conducted in 1970, and 784 of their children (n = 784). The indicators they used to measure progress included socioeconomic status, language use, neighborhood integration (i.e., residential segregation), educational attainment, and a host of personal behaviors and choices that reflect civic participation and what the authors considered to be markers of assimilation into mainstream U.S. society. The findings from this study that are most pertinent to understanding the degree to which progress towards educational equity and integration has been made over a 35-year period are those related to socioeconomic status and education. In particular, they found economic progress to halt after the second generation. Similarly, they found educational attainment to stall among third and fourth generations, and attribute this limited progress to chronic underfunding in school systems that serve high concentrations of Mexican American students (Telles & Ortiz, 2008). Thus, regardless of the generational status of Latinos, the fate of immigrants, bilingual students, and students living in poverty are largely intertwined and felt across a generational spectrum that has witnessed stagnant educational attainment and mobility over the past 40 years.

The Transition to College

Previous research has suggested that mobility among low-income Chicano/Latino students occurs as a result of positive performance in the education system (Gándara, 1982; Gándara, 1995). Within the Latino community, education has long been considered the vehicle for economic and social mobility of individuals (see for example, Contreras & Gándara, 2006), but now the changing demographics in the United States require greater investment in the education of Latino students. Because that investment has been uneven at best, the prognosis for the economic well-being of the United States, in an increasingly multicultural, multilingual union, is unacceptably poor. Discourse in the education policy arena has focused largely on the

FIGURE 1.4. Percent of Students Transitioning from High School to College Immediately Following High School Graduation: Select Ethnic Groups, 1972–2007

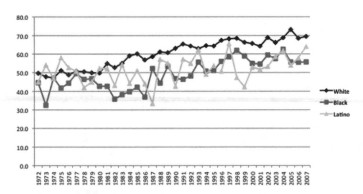

Source: U.S. Department of Commerce, Census Bureau, Current Population Survey (CPS), October Supplement, 1972–2007.

achievement gap, while the "opportunity gap" is rarely discussed. Chapter 2 outlines the key areas for improving opportunity—a rigorous curriculum, textbooks, highly qualified and bilingual teachers, facilities—so all children have an optimal foundation for learning and achievement.

While Latino demographic growth has more than tripled, very little progress has been made in the number of Latino students going to college after high school graduation. White students, by contrast, have experienced a sharp increase in the number who transition to college, despite a decline in K–12 enrollment over the past 30 years. The Latino student population grew from 6% in 1972 to 19.7% in 2005 (KewalRamani, Gilbertson, Fox, & Provasnik, 2007), whereas the White student population in public schools declined from 77.8% to 57.6% in the same period. Despite these growth trends, Latinos still lagged behind Whites in the percentage of students that transitioned to college. Latino enrollment in college immediately following high school rose from 45% to 54% during this same time, while the percentage of Whites transitioning to college post high school rose from 49.7% in 1972 to 73.2% in 2005 (KewalRamani, Gilbertson, Fox, & Provasnik, 2007). Figure 1.4 illustrates this historical trend.

Latino students who do enroll in higher education are most likely to attend community colleges, a segment of higher education that is openly accessible. In 2006, 58.3% of Latino students enrolled in community colleges (Li & Carroll, 2008). The primary concern with Latino students first enrolling in community colleges stems from the low rate of transfer to 4-year institutions among students of color and the increased time to earn a degree—a

FIGURE 1.5. Framework for Exploring Latino Student Achievement, College Transition, and Persistence Across the P-20 Continuum

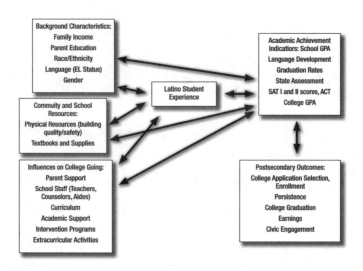

strong factor known to inhibit college persistence and graduation (Long & Kurleander, 2009; Cabrera, Nora, & Castañeda, 1993; Contreras & Gándara, 2006; Saenz, 2002; Wang, 2008). In their college decision-making process, Latino students are likely to consider cost, proximity to their family, the open-door policy, and the preparation they received in high school (Contreras & Gándara, 2006; de los Santos & de los Santos, 2003). Many students self-select themselves out of attending a 4-year institution even if they are qualified because they do not believe they can do well in this context based on their high school performance, or because of the lower cost associated with attending a community college.

Figure 1.5 illustrates the multiple influences on student academic achievement. Several factors contribute to the educational experiences and achievement among underrepresented students (Contreras, 2005a; Gándara & Contreras, 2009; Jencks & Phillips, 1998). The framework acknowledges the importance of individual background characteristics (Coleman, 1988; Garcia, 2001; Kao & Tienda, 1998; Tienda & Mitchell, 2006; Valencia, 2002; Valenzuela, 1999), community and school resources, and a systemic infrastructure for success—all factors that collectively contribute to student experiences in school and ultimately academic achievement (Gándara & Contreras, 2009; Nettles, Millett, & Ready, 2003; Yosso, 2006). These factors interact in a variety of ways to influence student achievement outcomes.

While the path of lower achievement begins early, there are opportunities for intervention and investment in Latino students at every step in the educational system, but the best hope for transforming the current crisis of underachievement and low college attendance rates into an opportunity will come from a recognition of the need for a paradigm shift in educating Latino students. Student success can be enhanced by capitalizing on a student's language and cultural background—what Yosso (2006) calls cultural wealth and Gándara and Contreras (2009) call "the Latino advantage." An education paradigm shift requires a move away from the current deficit model approach to one in which all agents in the education system acknowledge multiculturalism and bilingualism as an asset and strength.

Dropout Policies and Intervention

The issue of high school dropouts is a serious one that is just now starting to be viewed as a crisis among Latino and underrepresented students of color. As will be discussed in Chapter 2, 50% of Latino male students and 41% of Latinas drop out of high school, compared to 21% of White females and 27% of White males (Planty, Kena, & Hannes, 2009). Cutting its male graduation rate in half has considerable implications for the Latino community, in light of the diminished alternatives that exist in society for a man of color without a high school diploma. Complementing Orfield's (2004) *Dropouts in America,* which discusses several of the key issues associated with this problem nationally, Chapter 2 addresses the issue of dropouts among Latino students in particular, highlighting the role that public policy has played in contributing to this national crisis (e.g., exit exams, the criminalization of youth in schools, investment in the prison industry).

If we are concerned about the level of diversity in higher education, then the dropout crisis requires deliberate attention, investment, and contextual approaches to solutions. The issue of dropouts raises a larger question of where students go, particularly males, when they drop out of school (Saenz & Ponjuan, 2009). Increasingly Latino students have either turned to low-wage jobs or, among minority males, gangs or activities that result in incarceration. Scholars have described this phenonmen as the "school to prison pipeline" (Christle, Jolivette, & Nelson, 2005; Kim, Losen, & Hewitt, 2010). Latino convicts now represent 40% of federal prisoners, making them the largest ethnic population in prison. Yet in 2007 Latinos comprised approximately 13% of the adult population in the United States (Lopez & Light, 2009). Chapter 2 further describes national and state initiatives—both those that exist and those that are still needed—to address this growing problem and keep youth out of detention centers and in the classroom.

Testing and Accountability

High-stakes testing and accountability mechanisms continue to be the primary tool for education reform in the United States. Many states are grappling with low passing rates on statewide assessments and constrained resources to compensate for these gaps in achievement, particularly among Latino and African American students. The paradigm shift in education service delivery throughout the P-20 continuum that has resulted from this emphasis on outcomes and standardized exams has had punitive consequences for all stakeholders involved. The biggest losers in this high-stakes framework, however, are the students, as the numerous achievement and exit exams are being used to withhold high school diplomas and make grade-promotion decisions. While it is undoubtedly important to assess what and how well students are learning in schools, it is equally important to consider *how* these assessment and accountability mechanisms are being utilized and where the onus for the "achievement gap" is being placed.

Latino student achievement takes on increased importance in a time when every state is witnessing growth in its Latino population and closing the education gap is at the forefront of public discourse. In Washington state, for example, large gaps exist in the Washington Assessment of Student Learning (WASL) achievement exams, with only 23.5% of Latino tenth graders meeting the standard in math in the state in 2009. In one case, in the 2008–2009 academic year a mere 17% of Latino students met the math standard in a district where Latinos comprise over 86% of the student population (Office of the Superintendent of Public Instruction, http://www.k12.wa.us/). The results are similar for science, reading, and writing and they are likely to have a devastating impact on Latino students in the coming years, as the state continues to utilize assessment results as a graduation requirement.

No Child Left Behind and EL students

Under No Child Left Behind (NCLB), all states are required to monitor the progress of EL students while providing educational services to raise their achievement levels in school. Title I and Title III of the Elementary and Secondary Education Act of 1965 (ESEA), as amended and updated by NCLB, require each state educational agency (SEA) to develop a plan that specifically addresses how the state is establishing standards and objectives for raising the level of English proficiency.

NCLB mandates that all students, regardless of school context or background, be able to read and perform in math at grade level or better by 2014. The NCLB legislation identifies Limited English Proficient (i.e., LEP)

TABLE 1.1. SAT Test Takers Who Plan to Apply for Financial Aid for College, 2004 (percent)

	Other Latino	Puerto Rican	Mexican American	White
No response	7.2	5.9	6.2	8.9
Yes	75.8	80.5	80.0	63.5
No	3.6	2.3	2.4	7.5
Don't know	13.5	11.3	11.4	20.1
Total N	53,677	18,368	65,240	75,5207

Source: Data from the College Board, 2009.

concerns as a top priority. Based on several statewide exam results for EL students, many states are far from reaching this goal. In 2006, the U.S. Department of Education announced a new Title I regulation that gave states and local school districts flexibility on the assessment and accountability provisions for LEP students under NCLB. The new regulations award credit to states, districts, and schools for LEP student improvement in academic yearly progress (AYP) determinations, which are one framework for monitoring the progress among states' EL populations. However, the federal government does not play a strong role in monitoring assessments administered to ELs by states, particularly their validity and utility in helping states, districts and schools better understand the abilities, content knowledge and learning capabilities of their EL students (Abedi & Gándara, 2006; Duran, 2008). This state autonomy has resulted in a wide range of assessments for ELs in the United States, and, as will be discussed in Chapter 3, English Learners remain the most underserved and lowest performing group within the Latino student population. The overarching question addressed in Chapter 3 is whether NCLB is an appropriate accountability framework that should be continued, and, if so, whether the policy has resulted in positive outcomes for those students scoring in the lowest quartiles on statewide and federal assessments. Perhaps it is time to call for an accountability framework that does not place the onus of achievement primarily on the student and teacher, but addresses the larger systemic supports that foster progress in academic achievement.

Financial Aid

The increasing cost of college tuition, combined with limited opportunities for state and federal student financial aid, creates a significant barrier for Latinas/os in higher education. As a result, many Latino students have to work while in college, more than any of their peers: According to a study conducted by National Center for Education Statistics (NCES) researchers

(Horn, Nevill, & Griffin, 2006), 36.8% of the Latinos enrolled in higher education work full time (35 hours or more a week), compared to 31% of White students, and 21.8% of Asian American students.

Because Latino students are more likely to work in college, financial aid plays a key role in allowing students to pursue and focus on higher education. In addition to planning to work, all of the Latino subgroups are more likely than their White peers to apply for financial aid to attend college, as seen in Table 1.1. Eighty percent of the Mexican American and Puerto Rican SAT test-takers in 2004 planned to apply for financial aid, while 75.8% of the Other Latino category and 63.5% of White students intended to apply. White students were also more likely to mark "don't know" compared to the Latino subgroups (Gándara & Contreras, 2009). These data are consistent with a study conducted by Santiago and Cunningham (2005) that found that approximately 80% of Latino undergraduates applied for financial aid. However, the study also assessed average financial aid award amounts and found that while Latinos applied in record numbers, they received the lowest average financial aid award compared to their peers from other racial/ethnic groups.

Grants and scholarships are a decisive factor for Latino students as they decide on institutional type and location, and the number of hours they have to work while in school. The SAT data suggest that Latino students are well aware of their need for a combined approach to funding their higher education; this is an area that represents an option for investment to ensure that students who transition into higher education persist through to graduation. Chapter 4 examines the critical role of financial aid and tuition policies for Latino students and addresses the larger issues of rising tuition at public institutions, the personal trade-offs for taking out student loans, and the financial climate that forces low-income students to work long hours in order to afford rising college costs.

The DREAM Act

Immigrant students are often depicted as taking resources away from citizens in this country. The reality is that immigrant parents largely enter this country because they are seeking better life options for their children. Throughout the history of the United States, we have witnessed mean-spirited policies toward immigrant populations. The education sector is no different. From segregation to attempts to completely deny a public education to immigrant students, the education and the public policy sectors have played a direct role in how we incorporate or exclude immigrant populations from opportunities to learn—and as a result alienate them from the social fabric of this country.

Policies like the DREAM Act allow undocumented students to pay in-state tuition, since undocumented students are not eligible for many (if not most) forms of financial aid due to their legal status. Presently 10 states have passed a DREAM Act, and nationally this issue has led to heated debate on immigration reform. The plight of undocumented students in higher education is examined in Chapter 5, as these students continue to receive very little support as they pursue higher education. In my recent research, I found that many students were experiencing discrimination in their higher education institutions even if a DREAM Act was in place. One student framed the experience of many in trying to navigate a college's administration to secure employment as a work–study student:

> Even though I have those scholarships [a Costco scholarship] I am barely able to pay for tuition. I have to work. I have not been able to work [legally] because I am not documented. I tried to renew my work visa and they denied it after I paid the $400 to renew it for employment as a work–study student. The administrator said, "Well, that was just pure luck [the first time] and you are lucky we have not deported you."

These experiences are common among undocumented students, even when policies like House Bill 1079 (Washington) or AB 540 (California) are in place. As a result, this high-achieving student returned home during the summer to work in the fields and also in construction. Chapter 5 presents a case study of undocumented students in Washington state and describes the challenges of having undocumented status in the United States as a high-achieving college student. The students' stories convey an important American reality—a paradox of limited investment in the individual, accompanied by discrimination, exclusion, and oppression within both the workplace and halls of higher education.

Affirmative Action

As admission to selective colleges and universities remains largely based on quantitative indicators due to a number of contextual, institutional, and demand factors, it is important to assess the role that public policies play in access to higher education. Bans on affirmative action in states like California, Washington, Texas, and Michigan have been devastating for students of color attempting to navigate the college admissions process. In a time when Latino students comprise the majority of students in the K–12 system in states like California, Texas, New Mexico, and Florida, it is critical to understand the social, cultural, and political contexts that affect the educational success of these students as they pursue higher education. Affirmative action, born out of the civil rights movement, was one policy approach to address systemic inequities. Yet, in light of shifting policy climates, the concept of inequity has been turned on its head. No longer are definitions of inequity rooted in historical discrimination. Rather, the recent wave of legal cases related to affirmative action deal with the concept of *reverse discrimination*—namely, White students who claim that the historical and present context of discrimination, inequity, and exclusion in higher education is no longer relevant. The plaintiff in the *Hopwood* case for example, Cheryl Hopwood, claimed that affirmative action policies implemented at the University of Texas law school violated the equal protection clause of the constitution. Essentially, minority students took the slot of "more qualified" students like herself. The court concurred with this argument, which led to a series of anti-affirmative action initatives and cases to ban such policies in several key states with sizable minority populations. Such assumptions exemplify the extent to which white privilege dominates the current discourse on affirmative action and continues to threaten approaches to ensure underrepresented student access to higher education.

The fact is, affirmative action practices have been a prevalent feature within higher education even prior to the civil rights movement, through legacy preferences for children of alumni. In his book, *Affirmative Action for the Rich*, Kahlenberg (2010) examines the use of legacy preferences by higher education institutions in fundraising, and the implications for such preferences on the civil rights movement. Kahlenberg notes that while the civil rights movement served to remedy discrimination and exclusionary practices in multiple sectors, legacy preferences have no such justification. Rather, such practices unfairly advantage elites in this country (Kahlenberg, 2010; Schmidt, 2010; Lind, 2010). Yet we have not witnessed state legislation in the policy arena that challenge such preferential consideration in selective institutions. He notes that legacy preferences "explicitly classifies individuals by bloodline and does so in a way that compounds existing hierarchy" (Kahlenberg, 2010, p. 11). Despite the existence of legacy preferences in higher education, affirmative action remains at the center of controversy, illustrating the degree to which patterns of social hierarchy remain entrenched in university practices to favor the wealthy, and how we have not realized the full potential for affirmative action to serve as an equalizing tool for students from underreprestend, disadvantaged backgrounds.

Chapter 6 presents an overview of the anti-affirmative action policies currently in place, such as Proposition 209 in California and I-200 in Washington, and their impact on Latino and underrepresented student access to public higher education. Questions discussed in this chapter include: How have bans on affirmative action influenced institutional approaches to admissions and outreach? Who is admitted to college in this post–affirmative action era? And who are the winners and losers in the Post Affirmative Action era? Systemwide, institutional, and qualitative data are used to assess the overall impact of the ban on affirmative action in higher education in select states and the larger implications of these bans for underrepresented communities.

CREATING AN EDUCATION POLICY AGENDA THAT ADDRESSES LATINO STUDENT NEEDS

The book's final chapter revisits the overarching contradictions that exist in the education policy sector and the critical need to invest in Latinos on a national scale—that is, investing in Latinos is an investment in the present and future human capital of the nation. Chapter 7 also summarizes the opportunities that exist to improve the delivery of educational services and the findings outlined in the chapters concerning the differential opportunities to learn, testing and accountability, financial barriers, immigrant students, dropouts, and attacks on affirmative action policies designed to address past and current levels of discrimination and exclusion. The final chapter also explores the use of these councils as policy-making bodies with the potential to shape initiatives that support greater attention to the needs of Latinos and underrepresented low-income students.

As the country moves closer to a multicultural identity, the public policy sector must move the pendulum forward and support this transition by designing policies that are inclusive and proactive rather than regressive. The concluding chapter outlines recommendations for shaping constructive and deliberate education policies to raise student achievement and provide equitable resources without erasing or minimizing students' ethnic identity or language.

These recommendations will move education policy in a proactive direction to address uneven achievement and unequal access to higher education institutions, with particular emphasis on inclusion. Educational investment is the best option for the United States if it is to ensure a level of sustainability for all residents and remain a leader in multiple industries and institutions internationally. Innovation does not just happen; it is fostered. And investing in Latinos and communities of color rather than attempting to exclude or segregate them further is a step toward ensuring American innovation while strengthening the future demographic foundation of the United States.

CHAPTER 2

Falling Through the Cracks: Who Transitions to College and Who Doesn't?

Many Latino students continue to fall through the cracks of a leaking educational pipeline. The volume of students who drop out of high school represents a national crisis with considerable economic implications for low-income communities unable to break the cycle of poverty (Gándara & Contreras, 2009). This, of course, represents a missed opportunity for investing in our own national interests, because an educated population leads to healthy families, greater disposable income, civic participation, and reduced crime rates.[1] In addition, a college education is considered necessary to ensure meaningful participation in a skilled and technologically advanced global economy (Gándara & Contreras, 2009; Hanushek & Kimko, 2000; Levin, Belfield, Muennig & Rouse, 2007). While Latinos aspire to earn a college degree, many fall short of attaining this goal. In a poll on Latino education conducted by Univision and the Associate Press, Latinos were more likely than the general population to consider education to be extremely or very important (87% compared to 78%) (Alonso-Zaldivar & Tompson, 2010). In addition, 94% of Latinos said that they expected their own children to go to college. These data, derived from a nationally representative sample of over 1,500 Latino households, suggest that the desire for college attainment exists among Latinos. Now more than ever, transitioning successfully to college among Latinos is crucial to moving forward economically and socially in the United States. Latinos will need to contribute substantially to ensuring the overall economic well-being of this nation.

In Chapter 1, I introduced the paradox that stems from the proliferation of Latino students in schools and throughout the nation accompanied by minimal investment, anti-immigrant attacks, and poor education service delivery. The ramifications of limited attention and investment in the education policy arena exacerbates the low high school graduation rates, test scores, college readiness and college-going rates among Latino students.

This chapter discusses the role that the educational policy arena plays in contributing to this crisis and its potential for providing an avenue for policy development to better address the needs of Latino students (and their underrepresented peers) and prepare them for the postsecondary sector. Data for this chapter stem from the following sources: (1) survey and interview data from middle and high school teachers who participated in a statewide study on Latino achievement in Washington state, (2) graduation rate data from EdCounts using the Swanson CPI index model, (3) NCES data on high school graduation rates and transition rates, (4) data from the 2005 NAEP high school transcript study, (5) national data from the College Board on AP course enrollment, (6) national ACT data on college readiness indicators developed by the ACT, (7) data from the National Center for Juvenile Justice and (8) Integrated Postsecondary Education Data System (IPEDS) data on college graduation rates by gender and ethnicity. Together, these data sources are used to present an overview of the pathway to college for Latino students and the cracks that exist in the pipeline for these students that inhibit academic progression and success.

The navigational process for Latino students from the elementary and secondary to the postsecondary system contains several elements that influence student practices, aspirations, achievement, and outcomes. Figure 2.1 illustrates the various influences that impact students' progress throughout their education trajectory, including the policy arena, human resources, and the school resources that ultimately affect the pathway through school and into college and beyond.

This chapter discusses select policy issues that directly influence the transition to college for Latino students and ultimately influence college persistence, including (1) differential opportunities to learn in the K–12 sector, including the role of teachers; (2) graduation rates and policies around raising rates among underrepresented groups; (3) dropout policies and efforts; (4) course-taking access and policies; and (5) dual enrollment programs. These policy arenas have the potential to contribute to increasing the number of Latino students transitioning to higher education and successfully persisting through college and beyond. In addition, the issue of gender is discussed throughout to shed light on how appropriate targeted efforts by gender may alter the current Latino education paradox.

DIFFERENTIAL OPPORTUNITIES TO LEARN

The differential opportunities to learn that Latino students experience in the United States is evident through multiple indicators, especially the number of students that do not matriculate through high school and beyond.

Such differences help us to understand the widely documented "achievement gap" that exists between underrepresented students of color and their peers on standardized exams, persistence patterns, and overall educational outcomes. I contend, along with other leading educational scholars, that the framing of this issue is essentially the result of an opportunity-to-learn gap, or inequitable practices in education service delivery, such as variation in teacher quality, teacher perceptions, financial resources, facilities, curricular access, and culturally relevant curricular offerings and content (Conchas, 2006; Contreras et al., 2008; DeShano da Silva, Huguley, & Kakli, 2007; Flores, 2007; Gándara & Contreras, 2009; Guiton & Oakes, 1995; Ladson-Billings & Gillborn, 2004; Nieto & Bode, 2008; Rodriguez & Rolle, 2007; Stuart Wells & Serna, 2006; Valenzuela, 1999).

The opportunity gap is most pronounced among English Language Learners, the majority of whom speak Spanish in the United States (Fry, 2007; Gándara & Contreras, 2009; Gándara & Hopkins, 2010). In 2007, approximately 20% of youth between the ages of 5 and 17 (10.8 million) spoke a language other than English at home. And 5% of this group (or approximately 2.7 million students) spoke English with difficulty; 75 percent spoke Spanish (Planty, Kena, & Hannes, 2009). Further, the majority of Latinos in U.S. schools are the children of immigrants, and one in five of all school-age children will be the children of immigrants by 2020 (Fry, 2007; Gándara & Contreras, 2009). Yet, while the fastest growing segment of the population is bilingual and bicultural, seven states have policies in place that either ban or restrict native language use and instruction in public schools. In fact, this nation has a long history of restrictive language policies (Gándara & Hopkins, 2010). Gándara and Contreras (2009) argue that we are among the few developed nations in the world where speaking another language is considered a deficit rather than an asset or advantage to the student, despite well-documented research that proves the cognitive advantages of speaking another language (Hakuta & Bialystok, 1994; Valdés, 1996, 2001).

The Role of Teachers: The Case of Washington

Teachers play a pivotal role in providing students with opportunities to learn through setting the tone in classrooms and the pedagogical approaches they use to deliver subject content. Teachers also have the potential to serve as role models for students, with the ability to inspire students and cultivate a love for learning. Using survey and interview data from an Opportunity to Learn Study in Washington of Latino students in 14 middle and high schools in rural, urban, and urban ring districts (Contreras et al., 2008), this section highlights teacher findings from the surveys administered to teachers and interviews conducted among math teachers from October to November 2008.

FIGURE 2.1. Framework for Latino Student Navigational Processes Through P-20 Continuum and Policy Influences

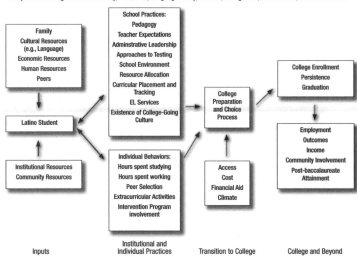

The teacher data collection occurred concurrently with student data collection in the middle and high schools. The research team attempted to survey all of the teachers in the schools visited. The teacher characteristics for the school districts reveal that the rural districts had a high percentage of teachers with less than 4 years of experience, which is consistent with the literature on teacher quality that has found Latino students more likely to attend schools with the least qualified teachers (Darling-Hammond, 1997; Gándara & Contreras, 2009; Gándara, Maxwell-Jolly, & Driscoll, 2005). In the large urban ring district, 31% of teachers also had less than 4 years of experience. Teachers in the entire state of Washington, however, have an average of 12.6 years of teaching experience. The issue of years of experience, however, calls into question teacher quality in districts that serve high concentrations of Latino students. The experience levels of teachers in districts with a high concentration of Latino students in Washington is consistent with studies that have also found that high-poverty, high-minority districts have the most inexperienced teachers compared to low-minority, low-poverty schools and districts (Gándara & Contreras, 2009; Gándara, Maxwell-Jolly, & Driscoll, 2005; Jencks & Phillips, 1998; Mayer, Mullens, & Moore, 2000; Valenzuela, 1999).

A total of 253 teachers participated in the survey, the majority of whom were female (55.4%) and White (83.4%). Only 8.3% ($n = 21$) of the teachers in the sample were Mexican American or Latino. There was also limited teacher diversity with respect to Asian American (*n* = 5), American Indian (*n* = 6), or African American (*n* = 1) teachers in the sample. The teacher responses are aggregated, and descriptive statistics are presented according to the themes covered in the survey protocol. In addition, 29 math teachers from the school sites were interviewed using a semistructured protocol that was consistent with the themes addressed in the survey. The protocol asked teacher opinions about the context for teaching, as well as Latino student opportunities, challenges, and contextual factors that influence learning and achievement. The central themes that emerged from the 29 interviews among math teachers are used to complement the survey findings here. Findings from the teacher data collection are very revealing about the context for educating Latinos in Washington State and provide a glimpse of educators' views toward a community that is rapidly altering the student composition within the state.

Context for Teaching

The study protocol sought to explore teacher opinions about thier context for teaching and working with Latino and EL students in their classes. Teachers who participated in the study believed they had the resources and materials necessary to provide relevant and appropriate instruction "most of the time" (55.4%). In addition, when asked if they had the opportunity to integrate culturally relevant materials into classroom instruction, teachers were likely to respond "frequently" (36.7%) or "sometimes" (38.7%), as seen in Table 2.1.

Few of the math teachers we interviewed described culturally relevant approaches and strategies to engage their Latino students in the classroom. Perhaps the narrow conception of multicultural education is in part to blame for the math teachers' limited discussion of their approaches to integrating culturally relevant content in the classroom (Banks, 1993, 2006). The five dimensions Banks (1993, 2006) addresses when describing the challenges to multicultural education, particularly "content integration" and "an empowering school culture and social structure," were not at the forefront of teacher concerns from the interview responses.

Teachers placed a strong emphasis on accountability, specifically the pressure they felt to raise achievement standards among underperforming students. State standards and meeting accountability requirements in general, such as Academic Yearly Progress (AYP), emerged as an important pedagogical objective for teachers. Over 95% of teachers surveyed believed that their classroom instruction was guided by state standards and either strongly agreed (43.5%) or agreed (52%) that standards played a significant

TABLE 2.1. Teacher Has Opportunity to Integrate Culturally Relevant Materials into Classroom Instruction

	N	Percent
Always	34	13.7
Frequently	91	36.7
Sometimes	96	38.7
Rarely	23	9.3
Never	4	1.6
Total	248	100.0

TABLE 2.2. Meeting WASL Standards Is a Priority Within School: Cross-Tabulation by School Type

Priority of Meeting WASL Standards	Urban	School Type UrbanRing	Rural	χ^2	Φ
Very High Priority	49.3%	49.4%	74.7%	16.16*	.25
	(35)	(41)	(71)		
Priority	49.3%	49.4%	25.3%		
	(35)	(41)	(24)		
Low Priority	1.4%	1.2%	0%		
	(1)	(1)	(0)		

* = $p \leq .01$. Group frequencies appear in parentheses below row percentages. $N = 249$.

role in their approaches to teaching. In addition, 90.1% of teachers either strongly agreed or agreed that meeting AYP for the subgroups was a priority in their school, and over 99% believed that meeting the Washington State Assessment of Student Learning WASL standards was a very high priority or a high priority (Contreras et al., 2008). A high school teacher from an urban school described the "intense" nature of accountability within her school:

> The WASL is challenging. We basically have to teach the test to try to get the kids to pass. We don't know everything on the test and we test to state standard. Our school, especially our math department is so in line with state standards that you can walk into any classroom any-time and the teachers could probably almost tell you what standards they are teaching. It's that intense.

These data illustrate the priority of the school and district to adhere to the state and national accountability frameworks. In addition, when these data were examined by school type, teachers from rural districts were more likely to report that meeting WASL standards was a priority at their school compared to urban and urban ring school districts (Table 2.2). Since the majority of Latino students in Washington attend school in rural districts, these data convey how Latinos are most likely to attend schools where accountability is likely to strongly influence teacher pedagogical approaches.

While the WASL emerged as a priority within the school, teachers responded that they were less likely to utilize the WASL exam results and data to inform their teaching approaches, with 41.2% responding "sometimes." It is clear however, based on the teacher survey and interview responses that describe the importance of testing, that the state standardized assessment was in fact influencing the teaching practices in their classrooms. For example, math teachers often mentioned the WASL as a central focus of their attention when implementing their curriculum. Several math teachers expressed a common sentiment among the teachers in the sample—that "teachers basically have to teach to the test so that the students can pass it." Teachers also talked about both the benefits of and the problems with the WASL and some believed that "the benefit is that now teachers are more aligned with the standards and everyone is on the same page." At the same time, concerns with the WASL were also communicated:

> The downside is when the kids don't pass [the WASL], and they are unsuccessful, they feel this sense of pressure and urgency . . . some of them get too discouraged and I can say I've seen kids drop out. They say "forget it."

While the WASL was clearly an emphasis for all math teachers in the classes we visited, a common concern expressed by the teachers was the impact of the exam on their Latino students. The WASL in Washington also served as a high school exit exam for students unable to pass.

Due to the heavy emphasis on raising WASL achievement in schools, teachers were often involved in either before- or after-school learning activities with their students (65.9%), illustrating their commitment to their students and to raising achievement. And when teachers were asked about the multiple approaches they used to support struggling students in their classes, the most popular response was "uses individualized instruction" (72.7%), followed by "provides individual assistance outside of class" (71.9%) and "reviews the key concepts for the entire class to address the needs of struggling students" (70.4%). For bilingual students or EL (English Language) students, it is not likely that they were receiving the same level of academic support due to the language barrier between Spanish-speaking students and their teachers. For the English-speaking Latino students, it appears that avenues did exist for support and assistance with their schoolwork before, during, and after the school day.

The policy context in Washington State is a move toward formative assessment through the newly developed High School Proficiency Exam (HSPE). While the current context of assessments have changed in Washington, the new Measurement of Student Progress (Grades 3–8) and High School Proficiency Exam (first implemented in 2010) replaced the WASL. HSP remains an exit exam at the high school level. The state is also moving towards implementing end of course exams in reading, writing, science and two math exams to graduate high school. It is too soon to tell whether this new assessment structure will have the same effects for teachers and students. Results from the first year of implementation show even lower scores for Latinos in several districts.

English Learners in Middle and High School

As Chapter 1 pointed out, the majority of English learners (ELs) in public schools today speak Spanish and this population continues to grow in states beyond the southwest. EL students are also the most underserved segment within the K–12 population, particularly in states that have not had a long history with Spanish speaking students nor an infrastructure to support their academic needs. Washington is an example of a state that has yet to adapt to the changing student population, both ethnically and linguistically.

The survey protocol from my study in Washington State attempted to explore teacher views and practices with respect to the education of Latino and English Learners in their classrooms. Most of the school sites used an "inclusion model," or full immersion, which was articulated differently to the research team across school sites. When the math teachers interviewed were asked who instructed their EL students, some of the teachers explained that there was an EL resource teacher. But it was also common for math teachers to explain how their "bilingual students in the class assisted their fellow peers with translating the lesson." One teacher explained, "My strategy for working with them is I pair my ELL students with each other, with other bilingual students." Other teachers explained that they "relied heavily on [a] paraprofessional to be able to translate and deliver the lesson, based on what [they] were teaching, to the ELL students." The problem with pairing EL students with fellow bilingual students, or the paraprofessional is the obvious fact that Spanish-speaking students and paraprofessionals do not possess comparable content knowledge to the math teacher. Thus, EL students have limited access to full instruction from the qualified teacher in the classroom. This lack of access to the math content in the classroom inhibits EL opportunities to learn.

A very small percentage of the teachers in the sample felt highly prepared (11%) to support their EL students in the subject content of their classroom.

Many teachers responded that they considered themselves to be "moderately prepared" for this task, and an additional 14% felt "inadequately prepared." Even fewer teachers felt that they "always" had the support they needed to provide relevant instruction for EL students (4.8%). Many teachers felt they had support "most of the time" (35.1%) or "sometimes" (39.1%). These findings suggest that greater professional development for teachers of English Learners, regardless of the model used in the school, is needed to raise the ability of teachers to support their EL students in the subject content they are delivering in their classrooms (Table 2.3).

Teachers in the school sites were most likely to meet with other teachers and specialists to discuss the academic needs of their EL students and identify appropriate instructional strategies for EL students "a few times a year" (35.6%), with 11.6% having meetings to discuss EL student needs once a year. Another 21.5% of teachers responded that they "never" met with other teachers or specialists to discuss the needs of their EL students in their classroom (Table 2.4). These data are disconcerting, because EL students are the lowest performers in the state of Washington on the WASL. With very little attention or active efforts to improve the approaches for meeting the academic needs of EL students, this population is likely to continue along a path of low performance both in school and on standardized measures of assessment.

A Mexican American/Chicana teacher from western Washington with 23 years of experience conveyed the importance of recruiting bilingual teachers:

> Hiring more ELL teachers to serve ELL students in an ELL setting for reading, writing, math, integration, and inclusion opportunities by combining students for art, PE, music, and library is needed. When students are all mixed together all day without appropriate support materials, everyone loses and instruction becomes one size fits all.

Many teachers were concerned about the effect of having a limited supply of bilingual teachers in their school on the pedagogical approach delivered to EL students. The bilingual teachers in particular expressed their concern over students not receiving appropriate instruction, which would stifle future achievement patterns. These data are similar to findings from teachers in states with growing Latino populations, where teachers are concerned about their abilities to serve EL students optimally without the resources or an infrastructure to provide the additional academic support that these students require to become fully biliterate (Gándara, Maxwell-Jolly, & Driscoll, 2005; Thomas & Collier, 1997).

TABLE 2.3. Teacher Has Support Needed to Provide Appropriate and Relevant Instruction to EL Students

	N	Percent
Always	11	4.8
Most of the time	81	35.1
Sometimes	91	39.4
Rarely	44	19.0
Never	4	1.7
Total	231	100.0

TABLE 2.4. Teacher's Frequency of Meeting with Other Teachers or Specialists to Discuss the Academic Needs of EL Students in Their Classroom

	N	Percent
Once or more a week	28	12.0
Once or twice a month	45	19.3
A few times a year	83	35.6
Once a year	27	11.6
Never	50	21.5
Total	233	100.0

Teachers as Role Models and Sources of College Information

In many of the schools we visited, regardless of the geographical location, discussions around college happened most often between the teachers and their students. Some of the teachers showed research team members learning plans, a well-documented best practice in the state of Washington among middle and high school students. In these learning plans, many teachers said that they "used the individual student learning plan to not only talk about the students' achievement in their classes, but to also use it as a guide for the students to begin to think more long term about their life goals and college, of course." Ninety-eight percent of teachers responded that they talked to their students about goals and their aspirations for the future. Since the majority of Latino students responded that the teacher was the primary source of college information (44%) compared to the school counselor (28%), the teacher plays a critical role in transmitting college information and signals to students.

The teacher also has the potential to serve as a barrier, influencing student aspirations about college by sending individual signals or straightforward messages about a student's aptitude for college, thereby limiting aspirations among students from select backgrounds. For example, one of the more surprising responses from the teacher survey results relates to teacher perceptions of their Latino students. Over 65% of the teachers surveyed believed that 25% or less of their Latino middle or high school students would attend a 4-year college in the future (Table 2.5). Some teachers explained that their students were drawn into the agricultural workforce at an early age. A male middle school math teacher from a small rural district described his perception of his Latino students' attitudes toward school:

> These [Latino] kids aren't seeing past working. They see that their parents pick cherries in the field and they think that this lifestyle is OK. A lot of them know they have a job in the orchard. So they do not strive to want more because they do not know beyond what they see.

With these low expectations of their eighth- or tenth-grade Latino students, it is difficult to know how these beliefs translate into investment, time, and attention toward Latino students in the classroom. Researchers have found that nonminority teachers often possess lower expectations for their underrepresented students, which influences their efforts to assist struggling minority students or provide them with the necessary academic support to raise achievement (Delpit, 1995, 2001; Hale-Benson, 1986; Haycock, 1998; Nieto, 1996; Rousseau & Tate, 2003; Ladson-Billings & Tate, 1995).

When asked during the teacher interviews about their perceptions of their students and the likelihood of their Latino students going to college, a number of teachers described how their Latino students wanted or needed to work right after high school or how "Latino students had no motivation." One high school teacher from a large rural district explained:

> The other issue I see with minority [Latino] students here, and I'm not sure if it is a cultural issue regarding race or poverty, but the kids don't think a lot about the role of education in their future and it affects their decisions as far as the classes they take, how much they value a given class that is outside of their natural interest, and their motivation in class.

It was common for the teachers we interviewed to consider the low achievement levels they witnessed among Latino students to be a result of individual motivation—or lack of motivation—rather than discussing the ways in which they are exploring or modifying their individual approaches to pedagogy and content delivery to better engage students and positively influence achievement.

TABLE 2.5. Percent of Latino Students That Teacher Believes Will Attend
4-Year College

Response	N	Percent
Less than 25%	89	37.7
25%	65	27.5
Half—50%	70	29.7
75%	11	4.7
Over 90%	1	.4
Total	236	100.0

Interaction with Parents

Teacher interaction with parents to discuss student progress, effort and experiences in school is well documented as a best practice in raising student achievement (Delgado-Gaitán, 1994; Goldenberg & Gallimore, 1995; Trumbull, Rothstein-Fisch, Greenfield, & Quiroz, 2001; Valdés, 1996). Parents play a critical role in motivating their children to aim high educationally, as seen in the very high Latino aspirations revealed in our parent survey results. There was a wide range of communication frequency among teachers speaking to parents in the survey results. Communication ranged from once every 6 months to once a month. The survey protocol further asked about the nature of this interaction, with teachers responding that the most frequent type of interaction was the parent–teacher conference (53.3%) or a parent night (17.8%) (Contreras et al., 2008). Both of these school events, by design, happen relatively infrequently during the school year and are activities required of all schools and teachers in the state.

There were also differences by school type that are important to note. Based on a chi-square test of independence to examine the relationship between school type and the nature of teacher interaction with the parents of Latino students, rural teachers were more likely to report that parent-teacher conferences were the primary mode of communication, while urban teachers were more likely to report parent interaction occurring for discipline issues and school-wide parent nights [χ^2 (10, N = 148) = 27.04; p <.05] (Table 2.6).

Further, when teachers were asked whether they sought input from Latino parents and how often, teachers in urban schools were more likely to report seeking input from Latino parents once per academic year while teachers in rural schools were more likely to report seeking input once every 4 to 6 months [χ^2 (10, N = 211) = 25.30; p <.05] (Table 2.7). These variations by school type suggest that urban teachers were less likely to be aware of how to approach Latino parents and made less effort to seek input on how to change their own outreach and communication efforts to better en-

TABLE 2.6. Nature of Teacher Interaction with Latino Parents: Cross-
Tabulation by School Type

Nature of Contact with Latino Parents	Urban	School Type Urban Ring	Rural	χ^2	Φ
Parent Teacher Conference	26.9%	59.5%	71.2%	27.04*	.43
	(14)	(22)	(42)		
Discipline Issue	13.5%	5.4%	6.8%		
	(7)	(2)	(4)		
Parent Night	30.8%	18.9%	6.8%		
	(16)	(7)	(4)		
After School Program	3.8%	2.7%	3.4%		
	(2)	(1)	(2)		
Community Organization	0%	0%	1.7%		
	(0)	(0)	(1)		

* = $p \le .05$. Group frequencies appear in parentheses below row percentages. $N = 148$.

gage the parents of their Latino students. Teachers often discussed the difficulty in relating to parents, conveying their own preconceived notions about
Latino parents. An urban middle school teacher who teaches ESL describes
the difficulty in working with Latino parents:

> Understanding the expectation of teachers in the school is a challenge.
> They [Latino parents] have, like any third world country people, the
> belief that sending a student to school means that the school will take
> care of everything.

Labeling Latino parents as "third world" or having a "lack of understanding" of the U.S. education system likely influences teachers' efforts to
interact with Latino parents more frequently other than the required parent-
teacher conference. What is even more problematic is that this teacher in
particular is an ESL teacher who works with EL students and did not further discuss the ways in which she has attempted to engage Latino parents
directly in the education of their children. If teachers interacting most often
with Latino EL students have these perceptions of Latino families, it may
serve as a barrier to fully utilizing parents to support their efforts with their
students (Perez Carreon, Drake, & Barton, 2005). Table 2.7 shows how ur-

TABLE 2.7. Frequency of Teacher Interaction with Latino Parents about Student Experiences in School: Cross-Tabulation by School Type

Frequency of Teachers Seeking Input	School Type			χ^2	Φ
	Urban	Urban Ring	Rural		
Once a week	1.8%	1.4%	3.5%	25.30*	.34
	(1)	(1)	(3)		
Once a month	14.0%	10.1%	18.8%		
	(8)	(7)	(16)		
Once every two months	12.3%	24.6%	21.2%		
	(7)	(17)	(18)		
Once every 4-6 months	19.3%	24.6%	38.8%		
	(11)	(17)	(33)		
Once an academic year	35.1%	21.7%	8.2%		
	(20)	(15)	(7)		
Other	17.5%	17.4%	9.4%		
	(10)	(12)	(8)		

* = $p \leq .05$. Group frequencies appear in parentheses below row percentages. $N = 211$.

ban school teachers, in particular, are more likely than urban ring and rural school teachers to connect with parents once an academic year.

The overall impression of the teacher participants with respect to working with parents was the need to communicate with Latino parents about the importance of school. Many teachers said that not "understanding the Mexican/Latino culture well enough" and not speaking Spanish limited regular and personal interaction with parents. When teachers were asked whether parents were offered Spanish translation at their school for example, less than half of the teachers in urban and urban ring school districts reported that their school always accommodated Latino parents, compared to over 68% of teachers in rural school districts. One math teacher explained the limitations of not reaching out to Latino families:

The biggest problem I think on campus is that we don't have very big connections with families. So having parent involvement open-houses in conferences, we just had them last week . . . where we had every student required [to attend], this was the first time that we had it required so I think that is why that we saw a lot of the Latino parents participate. But then, once they are actually going and meeting with teachers and talking to them individually, I feel like we don't as a school know very well how to connect with those communities and make sure that they feel we want them to participate and that we offer times and opportunities where it makes sense for them to participate with the school.

Many teachers expressed concerns related to communication and the fact that the majority of Latino parents speak Spanish. Although the state requires districts to provide translation services to parents, the practices within districts vary widely, with many districts failing to provide a bilingual translator for parent meetings and at public events for parents. The failure of schools to offer a translator for Latino parents, further limits their levels of engagement and ability to serve as partners in the process of educating Latino students (Delgado-Gaitán, 2001; Contreras et al., 2008).

Greater communication could potentially raise collaborative efforts between teachers and Latino parents, and raise both cultural awareness and expectations for parents in the process. A common frustration among teachers in all settings, for example, was the fact that during the holidays (after the crops are picked in the rural districts), Latino parents would take their children to Mexico for an extended period of time, up to two months. Teachers believed that this "made it very difficult for students to either catch up or remain at grade level." One EL teacher recommended a "program that would educate parents about the U.S. education system, especially for immigrant parents" as an approach to educating and engaging Latino parents.

Teachers further expressed the need for greater attention to the needs of EL students in their schools. They explained that it was very difficult to know if students were making progress and in what areas they needed further assistance, largely due to the language barrier. Some teachers expressed "feeling bad" that they didn't speak Spanish in a school that was over 90% Latino yet had only one Latina teacher (recently hired that year) who was shared between the middle and high school. Teachers explained the need for teachers who understood the students' cultural background. A Chicana/Mexican American elementary school teacher from rural eastern Washington explained:

Latino students need teachers they can connect with. They come to school only to learn that all they have known all their lives is wrong or taboo. They begin to reject their cultural values and language only to be replaced by the English language and American values. And when they begin to see that they still are unable to please, they begin to re-

TABLE 2.8. Cross-tabulation of School Type and Frequency of Spanish Translator or Bilingual Aid Available for School Events

School Accommodates for Latino Parents	Urban	School Type Urban Ring	Rural	χ^2	Φ
Always	46.2%	41.0%	68.2%	20.31***	.30
	(30)	(34)	(60)		
Most of the time	36.9%	39.8%	23.9%		
	(24)	(33)	(21)		
Sometimes	12.3%	15.7%	5.7%		
	(8)	(13)	(5)		
Rarely	1.5%	3.6%	2.3%		
	(1)	(3)	(2)		
Never	3.1%	0%	0%		
	(2)	(0)	(0)		

***= $p \le .001$. Group frequencies appear in parentheses below row percentages. N=228.

ject it all and turn to gangs or are complacent with minimum wage jobs and they *quit* school unfortunately.

Finally, another recommendation expressed by teachers was the need for more professional development on cultural competency and "understanding poverty" training. As one teacher commented, "I know many of these students have problems; I just don't understand those problems." Many teachers equated low-income levels with problems at home or problems that impede learning, conflating the issue of socioeconomic status with a child's ability to achieve (Rist, 2001). These comments were more frequently made in schools that had either no Latino teachers or few bilingual Spanish-speaking staff to assist teachers in understanding cultural norms and approaches to communicating with Latino parents and students. These findings suggest that teachers in Washington State, one of the 16 states with the highest concentration of Latino students, experience a cultural and linguistic disconnect with their Latino students and families. The findings have larger implications for states with growing Latino populations, as they provide a glimpse of the challenges and opportunities that a growing number of states will have in fostering an environment where optimal opportunities to learn are provided to Latino students in the school context.

GRADUATION RATES AND POLICIES

The differential opportunities to learn described above significantly contribute to uneven graduation rates between Latino students and their peers. Graduation rates are considered a better measure of student outcomes due to the variability in school and district reporting and tracking for students who drop out. The Cumulative Promotion Index (CPI; see Swanson, 2004a) utilizes a cohort approach to predict the likelihood of students who began high school in the ninth grade completing high school within 4 years.[2]

The high school graduation rates in 2007 for White and Latino students in states with the highest concentration of Latinos are presented in Table 2.9. The data are disconcerting for Latino students, particularly Latino males, who are the least likely (half nationally) to graduate from high school. In nine of the sixteen states presented, less than 50% of Latino males in the Class of 2007 graduated high school.

Unlike Swanson's graduation rate calculation based on the CPI, which shows sizable percentages of students who do not graduate from high school, the federal dropout rates based on NCES calculations are considerably lower. These calculations are based on the Common Core Data (CCD) calculations and on school district reporting, which typically represents the October 1 head count.[3] The 4-year graduation rates therefore convey differences between the models used by NCES and Swanson (2004a; Swanson & Chaplin, 2003). The graduation rates for the 2006–2007 cohort were 62.3 for Latinos and 80.3 for Whites using the national federal calculations that are based on the CCD system (Stillwell, 2009). Both rates are higher than the aggregate graduation rates in Table 2.9. And the event dropout rate for Latinos for the 2006–2007 year was 6.5 percent, while the rate for White students was 3 percent (Stillwell, 2009). Such low event dropout rates reported by the federal government are in part responsible for the hesitancy to rely on dropout rates rather than cohort graduation rates (Orfield, Losen, Wald, & Swanson, 2004; Swanson, 2004a). The message is clear, however, with respect to lower graduation rates and higher dropout rates among Latinos—that these data are not promising for a group that will be a majority of the workforce in the coming decades. Furthermore, Levin and colleagues (2007) found that raising high school graduation rates would save U.S. taxpayers exponentially per graduate. They identified the cost of five leading interventions, calculated their costs, and added up the lifetime public benefits of high school graduation in their model. Among their key findings was that the net public economic benefit per high school graduate would be $127,000, over 2.5 times greater than the estimated costs of the initial investment (Levin et al., 2007).

TABLE 2.9. High School Graduation Rates by Subgroup and Gender Across States with Highest Concentration of Latinos, Class of 2007 (percent)

	Statewide	White Total	Latino Total	Latino Males	White Males	Latinas	White Females
Arizona	68.2	74.1	60.3	54.9	71.5	65.1	76.3
California	62.7	78.2	57.0	52.1	74.8	61.5	81
Colorado	73.2	79.8	53.7	47.9	75.9	59.2	82.8
Florida	62.1	67.5	58.4	53.4	64.1	63.5	71
Georgia	57.8	65.5	42.8	38.5	61.8	45.9	69.2
Illinois	74.6	82.7	57.4	51.6	80.2	63.4	83.7
Massachusetts	77.3	82.6	53.1	47.3	79.8	58.1	84.3
Nevada	41.8	50.4	29.9	26.8	46.3	33.6	54.2
New Jersey	83.3	87.9	66.1	61.3	86.1	66.4	87.5
New Mexico	54.9	62.6	50.3	46.8	58.9	52.6	65.3
New York	70.6	80.5	49.1	44.2	77.7	52.9	82.1
North Carolina	57.8	64.1	43.5	40.2	61.4	46.3	66.9
Pennsylvania	77.6	83.3	49.8	43.8	81.1	54.6	83.5
Texas	65.1	76.0	55.6	51.9	73.4	58.2	77.4
Virginia	69.9	75.9	58.0	51.9	72	62.3	80.1
Washington	67.9	71.6	54.7	46.7	67.7	59.3	75.2
U.S.	68.8	76.6	55.5	50.6	73.7	59.4	78.8

Source: Ed Counts data system, 2010 (http://www.edweek.org/rc/2007/06/07/edcounts.html). Generated August 10, 2010. The data selected are based on the CPI Index, developed by Chris Swanson.

Latina and Latino youth are far less likely than their White peers to graduate from high school, which ultimately limits future life and employment options. Some reasons and factors for this crisis in high school graduation rates include early disengagement with school, disconnection with curriculum content, limited academic support, low grades, being held back a grade, teenage pregnancy, work, and poverty. For Latinas, the most prevalent factor contributing to dropping out of high school is pregnancy. Latinas have the highest teen pregnancy rates and teen birth rates compared to other ethnic groups. In fact, approximately 53% of Latinas get pregnant before the age of 20 (Hamilton, Martin, & Ventura, 2007), which has larger implications for limited social mobility and long-term poverty. While Latinas have higher graduation rates than their Latino male counterparts, the graduation rate data illustrates a significant gap between Latinas and White females. Latinas therefore remain very much at risk of dropping out of high school compared to their peers.

Many male Latino dropouts opt to work in low-skilled, low-paying jobs, while others enter the juvenile justice system. However, a recent study by Sum and colleagues (2009) found that Latino dropouts were more likely to be employed than any other racial or ethnic group. Fifty-three percent of Latino dropouts were employed, compared to 31% of African Americans, 43% of Asian Americans, and 46% of White high school dropouts (Sum et al., 2009). These relatively higher employment rates among high school dropouts suggest that the primary reason for dropping out of high school is poverty and that the alternate path to school for many Latino males is the workforce (Saenz & Ponjuan, 2009). The problem with Latino male workforce patterns, however, is that without a higher education, many Latinos tend to work in lower-paying jobs that afford limited economic mobility, security, or health benefits (Maldonado & Farmer, 2007; Saenz & Ponjuan, 2009).

For Latino males, who are less likely to graduate from high school than their female peers, this crisis requires urgent attention. While the alternatives to dropping out include working or even attending a community college to learn a skill set, many states have witnessed increases in Latino youth in the juvenile justice system. In fact, across racial and ethnic lines, incarceration rates are highest among high school dropouts (Sum et al., 2009). In many states, the Latino incarceration rate exceeds their proportional representation in the public school system. Incarceration therefore appears to be a viable explanation of the pathway that some Latino males take when they drop out of school.

The composition of the juvenile population in the states with the highest Latino concentration shows the sizable percentages of Latinos in the juvenile justice population (Table 2.10). These data are particularly problematic because they also represent states where Latinos constitute a growing majority of the K–12 population. In a state like California, the fact that Latino males constitute over half of the juvenile justice population is disconcerting given the overall growth in the state's Latino population; this represents a more challenging population to transition into higher education and the workforce. In addition, there is a high correlation between juvenile justice incarceration and adult incarceration among men of color (Mears & Travis, 2004). So students in the juvenile justice system are more likely to continue on the path towards incarceration rather than college graduation. In *The New Jim Crow*, Michelle Alexander (2010) describes the mass incarceration of African Americans as a reflection of a racial caste system, where the criminal justice system, which targets communities of color, is a contempo-

TABLE 2.10. Juvenile Justice Population in States with Highest Latino Concentration, 2009

	White	Latino	Black	Total
United States	56.8	22.5	14.9	38,138,171
Arizona	43.3	43.7	5.2	885,522
California	31.2	50.1	6.7	4,832,846
Colorado	60.7	29.8	5.5	628,226
Florida	49.9	26.5	20.5	2,080,260
Georgia	51.1	12.7	32.7	1,320,969
Illinois	55.5	22.2	17.6	1,623,694
Massachusetts	72.0	13.6	8.3	732,100
Nevada	44.7	38.8	9.2	349,931
New Jersey	54.4	21.5	15.3	1,047,728
New Mexico	29.3	55.3	3.4	259,682
New York	53.0	21.7	17.5	2,260,365
North Carolina	59.0	13.1	24.2	1,165,235
Pennsylvania	74.0	8.8	14.0	1,418,753
Texas	37.2	47.1	11.9	3,529,857
Virginia	60.7	10.7	22.6	942,985
Washington	66.8	17.6	5.8	802,654

Source: Puzzanchera, C., Sladky, A. and Kang, W. (2010). "Easy Access to Juvenile Populations: 1990-2009." Online. Available: http://www.ojjdp.ncjrs.gov/ojstatbb/ezapop/

rary form of racial control in the United States and a pressing civil rights issue. Latinos, given their growing composition in the juvenile justice and prison systems, are also subject to the new form of Jim Crow that Alexander describes, a path that may be altered in part through educational equity and opportunity.

High School Dropout Policies to Encourage School Attendance

One of the primary policy approaches states have used to keep students in school has been to allow 16- and 17-year-olds to drive. However, because dropout rates begin as early as middle school, such policies are likely to have less of an impact on students who leave school prior to the age of 16. Seventeen states limit driving privileges based on compliance with school attendance requirements, and four states make driving privileges contingent upon a combination of academic performance and attendance. Kansas, Louisiana, and Oregon will revoke driving privileges based on infractions of school rules, including suspensions, expulsions, and violations of public safety. Illinois and Indiana combine attendance requirements with student behavior patterns, while Tennessee is the only state that makes teenage driving privileges contingent upon attendance, satisfactory progress in school, and student behavior (Colasanti, 2007). These state policy efforts are considered an attempt to attach real consequences for teens not attending school or at risk of dropping out, based on attendance patterns, the number of expulsions, and progress made in school (Colasanti, 2007). It is still unclear, however, whether these driving-related policies have curbed dropout rates for Latino and other underrepresented students because limited data exist on pairing school data with DMV records, and oversight costs are likely to be a lower priority in school districts that do not have the resources to follow their students who drop out of school altogether. In addition, inaccuracies exist in how school leavers are coded altogether (Contreras et al., 2008). Thus, monitoring such policies are difficult without longitudinal, accurate data systems that follow the student through their P-20 enrollment patterns.

Additional state policy approaches include expanded learning opportunity (ELO) policies that states have adopted to address the dropout rates of their high school students. These learning opportunities include after-school programs, graduation coaches, and extending the school day for low-performing schools (Harris & Princiotta, 2009). Georgia, for example, has a Graduation Coaches Initiative whereby students at risk of dropping out are identified and paired with a combination of a coach and after-school learning programs to increase their performance and engagement. Other states are home to a host of successful after-school programs that promote student persistence, engagement, and high school graduation. However, the challenge with these programmatic efforts is that they are piecemeal and do not provide systemic reform for holistically addressing the dropout issue (Gándara & Contreras, 2009).

THE PATHWAY TO COLLEGE

Several factors influence a student's successful progression through school. College-bound students are often exposed to what Stanton-Salazar and Spina (2005) call "fortuitous relationships." Such relationships may be peers, teachers, parents, or mentors who provide a student with knowledge about the college process or the preparation necessary to transition to college. Mehan, Villanueva, Hubbard, and Lintz (1996) found that one of the primary benefits of intervention programs such as AVID is the relationship building that occurs among the program participants. Students are exposed to peers on a college-bound path, with similar interests and motivation, who are likely to influence that student in school and in extracurricular environments. As Gándara and Contreras (2009) discuss in their overview of successful intervention programs for Latino students, the problem with intervention programs is that they are not systemic and once the program ends for a student, so do the benefits of the intervention. Thus, longer-term systemic intervention is necessary to ensure that programmatic efforts are present for the student throughout their entire educational experience.

Figure 2.2 presents a framework for understanding the factors that influence Latino students as they navigate school. Unlike the pathway figure seen earlier in this chapter (Figure 2.1), this diagram illustrates the multitude of influences that occur simultaneously for students. Here the importance of peer networks, human resources, community resources, and an institutional infrastructure for success cycles around the student, influencing his or her ability to successfully navigate school. These elements are critical to ensuring the successful progression across the education continuum. The literature on transition to college (Bangser, 2008; Deli-Amen & Lopez-Turley, 2007; Kao & Tienda, 1998; McDonough, 2004) indicates that a myriad of influences affect students as they navigate their school context.

The constructs presented in Figure 2.2, such as supportive peer networks or access to curriculum, illustrate possible factors that students might encounter at various stages in their development as they navigate their school context.

Figure 2.2 presents critical elements for student support, engagement, information, and success—all potentially occurring simultaneously in an ideal student experience. Jeannie Oakes (2002) outlines six key factors that can make a substantial difference for students not only in graduating from high school but also in being prepared and competitively eligible for 4-year universities:

- A college-going culture
- A rigorous academic curriculum
- High-quality teaching
- Extra support
- A multicultural college-going identity
- Family connections and social networks

These factors are consistent with the framework I present in Figure 2.2, where access to infrastructure, adult human resources, community resources, and peer networks serve to create the conditions for academic preparation, awareness, and the motivation to transition to college. Students may not have access to all of these factors in their school, home, or community contexts, but a combination of these serve as a plausible approach to

**FIGURE 2.2. P-20 Framework for Latino Student Supports in Navigating
School and Preparing for College**

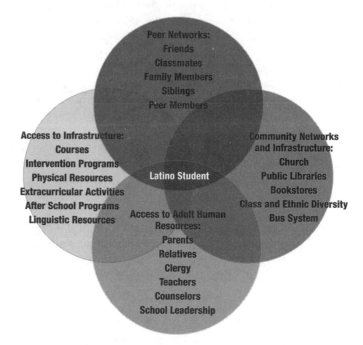

increasing student achievement, engagement, and a college-going culture
among underserved students.

Exposure to a school infrastructure for success (e.g., courses, teachers)
is perhaps one of the most challenging features for improving student outcomes, because it is largely intertwined with the larger issue of school equity and access to financial and human resources. In addition, curricular
resources such as math courses that support college readiness (e.g., calculus)
in high school contribute to a student's likelihood of transitioning to college
enrollment and success (Long, Iatarola, & Conger, 2009; McCormick &
Lucas, 2011). However, quality mathematics instruction is critical to the
success of such course offeringss and their ability to prepare students to be
college-ready (Long, Iatarola, & Conger, 2009).

According to the 2005 NAEP high school transcript study, the gap between completing a curriculum level at or above midlevel rigor diminished
from 1990 to 2005, although White students are still more likely to complete a midlevel and rigorous high school curriculum (NCES, 2007). In addition, the most significant differences that did exist by ethnic group were

FIGURE 2.3. Highest Level of Mathematics Course Completed, by Race/ Ethnicity, 2005 (percent)

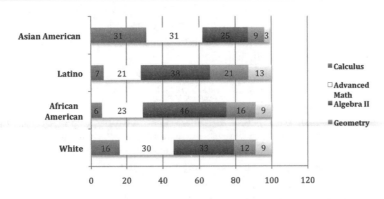

Source: U.S. Department of Education, Institute of Education Sciences, National Center for Education Statistics, High School Transcript Study (HSTS), 2005, p. 29.

in access to and course-taking patterns in mathematics and science courses. Asian American students were the most likely group to complete calculus and advanced math classes (62%) compared to their White (46%), African American (29%), and Latino peers (28%). Latinos were the least likely of the ethnic groups to complete advanced mathematics courses (NCES, 2007). Taking advanced-level mathematics is one of the most commonly used predictors of college enrollment and success (Dougherty, Mellor, & Jian, 2006; Geiser & Santelices, 2006; Gonzalez, O'Connor, & Miles, 2001; Morgan & Maneckshana, 2000). These data are therefore troubling beyond the impact they have on high school achievement or the content knowledge students are exposed to in school. Limited advanced-course-taking patterns in mathematics not only serve as a signal to colleges about student aptitude for college level work, but also influences the likelihood of Latino students transitioning to and persisting in college. In addition, students enrolled in AP courses often get a boost for taking such courses in their school context because these courses serve as a signal to admissions officers about the rigor of a student's high school course of study.

Figure 2.3 illustrates uneven advanced-mathematics-course-taking patterns for Latino students and their underrepresented peers compared to White and Asian American students.

Because access to honors and Advanced Placement (AP) courses in high school, for example, remains uneven and inequitably distributed across school districts (Oakes, Mendoza, & Silver, 2004; Solorzano & Ornelas, 2004; Contreras, 2005a), underrepresented students are consistently denied the opportunity to engage in a college-going curriculum and culture in high school. Access to curriculum in high school also determines the nature of the courses students can enroll in as they transition to higher education. If a student takes a college-going curriculum and is academically prepared, he or she is less likely to be required to take remedial courses that increase the time and costs to earn a college degree.

Figure 2.4 illustrates the percentage of AP examinees versus the percent of high school seniors in the United States for the class of 2009 by race/ethnicity.

The AP data illustrate a lack of parity between the percent of students taking AP exams versus the representation of racial/ethnic groups in the greater K–12 population in 2009, with the exception of Asian American students. It is important to note that access to AP classes alone does not lead to high passing rates on the AP exams (Contreras, 2005b) and must be accompanied by quality instruction, tutoring, and curricular resources to raise student achievement. For example, in 2009, 14.3% of Latino students passed an AP exam with a score of 3 or higher. These data suggest that efforts to increase not only access to AP classes but also the academic supports to do well in such classes must accompany a rigorous curriculum (College Board, 2010).

The college readiness benchmark scores, calculated by the American College Testing (ACT) program, provide yet another indicator of student preparation for college. The benchmark scores represent the minimum scores needed on the ACT subject tests that would indicate at least a 50% chance of earning a B or higher or a 75% chance of earning a C or higher in what the ACT calls "corresponding credit bearing courses." The four course subject areas include English composition, algebra, social science, and biology; scores range between 18 and 24 depending on the subject area and are based on actual college student performance.[4]

Figure 2.5 shows college readiness data for the graduating class of 2009 across the four subject areas with benchmarks established by the ACT to predict college performance in select content areas. Additionally, it conveys low college readiness levels across all ethnic groups, with Latino, African American, and American Indian students possessing the lowest benchmark scores.

The high school transcript study (NCES, 2007), College Board data on AP course taking, and the ACT college readiness scores all show limited preparation among underrepresented students, including Latinos. Unfortunately, these data are not disaggregated by EL status, where Latino students represent the majority of this subgroup nationally. Disaggregating this data for Latinos is relevant to understanding patterns of achievement and college readiness.

FIGURE 2.4. Race/Ethnicity of AP Examinees in the United States (percent), 2009

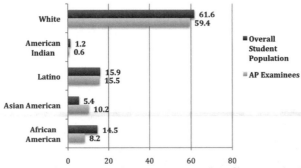

Source: The 6th Annual AP report to the Nation, National Profile 2009. The College Board, 2010.

FIGURE 2.5. Percent of Students Meeting ACT College Readiness Benchmark Scores by Race/Ethnicity (Four Subject Areas), Class of 2009 (percent)

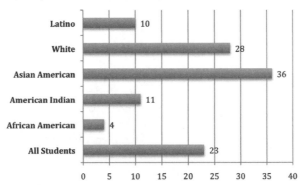

Source: ACT Profile Report—National: Graduating Class 2009.

WHO GOES TO COLLEGE AND WHO GRADUATES?

When Latino students do make it through the doors of higher education and enroll in college, there is the assumption that since they have made it this far they are likely to graduate. The reality for Latinos and their underrepresented peers, however, is high attrition rates in college, particularly if they begin higher education in 2-year institutions (de los Santos & de los Santos, 2005; Flores, Horn, & Crisp, 2006; Gándara & Contreras, 2009). Figure 2.6 shows that less than half of Latinos who enter 4-year institutions will graduate with their college degree within 6 years. So of the 55% of Latinos that graduate from high school, only 64% go on to higher education, with

FIGURE 2.6. Percentage of Students Seeking a Bachelor's or Equivalent
Degree at 4-year Title IV Institutions Who Completed a Bachelor's or
Equivalent Degree Within 6 years, by Race/Ethnicity and Control of
Institution: Cohort Year 2000

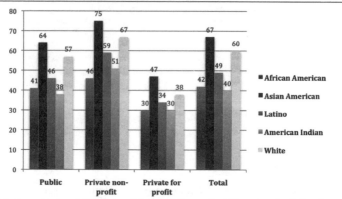

Source: U.S. Department of Education, National Center for Education Statistics, Integrated
Postsecondary Education Data System (IPEDS), Spring 2007, Graduation Rates component.

approximately 40% enrolling in 4-year institutions. Of this 40%, only 49%
will earn a college degree. Not only does the pool of students at each level
diminish, but those that earn their college degrees represent less than half of
the already small percentage that entered college to begin with.

The gender difference between Latino student graduation rates from
public institutions presents an area of further concern. Latinas are more
likely than their male peers to graduate from college, which is consistent
with the trend across ethnic groups of women outpacing men in college
graduation rates. However, even though the Latina rates for college graduation are higher than those of their Latino peers, less than half of Latina
students graduate from college within 6 years, and only 41.1% of Latinos
completed their bachelor's degree at a public institution (Table 2.11).

Both genders require concerted effort and attention to raise achievement
rates, preparation, college transition, and graduation rates. The approaches,
however, are likely to vary because Latino and Latina students navigate
school differently and have distinct challenges with their own approaches
and pathways of resistance within the school structure (Cammarota, 2004).
For both Latino men and women, the primary challenges to college graduation appear to be financial limitations, language barriers, lack of parental
support, and institutional climate, which ultimately influences student integration and success in higher education (Cabrera, Nora, & Castañeda,
1993; Hurtado & Ponjuan, 2005). Furthermore, actual student experiences
in higher education are the strongest predictors of perceived racial hostil-

TABLE 2.11. Percentage of Students Seeking a Bachelor's or Equivalent Degree at 4-Year Title IV Institutions Who Completed a Bachelor's or Equivalent Degree Within 6 years, by Race/Ethnicity, Control of Institution, and Sex: Cohort Year 2000

Characteristic	Total	White	Black	Latino	Asian/ Pacific Islander	American Indian/ Alaska Native
Total	57.5	60.2	42.1	49.1	66.7	40.2
Public	54.8	57.1	40.8	46.0	64.1	37.5
Male	51.3	53.8	34.1	41.1	60.0	33.6
Female	57.7	59.9	45.2	49.7	67.8	40.5

Source: U.S. Department of Education, National Center for Education Statistics, Integrated Postsecondary Education Data System (IPEDS), Spring 2007, Graduation Rates component.

ity on campuses, which also influence Latino student persistence patterns (Hurtado & Ponjuan, 2005). For Latino men in particular, the campus climate has a strong impact on persistence (Figueroa, 2002; Saenz & Ponjuan, 2009). Figueroa (2002) found, however, that with a strong infrastructure of support, which includes supportive peer networks, staff networks, and institutional resources, Latino men are more likely to flourish and succeed in higher education compared to Latino students without these supports.

CONCLUSION

The transition to college for Latino students represents a tenuous path at best, with few Latinos college-ready due to a variety of school, economic, and human resource factors within their school and community contexts. As a result, the persistence rates for Latinos in higher education are lower than those of their peers, regardless of institutional type (see Figure 2.6).

While there are cracks in the education pipeline, there are select areas for education policy intervention to raise college transition and college graduation rates. With the right set of opportunities to learn in school—including physical and human resources, particularly high-quality teachers who believe in the academic aptitude of Latino students, bilingual teachers to meet the needs of ELL students, access to curricular offerings and academic supports, and a school structure that serves to empower students (Banks, 1993)—college transition, preparation and graduation rates are likely to drastically improve from their current levels. We have known for some time the factors that lead to educational success and achievement—we have yet to actualize these solutions in a systemic manner across the P-20 educational continuum. As a result, we continue to lose close to half of Latino students in high school. And of those Latinos who do transition to college, half will not graduate. The Latino students most likely to graduate are those that attend highly selective institutions (Carnevale & Rose, 2003). However, Latinos do not represent significant proportions of the student bodies at these institutions.

These data have shown the need for ongoing academic support in school to increase the pool of students who actually make it to their college graduation and beyond. Ongoing academic support will require reframing current approaches to educating Latino and poor students as well as establishing tangible goals to support and invest in students through every stage of the education system (Gándara & Contreras, 2009).

Chapter 3 looks specifically at the issue of testing and accountability and the role that education policies related to the current accountability framework play in shaping Latino student experiences in school. Accountability is an area of public policy that is poised for reframing. Shaping the debate on how to assess achievement and utilize results to improve education service delivery to all students is critical to Latino student success and persistence.

Educating Latino Students in an Era of High-Stakes Testing, Accountability, and Assessment

High-stakes testing and accountability mechanisms have become a primary tool for education reform in the United States. Many states are grappling with low passing rates on statewide assessments and constrained resources to compensate for these gaps in achievement, particularly among Latino and African American students. Thus, a paradigm shift in education service delivery has occurred throughout the P-20 continuum, with an emphasis on outcomes and standardized exams as well as punitive consequences for all stakeholders involved. The biggest losers in this high-stakes framework, however, are the students—a myriad of achievement and exit exams are utilized to withhold high school diplomas and make grade promotion decisions. While the content that Latinos are learning in schools is necessary and important to assess, it is equally important to consistently evaluate *how* these assessment and accountability mechanisms are being utilized and where the onus for the achievement gap is being placed.

Given the current accountability framework for education, with 26 states now requiring exit exams,[1] the emphasis on student learning outcomes for schools is clear. A multitude of state-level assessments like the WASL in Washington (now the Measurement of Student Progress and High School Proficiency Exam), CST in California, TAKS in Texas, and AIMS in Arizona, to name a few, illustrate the continued if not increasing emphasis on accountability mechanisms for students and schools. Close to half of Latinos in public schools attend high-poverty schools with teachers who have high turnover rates and inadequate qualifications. Latino students are also more likely to attend schools in states that have exit exams (Center on Education Policy, 2010). Thus, high-stakes testing is a prevalent feature directly tied to education service delivery for Latino students in the United States. A growing concern with the current policy framework is the trend among schools and districts to "teach to the test" to improve exam scores to acceptable levels, which raises the following set of questions: What challenges do high-stakes tests create for educating Latino students? What challenges are embedded in the current policy framework, and are they fostering an increase in the number of Latinos being "left behind" or dropping out from school? Do high-stakes tests address the issue of resource inequities? Finally, what approaches to assessment may be more beneficial to meeting the needs of Latino students?

While this chapter cites several critiques of the high-stakes nature to the current accountability framework, it acknowledges the important role of assessing student learning and progress as a means of *improving* the opportunities that Latino students have to learn in the education system in the United States. Some of the well-documented critics of high-stakes exams (Nichols & Berliner, 2007; Valenzuela, 2005) also value the role that assessment plays as a measure of understanding the gaps in education that Latinos and other minority students experience in this country.

This chapter provides an overview of the current context of accountability in the United States and the role that high-stakes testing plays in the education of Latino students. The data utilized in this chapter come from the following sources: National Assesssment of Educational Progress (NAEP) test score data from the National Center for Education Statistics; a case study conducted among Latino middle and high school students, parents, and teachers in Washington State; AIMS data from the Arizona Department of Education; and exit exam data from the California Department of Education.

The chapter concludes by providing policy considerations, as educators and policy makers alike continue to grapple with low Latino student performance on state and federal exams and their implications for Latino student success along the P-20 continuum.

CONTEXT FOR ACCOUNTABILITY

The issue of assessment and evaluation of student learning has historically been based on the premise that the function of testing is to improve student learning and ultimately raise achievement levels. Measuring student progress has been a prevalent feature of the American public education landscape with respect to policy and practice.

However, the increased role of the federal government in public education service delivery is a relatively recent phenomenon, as states have primarily controlled approaches to schooling in the United States (Beadie, 2004; McGuinn, 2006; Kirst, 1984). The Smith Hughes Act of 1917 was among the first pieces of legislation by the federal government to allocate funding to K–12 schools to teach agriculture. And the 1954 Supreme Court decision in *Brown v. Board of Education* represents the first federal attempt to desegregate schools in America. *Brown* found segregated schools to be a violation of the Fourteenth Amendment; it was one of the early attempts to provide all students with access to an equitable education and a comparable foundation for academic achievement.

The concern for student achievement is evident throughout history, as the United States has attempted to remain competitive if not ahead of other developed nations. The launching of *Sputnik* in 1957, for example, initiated an era of science education reform, as political leaders in the United States worried about losing ground in the field of science and being second to the Soviet Union in space exploration. The successful launching of the Soviet spacecraft led to nationwide efforts and federal investment through the Office of Education's National Defense Education program[2] in the late 1950s and 1960s, supporting collaboration between notable science professors and classroom teachers on curriculum development and revision, science standards, and the development of science labs in schools (Rutherford, 1998). *Sputnik* also led to greater attention to science, with over 15 years of investment by the federal government, and largely placed the responsibility of raising the nation's level of competitiveness in science on schools; however, individual schools were not singled out or penalized for the lack of student knowledge of science concepts. Rather, the concerns raised by the federal administration to remain internationally competitive encouraged greater attention to the field of science in K–12 schools.

Several pieces of legislation followed *Sputnik,* in part due to pressures emerging from the civil rights movement, and served to complement the Civil Rights Act of 1964, enacted during the Johnson administration. The Elementary and Secondary Education Act (ESEA) of 1965 served as the foundation for a more direct relationship between the federal government and state education systems. ESEA in particular was a key element of the War on Poverty under the Johnson administration and sought to address school inequalities in the United States by creating a special funding allocation, Title I, for schools to better meet the needs of low-income children in the United States. ESEA also marked the beginning of Head Start. ESEA was amended in 1968 to establish Title VII, and the Bilingual Education Act was enacted to address the needs of bilingual and multicultural children with limited English skills. One important result of these federal policy approaches was the creation of categorical aid programs that directly relate to the national policy arena (e.g., poverty, economic competitiveness), features that remain prevalent elements of current educational policy initiatives such as No Child Left Behind (NCLB).

The National Assessment of Educational Progress (NAEP), which dates back to 1969, was among the early attempts to measure student achievement in grades 4, 8, and 12. Otherwise known as "the Nation's Report Card," NAEP assesses student knowledge in reading, mathematics, science, writing, U.S. history, civics, geography, and the arts from a subsample of the school-age population. NAEP expanded to provide state-level assessment in 1990, to assess how states are performing among student subpopulations.

The 1983 publication of the report *A Nation at Risk* by the National Commission on Excellence in Education spawned an even greater emphasis on accountability and raised concern that the students attending U.S. schools were not prepared to meet the demands of the workforce or to be leaders in the key industries that fuel the American economy. The report reflects the framework for education reform today, one rooted in fear of "falling behind" as a world leader and the need for greater accountability among schools and colleges. The report uses the term *mediocrity* to describe the students and their preparation: "The educational foundations of our society are presently being eroded by a rising tide of mediocrity that threatens our very future as a Nation and as a people." (p. 5). *A Nation at Risk* was in large part a direct response to the Cold War era under the Reagan administration and led to increased federal investments in public education. The broad areas of reform outlined in the report include: (1) content of the curriculum to include emphasis on the core subjects; (2) standards and expectations; (3) time-on-task learning the new basics; (4) teaching; and (5) teaching leadership and fiscal support. The "content" area includes five "new basics" that essentially outline "the following curriculum during their 4 years of high school: (a) 4 years of English; (b) 3 years of mathematics; (c) 3 years of science; (d) 3 years of social studies; and (e) one-half year of computer science. For the college-bound, 2 years of foreign language in high school is strongly recommended in addition to those taken earlier" (p. 5). *A Nation at Risk* led to a greater emphasis on standards as well as attention to high school graduation requirements, and reinforced the need for students to learn what the report called "the new basics."

Following *A Nation at Risk*, a shift also occurred from expasizing curriculum content, as seen in the wake of *Sputnik*, to placing greater importance on the outcomes of student learning. This paradigm shift can also be seen through Goals 2000 in 1993, a bill that sought to increase the federal level of influence over states and local reform efforts by providing incentives to states to implement standards-based reforms (McGuinn, 2006).

Following Goals 2000, the Elementary and Secondary Schools Act of 1965 was up for reauthorization and led to the Improving America's Schools Act (IASA) in 1994. IASA became part of the Clinton administration's effort to reform U.S. schools and built on the efforts of Goals 2000 to align existing federally funded education programs with state standards. IASA required annual student assessment and encouraged a single state accountability system, but it did not penalize states for not having a single statewide accountability system, as was the case with No Child Left Behind. The increased emphasis on state standards, the alignment of assessments with standards, the option for Title I schools and districts to establish charter schools, and IASA introduced the notion of "adequate yearly progress" that states were to define based on student performance on state assessments (McGuinn, 2006). IASA and efforts by the Clinton administration to move schools closer to creating state and federal standards can be described as providing a narrower framework for federal intervention in K–12 education to raise achievement in low-income schools.

NO CHILD LEFT BEHIND

The alarmist language of "falling behind" presented in *A Nation at Risk* in 1983 and IASA in 1994, together served as a foundation for the political discourse for education reform that dominates the present context for accountability, namely the No Child Left Behind Act of 2001, which became law in 2002. No Child Left Behind, a product of the Bush administration, has expanded the themes and concerns raised in *A Nation at Risk* and IASA, and it further expands the federal role in education reform by applying an accountability framework for all states. No Child Left Behind outlined the following priorities to be funded under Titles I-VII federal funding programs:

1. Improving the academic performance of disadvantaged students
2. Boosting teacher quality
3. Moving Limited English Proficient students to English fluency
4. Promoting informed parental choice and innovative programs
5. Encouraging safe schools for the 21st century
6. Increasing funding for impact aid
7. Encouraging freedom and accountability (NCLB, 2001).

No Child Left Behind (NCLB) represents a top-down approach to education, with the federal government mandating reform and placing emphasis on testing and outcomes, while teachers and school staff are left to develop approaches to raise student scores without overshadowing daily instruction (Moran, 2000). Many researchers and practitioners are claiming that the policy has not held up to its promise of "leaving no child behind" and that it has contributed to a greater number of students being left behind, penalized, and underserved (Nichols, Glass, & Berliner, 2006; Valenzuela, 2005). Under NCLB, states must develop a statewide accountability system to measure "adequate yearly progress" (AYP). By 2014, all students are supposed to test at the "proficient level" in reading and math.

NCLB is part of the accountability movement that has led to the development of ongoing measures that are designed to create statewide assessment systems to measure student performance and address areas for improvement among students not performing at passable rates. This approach to assessment has adversely impacted Latino students in the K–12 schools, as it has led to statewide and local approaches that focus on outcomes (test performance) rather than also taking into consideration the inputs necessary for optimal learning and achievement. This framework has extended into the Obama administration, with an even greater emphasis on outcomes, where testing continues to be front and center of defining student success. The underlying assumptions of the present accountability framework are that attaching consequences to education reform will raise student achievement. The approach does not solve the *education* and *opportunity gap* that exists for Latino students.

Using assessments to retain or promote students and withholding a student's diploma for not passing an exit-level examination are examples of how the current NCLB accountability framework emphasizes outcomes rather than the inputs (e.g., curricular resources, teacher professional development, physical resources) that students are exposed to in school (see Valencia, Villarreal, & Salinas, 2002). This approach also serves as an example of how assessment, as it is currently being used, is perhaps doing more harm than good for students and education stakeholders alike (see Nichols & Berliner, 2007). Valencia and colleagues (2002) discuss how Senate Bill 4 in Texas[3] went into effect in 2002 as an extension of the NCLB accountability framework and requires third graders to pass a reading exam (in English or Spanish) to be promoted to the fourth grade. SB 4 raises concern over the detrimental impact of this high-stakes accountability educational statute for Latino students, as many Latino students are likely to represent the largest portion of students retained.[4]

Studies have confirmed that students who are retained are more likely to have lower achievement levels (Holmes, 1989; Valencia et al., 2002) and to drop out of high school (Brooks-Gunn, Guo, & Furstenberg, 1993; Rumberger, 1995; Valencia et al., 2002; Warren, Jenkins, & Kulick, 2006). For example, Warren and colleagues (2006) explored the role of high school exit exams on completion rates and found that the more difficult state exit exams did in fact lead to lower high school completion rates and higher rates of GED test taking.

As a result of NCLB, states continue to create statewide assessment mechanisms as well as exit exams for high school graduation but have not adequately addressed the root causes of lower passing rates among students of color, including Latinos. In many states, NCLB has led to high failure rates among Latino and African American students from high-poverty areas, leaving students from the most disenfranchised communities without a high school diploma upon exiting high school, and raises concerns about their life options beyond secondary education. ESEA and subsequent congressional acts have fallen short of their goal of addressing the academic needs of poor and minority children in school via categorical aid such as Title I.

The inequitable practices in the K–12 system have led to landmark cases on behalf of students who have been subject to unjust practices in school through the use of testing. In the case of *Debra P. v. Turlington* (1984) in Florida, African American students questioned the high school graduation test required for a diploma on the basis that the exam was being administered without notice to students and used to segregate African American students into remedial courses. The court ruled on behalf of the students, requiring schools to provide adequate notice regarding both the test administration schedule as well as exposure to the curriculum that reflects the content of the exam.

The state of Texas, perhaps one of the leading states in this high-stakes accountability framework for education, is also the furthest along in legal action against high-stakes tests. The Mexican American Legal Defense and Educational Fund (MALDEF) filed a class action suit against the state, in *American GI Forum v. Texas Education Agency* (2000), stating that the TAAS (Texas Academic Assessment System) graduation requirement discriminates against Latino and African American students and violates their due process, as they have unequal access to resources in schools. The court ruled that while the exams do appear to negatively affect Latino and African American students, this was not the "intent" of the TAAS exam. Rather, it was designed to motivate students to learn and perform on such exams (Moran, 2000; Valencia et al., 2002). While the ruling in this case was largely a defeat to challenges of exit exams in Texas, it raises the important issue of whether the legal system in other states may be a venue for such action. In *American GI Forum v. Texas Education Agency* (2000), one important acknowledgment the courts made was the fact that the TAAS exam did in fact have a disparate impact on Latinos and African Americans, as they achieved far lower passing rates than their White peers.

In *Valenzuela v. O'Connell* (2007), the Alameda County Superior Court first ruled against maintaining the California High School Exit Exam (CAHSEE) as a condition of graduation for the class of 2006. The ruling suspended the CAHSEE as a requirement for graduation. State Superintendent of Public Instruction Jack O'Connell, however, asked the California Supreme Court to appeal the Alameda County court decision and uphold the exit exam. The California Supreme Court ruled in favor of O'Connell in 2007, mandating the implementation of the CAHSEE by all schools and districts in the state of California. While the arguments included a discussion of the differential passing rates for low-income and minority populations, the trend is to place the onus of an inequitable education and preparation on the student in states where exit exams are in place.

This trend is likely to exacerbate higher dropout rates and a greater level of disengagement with school among students failing such exams after repeated attempts. The underlying question we should be asking is: Why are these students failing to pass state exams and what can be done to improve these outcomes? Are there other options for measuring student progress and success that do not place the onus of achievement solely on the shoulders of students? NCLB requirements and subsequent statewide exit exams that have evolved across 28 states as a result of meeting NCLB requirements move away from the initial intent of ESEA. NCLB calls for accountability without the emphasis on collective responsibility and adequate resource allocation to raise achievement in schools and for underrepresented populations in greatest need of academic supports.

THE ACHIEVEMENT GAP AS A REFLECTION OF THE EDUCATIONAL OPPORTUNITY GAP

Uneven achievement levels between Latinos and their White and Asian American peers are largely a result of the differential inputs in education services that Latinos receive as they progress through the public school system. A myriad of factors play a role in the educational status of Latino youth, including an uneven distribution of school and district resources, inequitable access to curriculum, lack of intervention and services for English Learners, coming from low-income households, and limited access to highly trained teachers (Gándara & Contreras, 2009; Rodriguez & Rolle, 2007). Students' experience in school plays a vital role in how they navigate the preK–12 system and beyond, receiving (or not) the tools to acquire academic, life, and social skills to navigate through life.

The majority of Latino students in the United States attend urban schools, and close to half of the Latino students have parents with less than a high school education (U.S. Census Bureau, 2009). According to the National Center for Education Statistics (NCES), 49% of Latino fourth-grade students were enrolled in schools with the highest measure of poverty (schools with greater than 75% of students eligible for free or reduced-price lunch), compared to 5% of White and 16% of Asian/Pacific Islander stu-

TABLE 3.1. NAEP Average Scaled Scores for Fourth Graders in Math, Selected Years, 2000–2009

Race/ethnicity	2000	2003	2005	2007	2009
White	234	243	246	248	248
Black	203	216	220	222	222
Latino	208	222	226	227	227
Asian American	‡	246	251	253	255
American Indian	208	223	226	228	227

‡ Reporting standards not met.
Note: Black includes African American, Hispanic includes Latino, Pacific Islander includes Native Hawaiian, and American Indian includes Alaska Native. Race categories exclude Hispanic origin unless specified. The NAEP Mathematics scale ranges from 0 to 500. Details may not sum to totals because of rounding. Some apparent differences between estimates may not be statistically significant.
Source: U.S. Department of Education, Institute of Education Sciences; National Center for Education Statistics; National Assessment of Educational Progress (NAEP) 2000, 2003, 2005, 2007, and 2009 Mathematics Assessment.

dents (NCES, 2010). The low-income levels of Latino students also translate into limited (if any) access to health care and lower levels of preschool enrollment. Thus, Latino students are more likely to enter school with greater needs and less preparation (Gándara & Contreras, 2009).

In addition, Latinos are more likely to attend schools that are segregated by race, poverty, and language; they now represent the group with the highest high school dropout rates (Frankenberg, Lee, & Orfield, 2003; Gándara, 2010; Gándara & Contreras, 2009; Gándara & Orfield, 2010). The segregated context of education that Latino students experience is perhaps part of the explanation for patterns of low achievement in schools, as Latino students are more likely to have differential inputs both within the school and in their communities to support their educational development. Table 3.1 presents the NAEP math scores for fourth graders from 2000 to 2009, which are considerably lower than those of their White and Asian American peers.

From 2003 to 2009, Latino students did not raise their achievement levels in the NAEP average test scores. The primary concern for Latino students, who constitute the majority ethnic group in many states, stems from a pattern of low achievement on standardized exams that is likely to continue as they progress through the primary and secondary grades and may also lead to lower scores on state-level assessments, including high school exit exams. The fourth-grade NAEP math data show that gaps in achievement, particularly between Latinos and Whites and between Latinos and Asian Americans, begins very early.

Statewide Standardized Exams

All states have some form of standardized exams to measure student performance in core content areas. As a federal requirement under NCLB, states are required to measure adequate yearly progress on statewide assessments. Thus, greater emphasis continues to be placed on statewide assessment mechanisms to meet NCLB requirements for student learning in the content areas of reading and math. In addition, Latino students are most likely to reside in states with a high stakes accountability framework, including the administration of exit exams. In the 2009–10 school year, 83% of all students of color in public schools, 78% of low-income students, and 84% of English Learners were enrolled in schools in states that had exit exams (Center on Education Policy, 2010).

In addition to the presence of exit exams, testing dominates the landscape in states with high concentrations and growing proportions of Latino students. In Arizona, 40% of the student population is Latino. The AIMS exam in Arizona is administered for grades 3–12 in the academic areas of reading, writing, and math. The 2009 scores for reading and math in Table 3.2 illustrate lower levels of performance among all underrepresented groups, with very minimal gains from the previous year.

The AIMS data illustrate a recurring issue for Latino students—lower performance on standardized achievement exams compared to their White peers across all grade levels. What is important to note for Arizona is the comparable sample sizes between White and Latino students at the elementary level and a considerable achievement gap between the two groups, with an 82% passing rate on math for Whites compared to 62% for Latinos at the elementary level. Further, the percentage of ELL students passing math in 2009 at the elementary level was 34%, the lowest across all groups. The passing rates for Latinos in math is considerably low, with 59% passing the AIMS. Since Latino students will constitute a large base of Arizona students at the high school level in coming years, these data raise a serious concern over the exit exam feature of the AIMS assessment system necessary to graduate high school.

In California, the same pattern emerges on the California Standards Test (CST) exam. Close to half of the students at the K–12 level in California are Latino (49%, with 24.2% English Learners) compared to 27.9% White, the second-largest ethnic group in the state (California Department of Education, 2010). However, achievement patterns differ significantly, with Latino students scoring far below their White peers on the CST, as seen in Table 3.3.

The California data mirror Arizona's pattern, with Latino students scoring far below their White counterparts on the CST exams over the 6-year period examined (2003–2009). While test scores have shown marginal im-

TABLE 3.2. AIMS Test Results, All Districts, Elementary and High School, by Ethnicity (2009)

		White	African American	Latino	Native American	Asian American	ELL
MATH % Meeting Standard	Elementary	82 (n =216,814)	59 (n = 28,966)	62 (n = 204,748)	51 (n = 25,978)	86 (n = 14,895)	34 (n = 54,152)
	High School	81 (n = 35,134)	57 4511	59 (n = 28,465)	48 (n = 4,384)	86 (n = 2,327)	20 (n = 4,008)
READING % Meeting Standard	Elementary	83 (n = 216,874)	64 (n = 28,965)	61 (n = 204,816)	53 (n = 25,985)	84 (n = 14,894)	26 (n = 54,175)
	High School	86 (n = 35,373)	66 (n = 4,540)	63 (n = 28,745)	53 (n = 4,398)	85 (n = 2,323)	16 (n = 4,075)

Source: www.ade.state.az.us, 2010.

provement in later years, this improvement has not mitigated the achievement gap between underrepresented students and their Asian American and White peers. The test data reveal a trend of lower performance on both math and English/language arts. As for exit exam performance among Latino students, close to half of the Latinos passed the exam in 2009 (see Table 3.4). In many other states with exit exams, the data are alarming, with Latino, American Indian, and African American students in particular having the lowest passing rates. It is important to note, however, that all groups have passing rates below 50%. These data are disconcerting and suggest that an overwhelming majority of California high school students are unable to pass the state exit exam. These data further reflect the failure to optimally educate Latino high school students. In addition to low overall passing rates for Latino students, EL students, in particular, have the lowest passing rates among the subgroups tested (Reardon, Atteberry, Arshan, & Kurleander, 2009).

There have been many claims about the adverse impact of exit exams, particularly research that contains interview data from students and parents directly about the effects that such exams have on a student's self esteem or the motivation to stay in school (Contreras et al., 2008). However, few studies have substantiated these claims with individual district-level data. In a study using data from four individual school districts in California, Reardon and colleagues (2009) explored the impact of exit exams on students in California by exploring the effects on persistence, achievement, and graduation. They found that low-achieving students subject to the California High School Exit Exam had lower graduation rates, resulting in at least an 11 percentage-point decline in graduation rates. They further found negative effects of the CAHSEE requirement disproportionately adversely affecting female students and students from underrepresented backgrounds. Finally,

TABLE 3.3. California Standards Test Results in English Language Arts and Math; Percentage of Students Scoring at Proficiency and Above by Subgroup (all students), 2003–2009

Subgroup	2003		2004		2005		2006		2007		2008		2009	
	Eng.	Math	Eng.	Math	Eng.	Math	Eng.	Math	Eng.	Math	Eng.	Math	Eng.	Math
African American	22	19	23	19	27	23	29	24	30	25	33	27	37	30
American Indian	31	29	31	28	36	32	37	35	39	34	40	36	44	39
Asian	55	60	56	60	62	65	64	67	66	67	69	70	73	72
Filipino	48	44	50	45	55	50	58	54	60	53	62	55	66	59
Latino	20	23	21	23	25	27	27	30	29	30	32	33	37	36
Pacific Islander	31	31	31	31	36	35	39	38	40	38	43	40	47	43
White	53	47	54	46	58	51	60	53	62	53	64	54	68	57
Eng. Learners	10	20	10	20	12	24	14	25	15	26	16	28	20	32
Economically disadvantaged	20	24	21	25	25	29	27	30	29	31	32	33	36	37

Note: These are aggregate data for students in grades 2–11 for language arts and grades 2–7 for math and represent the state totals.
Source: California Department of Education, 2006, 2010.

TABLE 3.4. California High School Exit Exam (CAHSEE) Results for Mathematics and English Language Arts (ELA) by Ethnicity, 2009 (percent)

Subject		All Students	African American	American Indian	Asian	Hispanic or Latino	White
Math	# Tested	12,387	891	27	212	8,259	592
	Passing	4,073 (33%)	257 (29%)	5 (19%)	98 (46%)	2,655 (32%)	209 (35%)
ELA	# Tested	12,910	644	26	813	8,507	610
	Passing	3,094 (24%)	136 (21%)	5 (19%)	165 (20%)	1,910 (22%)	163 (27%)

Note: The data represent all high school grades.
Source: California Department of Education, 2010.

the study concluded that no clear evidence exists for supporting the notion that exit exams serve as a motivating agent for raising achievement among low-achieving students across their four-district sample (Reardon et al., 2009).

An alternate approach to a comprehensive exit exam is seen in the case of Texas, where state policy makers phased out the TAKS as an exit exam in 2007 (SB 1031) and replaced the exit exam feature of the assessment with end-of-course exams in four core subject areas for grades 9–12. These end-of-course exams account for 15% of a student's grade and allow multiple pathways to graduation rather than relying on a single exit exam. The intent of the bill is to promote college readiness by establishing a college readiness diagnostic and allowing performance on Advanced Placement (AP) or International Baccalaureate (IB) college-level classes to substitute for end-of-course exams. Thus far Texas has witnessed an increase in passing rates, but progress for Latino students remains below their White and Asian American peers, consistent with national trends. In 2010, for example, 47% of Latino students passed the Algebra I end-of-course exam compared to 84% of Asian American and 71% of White students. And only 21% of LEP (Limited English Proficient, the majority of whom speak Spanish) students passed this exam. These data suggest that while multiple pathways are an important step forward in providing students with flexibility in illustrating academic competency for graduation, they do not solve the core issue of uneven inputs and academic preparation. Thus, similar problems remain with Latino and underrepresented students scoring lower on content exams than their White and Asian American peers.

ENGLISH LEARNERS IN THE ACCOUNTABILITY FRAMEWORK

As seen in the exit exam and select data for individual states, ELL students are the least likely to pass such statewide assessments. State assessment data illustrate how English Learners (EL) in this country are largely underserved in the K–12 system. Between 1979 and 2008, the number of school-age children who were bilingual increased from 9 to 21% (NCES, 2010), and of the students who spoke another language at home and were reported to speak English with difficulty, 75% were Spanish speakers (Aud et al., 2010). The disparate achievement levels of English Learners compared to their peers has been well documented and illustrates the largest gaps in achievement on statewide assessments (Fry, 2007; Gándara, Rumberger, Maxwell-Jolly, & Callahan, 2003). In the wake of English-only policies and efforts, such as Proposition 227 in California, schools are left with few options and minimal resources to adequately address the needs of English Learners in this country. While this student population requires the greatest investment to minimize test score gaps and raise levels of linguistic development, funding for EL programs is tenuous at best and varies widely across state and district contexts.

Arizona has been an ongoing battleground for the rights of EL students, with the *Flores* case, which was filed on behalf of EL students in 1992 and settled by the Supreme Court in June 2009. In the *Horne v. Flores* case, the Supreme Court reversed previous decisions from lower federal courts that upheld minimal resources and standards necessary for educating EL students. This decision is considered to be a setback for Latino students nationally, because the largest proportion of EL students in Arizona are Latino students. The case has larger implications for several states, with the majority failing to address the linguistic needs of Latino EL students and helping them to learn English while supporting their learning in the process. Many states have systematically ignored funding the educational supports necessary to raise EL achievement (Gándara & Contreras, 2009).

Gándara and colleagues (2003) cite a set of unequal resources that lead to the unequal outcomes we witness in student achievement among EL students in California. They present a range of inequitable conditions that EL students experience in California's schools, including inequitable access to highly trained teachers, limited professional development opportunities for teachers of English Learners, lack of appropriate assessments to measure EL achievement, lack of access to materials and curriculum resulting in a weak curriculum, and inequitable access to adequate facilities. This context for EL education, they contend, creates an unequal foundation for learning and explains the low achievement among this growing segment of the K–12 population in California (Gándara et al., 2003).

TABLE 3.5. Passing Rates on Exit Exams Among English Learners, Select States 2009 (percent)

State	Math		Reading Language Arts English	
	All Students	ELs	All Students	ELs
Arizona	70	20	74	16
California	33	26	24	15
Florida	81	47	57	12
Washington	45	8	81	36

Source: Arizona, California, Florida and Washington state departments of education.

For English Learners in this country, having to pass exit exams is likely to be an even greater obstacle because the programs for youth who need to learn English are underfunded, poorly staffed, and lack the appropriate resources within schools (Rumberger & Gándara, 2000; Gándara & Hopkins, 2010; Gándara & Contreras, 2009). Given this grossly deficient context for educating Latino EL students, exit exams further demonstrate even larger gaps in achievement. The passing rates for English Learners are therefore even lower for this group compared to their peers, as seen in the achievement levels on exit exams for select states in Table 3.5.

The low pass rates among EL students have serious implications for graduation with a diploma among this population. More importantly, these test results leave me questioning the curricular offerings and additional academic support services that English Learners are receiving in their high school context to raise achievement levels and master the English language.

PLAUSIBLE EXPLANATIONS FOR GAPS IN ACHIEVEMENT

Some researchers have attributed these differential achievement levels to the uneven inputs within schools, student curricular choices that mirror tracking, and limited social capital within the home and community (Jencks & Phillips, 1998; Nettles, Millett, & Ready, 2003; Zwick, 2004); others have attributed differential performance on standardized exams like state exams to testing biases that adversely affect communities of color (see Gould, 1995). This section presents the challenges that high-stakes tests create for educating Latino students as well as the challenges embedded in the current policy framework, including a discussion of resource inequities that inhibit progress toward achieving state and federal requirements.

Fulfilling the Stereotype

Claude Steele (1997) has developed the theory of "stereotype threat" to explain why many African Americans, as well as other students of color, may perform poorly or become disengaged with school. In his landmark study, Steele found that African American students scored lower on tests than other students after being told that other ethnic groups regularly performed better on the exam than African Americans; as a result of this pre-exam information, these students experienced performance anxiety and pressure that they might continue the previous patterns of low performance. Steele suggests that this belief of inferiority can lead to greater disengagement with school in general out of fear of living up to the stereotypes that exist regarding their ethnic group.

Given comparable educational experiences for African American and Latino youth, similar patterns have emerged for Latino students with respect to performance on standardized exams and disengagement in school. While the psychological impact of exit exams has yet to be revealed for Latino students, informal accounts from parents suggest that exit exams are adversely affecting Latino student motivation to graduate from high school due to a sense of hopelessness that they experience after failing initial attempts. Fear that they cannot pass the exit exam may contribute to higher levels of disengagement with school (Contreras et al., 2008).

In the state of Washington, for example, according to parent feedback given in the survey results of a statewide investigaion of Latino opportunities to learn, many parents conveyed the importance of expectations and information (Contreras et al., 2008). Parents were concerned that the climate in schools influenced student self-perceptions, which in turn influenced expectations. One parent said, "There are many problems in Eastern Washington relating to discrimination in the schools. There is a sense that Anglo teachers don't care if Latino youth fail."

In addition to the issue of stereotype threat on high stakes exams, even Latino high achievers are more likely to have a lower self-perception of their ability in the content areas of reading, writing, and science. For example, in a study conducted on the SAT test-taking pool of high school students, Latinos were less likely than their peers to rate themselves in the highest 10th percentile in comparison to their peers across all areas, particularly in math (Gándara & Contreras, 2009). These Latino students, while a self-selected sample, represent the likely college-going pool of students. Yet these high achievers, regardless of the fact that many had GPAs exceeding a 3.6, were more likely to rate themselves as above average or average rather than in the highest 10th percentile when asked to compare their ability to their peers on given subjects. These findings suggest that perhaps Latino students do not receive positive affirmation from adults or among their peers with respect to their ability in school (see, for example, Valenzuela, 1999).

Quality of Teachers

One of the key issues regarding the high-stakes nature of education service delivery for Latinos is teacher quality and experience. I have already noted earlier that Latino students are more likely to attend urban schools in high-poverty neighborhoods. Latinos are also more likely to attend schools with less qualified teachers. According to the Urban Institute, teachers in schools with high concentrations of English Learners are more likely to have "provisional, emergency, or temporary certification than are those in other schools" (Cosentino de Cohen & Clewell, 2007).

Not only are schools in more affluent areas better organized to provide more rigorous curricula, they also tend to have stronger teachers (Ferguson, 1998; Haycock, 1998). However, Haycock (1998) describes how children of color, regardless of their socioeconomic level, are more likely to be taught by teachers with lower test scores and less academic preparation than those who teach predominantly White children. The quality of the teacher, measured by certification, quality of institution from which the teacher received his or her degree, and test scores, has been shown in a number of studies to have a significant impact on student performance. Ferguson (1998) found that teachers with higher scores on basic skills tests for teachers and college entrance exams were more likely to produce significant gains in student achievement than their peers with lower scores (Ferguson & Ladd, 1996). Goldhaber and Brewer (1997), in an analysis of the National Educational Longitudinal Survey (NELS 88), also found a positive relationship between postsecondary degrees held by teachers in technical areas (math and science) and student achievement levels.

A study by the Education Trust (Peske & Haycock, 2006) examined teaching inequality for poor and minority students in Cleveland, Chicago, and Milwaukee schools and found large differences between the qualifications of teachers in high-minority, high-poverty schools. In particular, they found that more classes in high-poverty, high-minority schools are more likely to be taught by out-of-field teachers. This finding reinforces the already apparent fact that Latino, poor, and underrepresented students are less likely to attend schools with highly qualified teachers in comparison to more affluent schools with primarily nonminority students. Peske and Haycock (2006) also call for addressing teacher equity more directly by investigating the allocation and uneven usage of Title I money among districts.

They claim that some districts may be using funds that should be used for professional development, for salaries for teachers in Title I schools or who tend to be new to the field (Peske & Haycock, 2006).

Darling-Hammond (2000, 2010) also describes how teachers at successful schools tend to have strong academic credentials and who have been prepared to teach students with special needs, both of which enhance the success of the students in their classroom. Teachers with high levels of education and certification are also more likely to create "a strong coherent curriculum" through the processes of planning, their own professional development, and individual efforts to learn more about pedagogical approaches to best serve their students. They are also more likely to collaborate with their peers and develop a peer mentoring network, which allows them to share information and approaches to teaching. Conversely, in poor urban schools, there is high teacher turnover and limited resources to support teachers professionally (e.g., professional development opportunities). With the uneven access to qualified teachers, issues of high turnover in poor urban schools, and the fact that Latino students are less likely to be exposed to a coherent curriculum, reducing gaps in achievement represents a multifaceted dilemma.

School Inequity:
Access to Curriculum and Quality of Instructional Offerings

Differential access to curriculum and knowledge begins early. There is uneven access to quality preschool for Latino and underrepresented students, which places students on an unequal trajectory from the starting gate. In a study primarily focusing on Mexican immigrant children, Crosnoe (2006) discusses how the children from Mexican immigrant families had lower rates of learning in math compared to their native peers across races/ ethnicities, which represented a long-term risk for learning and achievement in school. Using the ECLS-K, which essentially assesses what children know before entering school, Crosnoe (2006) found differences in pre-K knowledge. He also describes how these initial differences become compounded or magnified in the process of formal schooling. While Crosnoe's findings were specific to Mexican immigrant children, he also found similar patterns of socioeconomic inputs across native Latino groups and comparable predicted achievement scores in math, although they were slightly higher than those of the Mexican immigrant children. His findings therefore are applicable to the umbrella Latino student group. His study conveys that attention in the earlier grades, particularly in math, is one effort worth investing in as a solution to reducing gaps in student achievement.

The particular school that a student attends can also have a significant impact on his or her academic achievement. Forty-six percent of Latino students attended high poverty elementary schools in 2008 (U.S. Department of Education, NCES, 2008). Latinos accounted for approximately 10 million students from urban, rural and suburban high poverty elementary and secondary schools (U.S. Department of Education, NCES, 2008). Schools in more affluent neighborhoods have been shown to provide more rigorous college preparatory and honors courses than schools in lower-income communities that largely serve populations of underrepresented students. For example, in a study of California schools, Betts, Rueben, and Danenberg (2000) found that only 52% of classes in the lowest-income schools met college preparatory requirements, while this figure rose to 63% in the highest-income schools. Similar patterns prevailed when the analysis was done by percent of non-White students enrolled in the school. Likewise, Betts and colleagues found that "the median high [socioeconomic status] school has over 50 percent more AP courses than the median low-SES school" (2000, p. 72). Based on analyses of the High School and Beyond database, Adelman (1999) concluded that the rigor of the curriculum to which students are exposed is more predictive of long-term academic outcomes than even the powerful variable of family socioeconomic status. That is, Adelman argues that the greatest amount of the variance in long-term academic outcomes among ethnic groups can be attributed to the differences in the groups' exposure to high-level curricula, particularly to advanced mathematics. Black and Latino students are least likely to take advanced mathematics courses because they are either not available in their schools or because they are less frequently counseled or "tracked" into them.

In California, where half of the K–12 population is Chicano/Latino, these curricular and school inequities are apparent and ultimately affect student performance on statewide assessments and the California High School Exit Exam. In an effort to directly address the school inequities that poor and minority students experience, *Williams v. State of California* (2004) sought to "ensure that every student in California is provided basic educational necessities, such as trained teachers, adequate textbooks, and minimally habitable facilities." The case, which argued that Latino and underrepresented students were grossly underserved in the California public education system, was filed by the American Civil Liberties Union (ACLU) Public Advocates, the Mexican American Legal Defense and Educational Fund (MALDEF), and other civil rights organizations, as well as the Morrison & Foerster LLP, firm on behalf of low-income underserved students. The case settled in 2005 in favor of the plaintiffs and led to greater state oversight of educational services and inputs that poor students of color receive in public schools. The specific bills that implemented the settlement agreement related to establishing minimum standards for school facilities; materials for instruction such as textbooks; teacher quality and appropriate training to teach EL students;

and financial resources to improve school facilities. Finally, all schools are now required to publish a School Accountability Report Card to ensure that they are in compliance with the requirements established by the Williams case. With the current financial crisis in California however, it is unclear whether the state will be able to maintain the promised resources to adhere to the settlement terms, and the degree to which schools and districts will be able to maintain oversight and implementation over time.

Financial Support for NCLB

The lack of resources and overall investment in schools, teachers, and students in large part explains the achievement gap between Latino students and their peers. Therefore we should not be surprised by the fact that under NCLB, the gaps in overall achievement are not significantly improving or closing among Latino, African American, and poor students when compared to their White, Asian American and middle to high income students.

The current accountability framework raises the overarching question of why we continue to accept and endorse the high-stakes nature of testing, particularly if we are not providing youth from poorer schools and neighborhoods with the necessary resources and supports to perform on these exams. Schools that have pronounced achievement gaps have not received a level of funding that would help them to achieve NCLB goals. And schools alone cannot solve the larger issue of poverty and its impact on children beyond the classroom (Gándara & Contreras, 2009).

While setting high standards and expectations for our students is essential, we also need to ensure that we provide schools with the resources to deliver the results we expect from them. According to the American Federation of Teachers (AFT), since the passage of No Child Left Behind, there has been a gap between the amount of funding Congress has promised and delivered for NCLB programs (AFT, 2007). Critics of NCLB argue that the Bush administration provided less funding than the education arena had expected. Table 3.6 shows the trends in funding that Congress authorized versus the amount actually appropriated for NCLB efforts under federal government allocations.

The gap from 2002 to 2007 between the amount that Congress had committed and the actual funding allocated is $40 billion dollars. Rather than investing greater levels of resources in students with the lowest passing rates on statewide and exit exams, the Bush administration allocated less resources for implementing NCLB requirements, further exacerbating achievement gaps for low-income students of color and EL students, groups

TABLE 3.6. NCLB Funding Allocations 2002–2007 (In billions of dollars)

Year	Funding Authorized	Actual Funding Appropriated	Gap
2002	26.4	22.2	4.2
2003	29.2	23.8	5.4
2004	32.0	24.5	7.5
2005	34.3	24.5	9.8
2006	36.9	23.5	13.4
2007	39.4	23.7	15.8

Source: U.S. Department of Education.

with the lowest passing rates on statewide assessments. The level of investment that occurred during the past administration suggests a shift in priorities by Congress and diminished the potential for schools and districts to achieve NCLB goals.

In 2009, with a change in the presidential administration, funding for education is seeing a notable increase, primarily through the American Recovery and Reinvestment Act of 2009, which allocated $140 billion to education through various initiatives such as Race to the Top, allowing states to compete for $4.3 billion in an effort to reform and overhaul state education efforts and raise statewide achievement among their lowest-performing student groups. Race to the Top, however, was only awarded to 11 states, none of which are states where Latino students are close to or over half of the K–12 population. The lack of regional representation in awards further demonstrates a limited understanding of the severe inequalities that Latino students face in schools, despite constituting a significant population in many states.

Other allocations under President Obama's stimulus package include $12 billion for Title I schools, $20 billion for school renovation, and a $79 billion grant program for states to avoid cuts to various programs and of various teachers. While the level of investment is a move in the right direction, with the Recovery Act representing unprecedented investment in education thus far, the funding is temporary and has not reached all states or districts. Nor does the funding focus on the core issue of badly needed reform, teacher diversification, cultural competency awareness and professional development, and EL professional certification incentives for a grossly underserved segment within the education system. A significant gap in funding remains if all schools are expected to provide the additional instruction and time to reduce achievement gaps among the lowest-performing schools and students.

CONCLUSION

The differential achievement levels between Latinos and Whites illustrate serious implications for the successful progression of Latino students beyond high school. The high-stakes accountability framework, while designed to address the gaps in achievement, has served to exacerbate the problem of uneven access by creating an outcomes-oriented model, one rooted in a deficit-model paradigm (see, for example, Valenzuela, 1999). It is no wonder that by the time Latinos get to the point of high school graduation—if indeed they make it—they have not received an education that prepares them for life beyond high school and success in higher education. The gaps in achievement discussed here clearly point to uneven inputs in education service delivery.

The growing importance placed on statewide exams requires ongoing analysis and evaluation, particularly with respect to the detrimental impact of these assessments on the educational progression of Latino students. While assessment is necessary and may be extremely useful to educators as well as the policy arena in knowing the achievement levels of students, how we use these measures needs greater attention and thoughtful action. The following recommendations are designed to provide tangible approaches toward changing the current punitive accountability paradigm to one of investment and shared responsibility for our collective future.

Recommendations

Provide schools with the resources to reduce the gaps that exist among Latino students and their peers. Policy initiatives designed to invest in and not punish students are the first step toward changing the high-stakes nature of education. For example, the city of Seattle has passed a Families and Education Levy, the most recent totaling $120 million, to invest in select schools in order to raise the achievement levels of students of color and low-income students not meeting the WASL standards. The Seattle Families and Education Levy has resulted in greater collaboration among teachers, administrators, service providers, and families, and it uses a holistic approach to education service delivery and dropout prevention.

Provide teachers with the necessary support and resources to modify curriculum and adhere to state content standards. Providing resources for the professional development of teachers is an important step toward validating and supporting their efforts to address the needs of Latino students.

Provide teachers with ongoing cultural competency professional development opportunities. Specific professional development of cultural competency will enable teachers to better understand the background, culture, and linguistic needs of Latino students. While the student population in the United States has experienced dramatic demographic changes, very little change has occurred among the teaching population, which remains largely White. Thus, professional development efforts would provide teachers with education on the culture, language, and history of the Latino students they serve.

Require Teacher Certification to include specific competencies for working with EL students. Creating specific teacher certification requirements to include core competencies for working with EL and bilingual students for all new teachers will better equip states with the abilty to serve a rapidly growing segment of K–12 populations in several state contexts (Contreras et al., 2008).

Provide English Learners at both the elementary and high school level with the necessary resources and strong curricular offerings to raise achievement. Expecting EL students to pass an exit exam when in many cases they do not receive services or additional academic support is inefficient public policy and tells us very little more than what we already know—that EL students need additional investment in education and a meaningful curriculum designed to accelerate learning (see also Gándara & Contreras, 2009).

Develop exams that measure the content of what is taught in schools. Continued efforts to align statewide assessments with state standards should remain a priority, as this approach is likely to provide the best measure of student learning for teachers and provide a mechanism for intervention. In addition, utilizing longitudinal data systems to measure the progress of all students, particularly EL students and those not performing at grade level, is an essential component to informing teacher practice and curricular content. Thus, teachers should play a role in providing direct feedback on these statewide assessments to ensure that they match the curriculum being taught in the classroom.

Do away with exit exams as a requirement for high school graduation. Ongoing assessment of student learning throughout grades K–12 is necessary to monitor student knowledge acquisition. However, withholding diplomas does more harm than good for Latino students and, as discussed, may lead to higher dropout rates (Valencia et al., 2002). Exit exams simply do very little to raise achievement levels, as seen in the case of the

CAHASEE (Reardon et al., 2009). In the 28 states that now have an exit exam in place, gaps in achievement remain pervasive for Latino and underrepresented students.

Establish multiple pathways to graduation rather than relying on a single pass/fail exam. As seen in the case of Texas (mandated through SB 1031), high school graduation may be achieved through passing end-of-course exams in addition to the statewide assessment. Students should be able to demonstrate knowledge in classes via their GPA in addition to performance on standardized exams. This multifacted approach to assessment provides students multiple avenues to earn a high school diploma. The move toward utilizing end-of-course exams in states like Texas, and more recently in Florida and Washington, represent a move in the right direction—exams that represent the academic content taught to students and an alternate pathway to graduation. The caveat, however, is the fact that such exams do not remove the existence of inequities in schools (e.g., in course offerences, teacher quality) and are likely to mirror previous patterns of low achievement among underrepresented and EL students.

Place value on locally developed and implemented assessments of student learning. While emphasis in the high-stakes accountability framework is on statewide assessments, placing greater value on locally developed and implemented assessments of student learning is a better way to measure progress and a more applicable approach for direct intervention. This also moves states and school districts away from the strong federal role in assessment and balances the "outcome" approach with one that may better adapt and react to student needs.

Blanket accountability policies like NCLB need to be evaluated as to whether they are adversely affecting students, teachers, schools, and districts. Have we set up a culture of fear within our schools? Assessment should be used to enhance learning, not point the finger at individuals who are falling behind. How do we shift the paradigm from a deficit model to one that focuses on the need for greater investment rather than punishment? We ask schools to make up for the socioeconomic differences, health disparities, and institutionalized barriers that exist in society without a fraction of the resources and level of investment necessary to accomplish the task. The gap in fiscal support authorized and delivered by Congress under NCLB tells a story of the failure to invest in Latino and underserved youth.

Greater attention must be placed on the serious crisis that exists in the education of Latino students—a 52% high school completion rate does a fairly good job of telling the current story, which is one of too little invested in a youthful and growing segment of the population. Indeed, assessments are one way that we can measure student progress. However, as seen with the data on passing rates for state-level assessments, the current accountability framework under NCLB appears to be further exacerbating the problem rather than fostering solutions to raise Latino student achievement. And since one in four U.S. residents will be Latino by the year 2050 (U.S. Census Bureau, 2008), the need to invest in this growing majority is critical for the economic infrastructure of the agricultural, technological, and business industries in the country (Gándara & Contreras, 2009).

The current story of Latino underachievement is one that must be addressed by multiple stakeholders and the policy arena. Testing and accountability measures explain only part of the current crisis and, as I have summarized, are contributing to the problem by using assessment to withhold diplomas and influence how education is delivered in schools. This story, while it is still in the process of being written for the growing numbers of Latinos in the K–12 system, has the potential to be altered rather than predetermined. And perhaps in this revised storyline, the Latino students who persist in the pipeline might not be depicted as the anomalies, but instead represent the norm, where a standard of high expectations and access to academic resources applies to all students, regardless of their racial, linguistic, neighborhood, parental education, and economic backgrounds. The stakes are too high for us to sit back and allow a punitive approach to dominate the education of our children.

CHAPTER 4

The Role of Financial Aid, Tuition Policy, and Affordability in Latino Higher Education Access

The rising cost of college places students who are the most economically disadvantaged at risk of dropping out of college or avoiding higher education altogether (Perna, 2004; Gladieux & Perna, 2005). College affordability is a key issue, in addition to academic preparation, that influences the transition to college for Latino students. According to the College Board, tuition and pricing over time have steadily increased, with the largest tuition increases occurring at public institutions (Baum & Ma, 2010; Baum & Steele, 2007). Affordability is both a concern and a barrier for Latino students and their families in pursuing higher education (Perna, 2004; Gándara & Contreras, 2009; Zarate & Pachon, 2006).

In *Refinancing the College Dream: Access, equal opportunity and justice for taxpayers,* St. John (2003) argues for applying a social justice framework to the principle of college access. That is, all students should possess equal opportunity to earn a postsecondary degree regardless of their socioeconomic status in this country, in part explained by tax efficiency. Applying John Rawls's (1971) theory of justice as fairness, he argues that each generation shoulders the responsibility to pass capital onto the next through educational opportunity (St. John, 2003). Financial aid is a key component toward ensuring that subsequent generations have the opportunity to acquire capital relevant to the marketplace, which ultimately leads to economic sustainability and mobility.

Financial aid is one of the primary mechanisms used by Latino students to address college affordability and represents an important aspect of college access and persistence for many high-achieving Latino students from low-income backgrounds (Cabrera, Nora, & Castañeda, 1992; Gándara & Contreras, 2009). Further, it is well documentd in higher education literature that financial aid, such as Pell Grants, influences college choice (Hansen, 1983; Manski & Wise, 1983; St. John, 2003) and persistence patterns among students (Cabrera, Stampen, & Hansen, 1990; St. John, Cabrera, Nora, & Asker, 2000; St. John et al., 2000). Many Latino students, given the low-income status and parent education levels are likely to rely on various forms of financial aid, in addition to working, to progress through college.

This chapter addresses the intersection among financial aid policy, tuition policy, and affordability that ultimately influences higher education access and degree completion among Chicano/Latino students in the United States. Data sources for this chapter include (1) an overview of relevant literature on financial aid and college access, (2) data from the National Center for Education Statistics (NCES), (3) data from the National Postsecondary Student Aid Study, and (4) data from a 2008 case study of Washington State on Latino student opportunities to learn. Together these data provide an important context for understanding the policy framework for tuition policy and trends, federal and state approaches to financial aid, and how these factor into affordability and college access for low-income underrepresented Chicano/Latino students.

SOCIOECONOMIC STATUS

The socioeconomic status of Latino students who attend public schools in the United States has historically lagged behind that of their White peers.[1] One common measure of socioeconomic status in the United States is attainment of a bachelor's degree. Many have argued in sociological and education bodies of literature (see for example, Bourdieau & Passeron, 1977; Coleman, 1988; Gándara, 1995; Gándara & Contreras, 2009; Stanton-Salazar, 2001, 2004), social capital is transferred to youth based on their level of exposure at home and in the community to activities and behaviors that support their intellectual development and ultimately affect their educational achievement in school (DiMaggio, 1982; Contreras, 2005b).

A closer look at parent education levels for students in the K–12 system (Figure 4.1) shows clear differences in BA attainment levels between Latinos and Whites, with Latino parents. In addition, Latino parents are most likely to have less than a high school education (Table 4.1). In fact, White parents are more than three times more likely to have a bachelor's degree than Latino parents. Such low education levels, particularly less than a high school education, suggest that Latino parents are not familiar with the requirements for college in particular or perhaps the postsecondary education system in general. Schools therefore play a key role in compensating for the socioeconomic differences that exist between Latino families and oth-

FIGURE 4.1. Percent of K–12 Students with Parents Who Have a BA or
Greater, 1979–2006

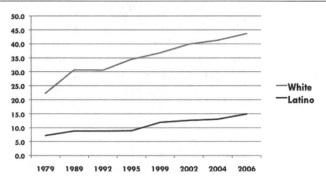

Source: NCES, 2009

er groups. And while schools cannot achieve this in isolation (Gándara &
Contreras, 2009), they have the opportunity to address specific educational
needs for Latino and EL students, relevant and rigorous content to assist
students prepare for and succeed in college.

The data on the poverty status of Latino families compared to Whites
further convey differential economic resources within the home (Table 4.2).
Examining poverty status among 5–17 year olds for select years from 1995
to 2006 illustrates how Latino families are three times more likely to be
considered poor (below the poverty threshold) or near-poor compared to
White families. These data suggest uneven inputs for Latino children as they
navigate the school system. Staff in the education system may not be fully
aware of the economic challenges of Latino students and their families or
the limited resources that exist within the home to purchase items that support and complement educational instruction (school supplies, art supplies,
instruments or music lessons).

While there are numerous resources within communities that cannot be
assigned dollar amounts—such as having a two-parent household, extended
family members and support networks, a dual-language home, or witnessing a strong work ethic—the educational and poverty levels of Latino families suggest large gaps in the financial means that Latino parents have to
expend substantial resources on rising educational costs.

A CASE STUDY OF WASHINGTON

We know from several data sources that Latino parents possess a strong
desire to see their child earn a college degree despite lower income levels

TABLE 4.1. Education Levels of U.S. Parents of 5- to 17-Year-Olds, Select Years, 1995–2006

Level	1995		1999		2002		2006	
	Latino	White	Latino	White	Latino	White	Latino	White
Less than high school	43.5	5.5	40.8	5.2	38.0	4.5	32.4	4.0
High school	25.4	28.5	26.3	26.2	27.7	24.2	28.8	22.0
Some college	22.3	31.4	21.1	31.8	21.7	31.3	23.8	30.3
BA degree or higher	8.9	34.5	11.9	36.8	12.6	39.9	14.9	43.7

Source: NCES, The Condition of Education, 2010.

TABLE 4.2. Poverty Status of U.S. Families of 5- to 17-Year-Olds, Select Years, 1995–2006

Level	1995		1999		2002		2006	
	Latino	White	Latino	White	Latino	White	Latino	White
Poor (Below poverty threshold)	39.8	12.1	33.6	10.8	28.8	9.5	26.5	9.9
Near-poor (families at 100% to 199% of the poverty threshold)	30.7	19.3	31.8	16.4	32.5	16.1	32.8	15.4
Nonpoor (families at 200% or more than the poverty threshold)	29.5	68.6	34.6	72.7	38.7	74.4	40.7	74.7

Source: NCES, The Condition of Education, 2010.

and education levels or a lack of familiarity with the U.S. secondary and postsecondary education systems (Gándara & Contreras, 2009). A case study conducted in Washington State on Latino students (Contreras et al., 2008) shows low parent education and income levels but very high aspirations for their children. In this study, the findings were consistent with the profiles seen for Latinos nationally, with Latino parents having considerably lower education levels, and Latino students more likely than their peers to have parents with less than a high school education. In fact, most of the Latino parents had "grade school or less" as their highest level of education. For example, 50.6% of their fathers had a grade school education or less, compared to only 15.2% their non-Latino peers (n = 245). A similar profile exists for the mothers' education level, with 38.8% of the mothers of Latino students having a grade school education or less. The parent education data, with most parents having less than a grade school as their highest level of educational attainment (Table 4.3), suggests that Latino families are likely to be in the lowest income brackets in their regional context. In addition, when parents were asked whether they rented or owned their homes, another marker of personal wealth, 63.2% of Latino parents reported that they rented their place of residence (n = 247).

Parent income data shows how 65% of the parent respondents made less than $39,000 annually. However, an overwhelming majority of Latino parents conveyed their intent to help their child pay for college, which indicates that Latino parents consider education a priority and are willing to offer whatever resources they have to support their child's educational efforts. However, with such modest income levels, disposable income for Latino families for educational expenses is likely to be limited. Thus, Latino parents therefore have economic constraints that inhibit their ability to significantly help their child with college costs. In addition, Zarate and Fabienke (2007), for example, have found that Latino parents lack knowledge about college costs as well as the multiple mechanisms or forms of financial aid available to assist their child pay for college.

Despite the barriers to college affordability that low-income levels present for Latino students (Gladieux, 2004), the hopeful nature of these students and their parents cannot be underestimated (Suarez-Orozco, Suarez-Orozco, & Todorova, 2008). The relatively high number of Latino students who aspired to college (79.7%) may be attributed to the hopeful disposition of first-generation students, whose families often came to the United States for educational opportunity and social mobility (Gándara & Contreras, 2009; Gándara, O'Hara, & Gutierrez, 2004; Gibson, Gandara, & Koyama, 2004; Grogger & Trejo, 2002; Suarez-Orozco, Suarez-Orozco, & Todorova, 2008). The majority of Latino students responded that they wanted to attend a 4-year institution after high school (60.2%), slightly more than their non-Latino peers (56.5%) in the sample. These findings convey how Latino student respondents in both the survey and focus groups were keenly aware of the benefits that a college degree is likely to have on their lives and future employment options.

In addition to planning to attend a 4-year college or university after high school, 64% of Latino students aspired to earn a bachelor's degree or higher. Over 22% of Latino and non-Latino students also expressed a desire to earn a graduate or professional degree as their highest level of education (Table 4.5). These high aspirations are also consistent with national data,

TABLE 4.3. Parent Education Levels

| | Latino | | Non-Latino | |
	Mother	Father	Mother	Father
Grade school or less	38.8 (n = 95)	50.6 (n = 121)	16.1 (n = 32)	15.2 (n = 29)
Some high school	35.1 (n = 86)	31.4 (n = 75)	16.1 (n = 32)	25.7 (n = 49)
High school diploma or less	13.9 (n = 34)	10.0 (n = 24)	20.1 (n = 40)	16.8 (n = 32)
Business or trade school	—	.4 (n = 1)	2.5 (n = 5)	2.6 (n = 5)
Some college	5.3 (n = 13)	2.9 (n = 7)	22.6 (n = 45)	15.2 (n = 29)
Associate or 2-year degree	2.0 (n = 5)	1.3 (n = 3)	7.0 (n = 14)	5.8 (n = 11)
Bachelor's or 4-year degree	2.9 (n = 7)	1.3 (n = 3)	10.6 (n = 21)	9.9 (n = 19)
Graduate or professional degree	2.0 (n = 5)	2.1 (n = 5)	5.0 (n = 10)	8.9 (n = 17)
Total	100.0 (n = 245)	100.0 (n = 239)	100.0 (n = 199)	100.0 (n = 191)

Source: Contreras et al. (2008).

TABLE 4.4. Latino Parent Income Levels (n = 247)

Income Level	Percent
Less than $10,000	7.6 (n = 17)
$10,000–19,999	18.4 (n = 41)
$20,000–39,999	39.0 (n = 87)
$40,000–59,999	20.6 (n = 46)
$60,000–89,999	9.9 (n = 22)
$100,000–179,999 or higher	1.7 (n = 4)
No response	2.7 (n = 30)
Total N	247

Source: Contreras et al. (2008).

but they convey a story where cracks in the education pipeline are real, where students are not prepared for higher education or simply fall short of their aspirations to transition to college and earn degrees.

While aspirations were high among Latino students in the Washington sample, specific questions and concerns arose during data collection around financial aid, particularly among undocumented immigrant students. Those

TABLE 4.5. Student Post–High School Aspirations, Washington

	Latino		Non-Latino	
	N	Percent	N	Percent
High school diploma or equivalent	36	15.5	18	9.2
Business or trade school	4	1.7	3	1.5
Some college	23	9.9	22	11.3
AA degree	21	9.1	18	9.2
BA degree	49	21.1	46	23.6
Some graduate or professional school	9	3.9	8	4.1
Master's degree	38	16.4	32	16.4
Graduate or professional degree	52	22.4	48	24.6
Total	232	100.0	195	100.0

Source: Contreras et al. (2008).

who were aware of HB 1079 (The DREAM Act in Washington) were most concerned about their ability to finance the cost of college because undocumented students do not qualify for in-state aid or federal financial aid. This presents a dilemma for students across the United States with similar legal standing and the need for greater financial options for a small proportion of high achieving and resilient college students, and will be further explored in Chapter 5.

Consistent with research on parental aspirations for their children (Goldenberg et al., 2001; Goldenberg & Gallimore, 1995), Latino parents in Washington also conveyed very high educational aspirations, with 46.2% wanting their child to earn a graduate or professional degree and 74.9% wanting their child to earn a bachelor's degree or greater as their highest level of education. In addition, 91.7% of parents indicated that they planned to help their child pay for college (Table 4.6).

These results are consistent with the findings from the Latino National Survey (Fraga et al., 2010), with 38.8% of parents responded that they wanted their child to graduate from college, and another 55% of parents who wanted their child to earn a graduate or professional degree (n=2815, based on the author's calculations).

The findings from the parent survey in Washington illustrate that Latino parents need information pertaining to their child's education and need to work with schools to become better engaged in the educational process of

TABLE 4.6. Highest Level of Education Parent Hopes for Child

High school grad	13	6.5
Business or trade school	1	.5
Some college	7	3.5
AA degree	29	14.6
BA degree	31	15.6
Some graduate school	2	1.0
Master's degree	24	12.1
Graduate (PhD) or professional degree (JD or MD)	92	46.2
Total	199	100.0

Source: Contreras et al. (2008).

their children. A clear disconnect exists between parent aspirations for their child and information about the processes, practices, and resources necessary for Latino children to transition to college. As one parent commented in a focus group: "We need more information about scholarships for the university. We have children with good grades but no information" (Contreras et. al., 2008, p. 57). While aspirations for their children are high, the low education, income, and literacy levels in English suggest that Latino parents in Washington are not well equipped to provide navigational support for their children. This presents an opportunity for schools, communities, and parents to create a network of support for Latino youth, where parents are supported, welcomed, and held accountable in the process of helping their children make informed decisions about the future. Both a challenge and opportunity exist for schools as well as policy makers to ensure that these students have the opportunities to fulfill such high aspirations and, in turn, better the livelihood of their communities and the state.

HISTORICAL AND POLICY CONTEXT FOR FINANCIAL AID

There are several key financial aid policies that have benefited students from low-income and diverse backgrounds. Financial assistance to attend college represents an even more critical aspect of the college access discussion, as the economy in both the United States and the world has changed over time, demanding a workforce with advanced training, depth of knowledge, and a skill set valuable to the marketplace. A college degree presently marks a minimal requirement for entry into middle class, higher-wage jobs, and has become a significant factor in predicting earnings (Kane & Rouse, 1995).

Perhaps one of the most notable federal pieces of legislation that established a precedent for programs which funded the costs associated with attending college, was the GI Bill, passed in 1944. The GI Bill was designed to help veterans acquire additional education and training that would enable them to compete in the workforce following their service in World War II. While this bill applied directly to military personnel, it served as an important model and precedent for student assistance and investment and led to the integration of servicemen and women into job sectors that may not have been open to them without a college degree or training. As a result of the GI Bill, over 8 million eligible veterans participated in education and training programs from 1945 to 1956, and college enrollments increased by 70% from pre–World War II levels (Chambers, 2000). In addition, with the Veterans Readjustment Act of 1966, such benefits were extended beyond veterans of war to those serving in the armed forces during peacetime. The GI Bill, through its direct federal aid for higher education, has been credited with expanding the middle class in the United States (Bennett, 1996; Chambers, 2000).

Another notable piece of legislation was the Higher Education Act of 1965, which specifically addressed the issue of affordability and opportunity for all U.S. residents. Under the Higher Education Act, Title IV of the act created the Trio Programs, including the Talent Search program, the Student Support Services Program, and the Ronald E. McNair Post-baccalaureate Achievement program, which provides disadvantaged college students with preparation opportunities for doctoral study. While these programs are not direct scholarship programs, they are student support programs that provide academic supports and educational opportunities for disadvantaged students from underrepresented backgrounds.

Figure 4.2 provides a timeline of key federal financial aid policies in the United States since the GI Bill.

The Basic Education Opportunity Grant (BEOG), established by the federal government in 1972, represents the first major need-based federal grant program for low-income students in the United States and a more central role for the U.S. government in ensuring equal educational opportunity to individuals seeking a postsecondary degree (Heller, 1999, 2001). Today this grant has been renamed the Pell Grant and was reauthorized as part of the Higher Education Act of 1980. Like its predecessor, Pell Grants provide financial assistance and pay for college-related costs for low-income students at the postsecondary level.

The 1992 Higher Education Amendments and the Taxpayer Relief Act further opened up opportunities for low-income students pursuing higher education. They provide tax breaks for students and parents with dependent children pursuing college with the HOPE scholarship credit and the Lifetime Learning Tax Credit.

FIGURE 4.2. Timeline of Key Federal Financial Aid Policies

1944 GI Bill (Servicemen's Readjustment Act)

1954 College Scholarship Service (CSS) created

1958 National Defense Act (PL88-452) which established the National Defense Student Loan Program (NDSL) and was the precursor to the Perkins Loan Program, the first Federal student aid program for low-income students

1964 Economic Opportunity Act of 1964 (established college work study, Head Start, Upward Bound)

1965 Higher Education Act of 1965 [authorized the Educational Opportunity Grant Program, Guaranteed Student Loan program (now Stafford Loan Program]

1966 Veterans Readjustment Benefits Act (extend GI Bill provisions to those serving in armed forces even in peacetime)

1972 Basic Education Opportunity Grant (is the origin of the Pell Grant)

1976 College Scholarship Service the Financial Aid Form (FAF)

1980 Higher Education Act reauthorized (Basic Education Opportunity Grant Program renamed and reauthorized Pell Grants)

1986 Michigan Education Trust, the first prepaid state tuition plan established

1992 Higher Education Amendments (requiring FAFSA to be free to public)

1997 Taxpayer Relief Act passed (Hope scholarship established, Lifetime Learning Tax Credit, Tax deductions for student loan interest)

1998 Higher Education Amendments (GEAR UP created)

2005 Higher Education Act of 2005 (part of Deficit Reduction Act of 2005, cut $12.7 billion from student aid)

2009 American Recovery and Reinvestment Act of 2009

2010 Post 9/11 GI Bill: Post-9/11 Veterans Education Assistance Improvements Act of 2010

Source: www.FinAid.org, 2009.

Fast forward to 2005, when significant cuts in financial aid were implemented under the Bush administration; at the same time, college costs were consistently rising, students were primarily left with the option of taking out loans as a viable option for college aid, working, or starting their postsecondary education in 2-year colleges. The Higher Education Act of 2005 cut approximately $12.6 billion from student aid and had significant implications for state aid programs that rely on federal aid for college students. In addition, the aid amounts that were raised were loan totals for qualifying students, with maximum loan amounts exceeding Academic Competitiveness Grants (which is $750 for first-year awards and $1,300 for second-year awards) (Higher Education Act, 2005, Section 8005). In addition, the first-year loan limit increased from $2,625 to $3,500 and the second-year loan limit went from $3,500 to $4,500 (National Association of Student Financial Aid Administrators, 2006). The implications of this act for higher education are likely to be far-reaching and set a precedent for greater reliance on student loans as an answer to rising college costs.

TRENDS IN COLLEGE PRICING

College affordability is a key issue that in many ways determines Latino and underrepresented student access to and success in higher education (Orfield, 1992; St. John, 2003 ; St. John, Cabrera, Nora, & Asker, 2000). Public institutions in particular have been the portal to opportunity for underrepresented students seeking bachelor's and postgraduate degrees. Affordability is a central concern in the current economic climate, where students continue to face rising tuition costs to compensate for state economic shortfalls.

Figure 4.3 illustrates the trends in college pricing during the past 30 years (select years) at public institutions. The trend illustrates an increase in tuition for in-state public institutions for both 2- and 4-year institutions, with the largest increases occurring at the 4-year level. Such increases have direct implications for affordability and access to colleges and universities, particularly for Latino and underserved students, who are more likely to come from families with lower median incomes and overall lower levels of socioeconomic status.

Over the past decade, in-state tuition and fees rose from 3.3% in 1990 to 5.6% beyond the rate of inflation at public 4-year colleges and universities (The College Board, 2010a). In addition, the greatest increases in tuition have occurred within the public sector, but the gaps are significantly large between the cost of attending public and private institutions (Baum & Ma, 2007; The College Board, 2010b). These changes come at a time when state appropriations for public higher education have diminished (The College Board, 2010a; Trostel, 2003; Trostel & Ronca, 2007). Trostel (2003) argues that the long-term effects of declining investment and support for higher education are lost opportunities for those who *would have* gone to college. Trostel and Ronca (2007) further argue that investing in higher education is a cost-effective economic tool for states and the nation because such expenditures maximize opportunities to invest in its population.

St. John (2003) takes the notion of opportunity a step further and calls for a refinancing of higher education, a social justice approach to funding higher education based on: (1) access for the majority; (2) an equal opportunity to enroll; and (3) justice for taxpayers. (p. 17). This approach to college financing takes into account equitable opportunities for accessing higher education as well as the per student taxpayer expenditures to address concerns about efficiency. Together, these dimensions provide a framework

FIGURE 4.3. Average Undergraduate Tuition and Fees for In-State Public Institutions, 2- and 4-year, Select Years 1985–2008

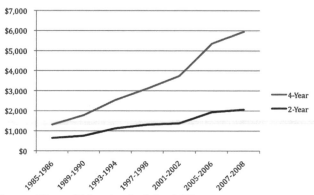

Source: Digest of Education Statistics, 2010.

for understanding the role of financial aid policy in college access, and the importance of equitable financing processes.

Financial Aid as a Response to Rising Costs

With the rising cost of tuition across higher education institutions in the United States as a response to state and federal economies, students are increasingly in need of financial aid options to afford a college education. The most common forms of financial aid include federal and state grants, scholarships, and loans. Federal and state grants, typically administered through Pell Grant funding, are designated for students from low-income backgrounds. Such programs have had the greatest impact on low-income and underrepresented student access since their inception. The trend in Pell Grant expenditures shows an increase in the number of Pell Grants and recipients over time. However, it is important to note that the average Pell Grant amount per recipient has remained relatively flat over the past 35 years (The College Board, 2010).

While the number of Pell Grants has risen, they make up a smaller proportion of the cost for attending both public and private institutions, as they had in the past. A decade ago in 1990, Pell Grants made up 45% of the cost for attending a public four-year institution compared to 34% in 2010 (Figure 4.4).

State Merit Aid

In addition to federal aid programs to assist students in financing higher education, there are also state merit aid programs such as the Georgia

FIGURE 4.4. Maximum Pell Grant as a Percentage of Tuition and Fees and Room and Board (TFRB) 1990–2011

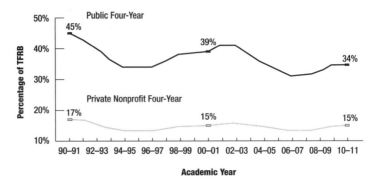

Source: The College Board, Trends in Student Aid, 2010.

HOPE (Helping Outstanding Pupils Educationally) scholarship, the Wisconsin Covenant, The PROMISE Scholarship in West Virginia, and The Washington Promise that provide scholarships to high-performing or competitively eligible students in their respective states. Seventeen states currently have statewide scholarship programs for students to attend college (Krueger, 2005).

One important critique of such state programs is that they do not widen access for the most economically disadvantaged students. (Heller & Marin, 2002, 2004; Marin, 2002; St. John & Chung, 2004). Rather, merit aid programs disproportionately benefit students from high-income families (Heller & Marin, 2004; Marin, 2002). And since Latino students are more likely to be from low-income families and have parents with less than a high school education, they do not fare well in securing many forms of state merit aid (Table 4.7).

Latino students are less likely to receive merit aid compared to their White peers, and when they do receive merit aid, the amounts are significantly lower than their white peers, who make up the largest group of students benefitting from grants greater than $6,500 (Table 4.7).

Merit, as it is presently conceptualized by state grant programs, is therefore narrowly defined and often based on academic indicators such as state standardized test scores (2 states), a combination of GPA and SAT/ACT test scores (10 states), or the top percentile of their graduating class (4 states) (Krueger, 2005). These eligibility standards, such as those that rely on test scores or the top percentile, reinforce the notion of inequity—that is, for low-income Latino students, standardized test scores, as discussed in Chap-

TABLE 4.7. Merit Only Grants by Race/Ethnicity, 2008

Race/ethnicity (with multiple)	White (%)	Black or African American(%)	Hispanic or Latino (%)	Asian (%)	Native Hawaiian / other Pacific Islander (%)
Total	61.8	14.0	14.1	5.9	0.7
$1-1,199	66.0	17.1	10.0	3.7	0.2
$1,200-2,999	74.6	10.1	8.8	2.9	0.3
$3,000-6,499	76.9	8.1	7.2	3.9	0.4
$6,500 or more	76.7	9.1	6.5	4.9	0.4

Source: The National Postsecondary Student Aid Study (NPSAS), 2008.

ter 3, are largely a reflection of inadequate preparation, resources, and inputs in the P-12 system. Thus, opportunities for minimizing racial inequity in college access are not optimized under merit aid state programs (Heller, 2002, 2008; Heller & Marin, 2002, 2004; Marin, 2002).

Trends in Financial Aid Need and Use

Trends in financial aid show fewer resources in the form of direct aid and scholarships and an increasing reliance on student loans to finance higher education. Students are taking out greater percentages of loans without the promise of a job following college graduation, leaving them with debt at the start of their entry into the workforce. Table 4.8 shows the percentage of full-time undergraduates receiving any type of financial aid by race/ethnicity for select years. The data illustrate a reliance on financial aid across all groups and an increase in financial need over time, with the highest levels of aid occurring in 2007–2008.

The higher percentages among underrepresented student groups suggest greater financial need and lower socioeconomic status, as seen in Chapter 2, with higher poverty rates and lower parent education levels among Latinos and underrepresented student groups.

Table 4.9 further illustrates noteworthy data with respect to student financial aid. The first is that Latino students are more likely to receive a lower total amount of financial aid than their White, African American, and Asian American peers. Second, they receive the lowest grant amounts compared to their peer groups, even though their need levels and low family incomes and poverty rates mirror patterns of other minority groups in the

TABLE 4.8. Percentage of Full-Time, Full-Year Undergraduates Receiving Financial Aid from Any Source by Race/Ethnicity: 1999–2000, 2003–2004, and 2007–2008

Race/Ethnicity	1999–2000	2003–2004	2007–2008
Total[1]	72.5	76.1	79.5
White	70.2	74.0	77.2
African American	88.2	89.2	91.9
Latino	78.7	80.7	85.2
Asian/Pacific Islander	60.9	66.1	68.3
American Indian/Alaska Native	81.1	81.9	85.2

[1] Total includes other race/ethnicity categories not separately shown. Race categories exclude persons of Hispanic origin.
Sources: U.S. Department of Education, National Center for Education Statistics, 1999–2000 and 2003–04 National Postsecondary Student Aid Study (NPSAS: 2000 and NPSAS: 04); 2007–2008 National Postsecondary Student Aid Study.

United States (Gándara & Contreras, 2009). Finally, for all groups, including Latino students, loan amounts are greater than grant amounts for all three years examined, suggesting a greater reliance on loans versus grants to pursue higher education (Hearn & Holdsworth, 2004; St. John, 2003). The concern with an increasing reliance on loans is the effect they have on persistence. Dowd and Coury (2006), for example, found that loans had a negative effect on student persistence. Students who did not borrow were more likely to persist than students who took out loans in college. Gladieux and Perna (2005) found similar results, with more than 20% of all borrowers dropping out of the cohort they examined. However, they acknowledged that well-documented risk factors, such as attending college part time or working full time, appear to have a greater impact on degree completion and persistence than borrowing alone (Gladieux & Perna, 2005).

These data are particularly relevant for Latino students, especially in looking at grant amounts, because Latino students have been found to be less likely to borrow for college, regardless of institutional type (Cunningham & Santiago, 2008). Cunningham and Santiago (2008), after conducting focus groups with Latino students, found that Latino students possessed an aversion to borrowing and based educational decisions on their current economic status, preferring a "pay as you go" approach to financing higher education (Cunningham & Santiago, 2008). Data from the National Postsecondary Student Aid Study (NPSAS), Table 4.10 shows that at every level, Latino students are most likely to have less than $5,000 (16%) or $10,000 (14%) cumulative debt for their undergraduate degrees, compared to their White peers that are more likely to have greater than $10,000 cumulative undergraduate debt. While this data does not

TABLE 4.9. Average Amount of Financial Aid Awarded from Any Source per Full-Time, Full-Year Undergraduate Student, by Type of Aid and Race/Ethnicity: 1999–2000, 2003–2004, and 2007–2008

Type of Aid and Race/Ethnicity	1999–2000	2003–2004	2007–2008
Any aid			
Total[1]	$9,300	$9,900	$12,470
White	9,500	9,900	12,860
African American	9,300	10,500	13,530
Latino	7,800	9,000	11,360
Asian/Pacific Islander	10,100	10,000	12,570
American Indian/Alaska Native	9,200	9,500	10,850
Grants			
Total[1]	$5,400	$5,600	$7,110
White	5,600	5,500	7,090
African American	5,100	5,700	7,040
Latino	4,700	5,400	6,500
Asian/Pacific Islander	6,400	6,700	8,760
American Indian/Alaska Native	5,700	5,400	6,680
Loans			
Total[1]	$6,000	$7,300	$9,480
White	6,000	7,400	9,790
African American	5,800	7,100	8,940
Latino	5,900	7,000	8,970
Asian/Pacific Islander	6,000	7,100	8,770
American Indian/Alaska Native	5,800	6,900	7,980

[1] Total includes other race/ethnicity categories not separately shown.

Note: All dollar values are in 2003–2004 dollars for 2004 data. Students may receive aid from multiple sources. Figures include PLUS loans (loans to parents). Data include undergraduates in degree-granting and non-degree-granting institutions. Race categories exclude persons of Hispanic origin, but ethnicity includes Hispanics/Latino.

Sources: U.S. Department of Education, National Center for Education Statistics, 1999–2000 and 2003–2004 National Postsecondary Student Aid Study (NPSAS: 2000, NPSAS: 04); 2007–2008 National Postsecondary Student Aid Study.

differentiate for institutional type, it suggests that Latinos are in fact more likely to utilize a pay as you go approach to financing higher education. And since many Latinos begin in community colleges, this may also be a factor in lower debt levels.

The fact that most Latino students who enroll in higher education start at community colleges is largely related to affordability (Fry, 2002; Flores, Horn & Crisp, 2006; Gándara & Contreras, 2009). The problem with start-

TABLE 4.10. Total Cumulative Amount of Debt for Undergraduate Degree by Race/Ethnicity 2008 (Percent)

	White	Black or African American	Hispanic/ Latino	Asian	American Indian/ Alaska Native	Native Hawaiian /Pacific Islander
Total Students	61.8	14.0	14.1	5.9	0.8	0.7
$1-4,799	58.4	16.6	16.0	4.4	1.0	0.7
$4,800-9,999	58.9	18.1	14.3	4.5	0.9	0.7
$10,000-18,999	63.2	17.0	11.6	4.1	0.7	0.6
$19,000 or more	62.9	18.9	10.2	3.9	0.6	0.5

ing college at 2-year institutions is that many Latino students do not successfully transfer from community colleges and are less likely to earn a college degree (either an AA or BA) than their White or Asian American peers.

The Importance of Information

The need for greater grant assistance rather than loans is an obvious yet historically difficult policy solution to achieve for all students. However, there are additional educational policy approaches that may result in more students being able to afford the cost of college. Early college planning is just as critical as having and sustaining high aspirations to achieve a college degree. Unfortunately, many Latino students, and their underrepresented counterparts, do not come from households where relevant information is known or early college planning occurs, as is the case of many middle-class households. In the case of Washington, where the majority of parents planned to help their children pay for college, it is unclear how many Latino parents actually do assist their child with college costs when the time comes for financial support (Conteras et al., 2008). Grodsky and Jones (2004), for example, using the 1999 National Household Education Survey to examine parent knowledge about college costs, found that less educated, low-income Latino parents were not only least likely to give a cost estimate of college costs; when they did, they tended to overestimate the cost of college tuition by two- or threefold. Their findings suggest that parent misperceptions of college costs may also influence student perceptions of affordability and ultimately their aspirations to pursue higher education.

Zarate and Fabienke (2007) conducted a national survey of Latinos on college information and financial aid and found that both Latino parents and students lacked information about college generally, but also lacked information about financial aid and college costs. In addition, they found that over 70% of the respondents had never received information or advice about college financial aid while they or their child was in the K–12 education system. The findings from the Grodsky and Zarate studies suggest the need for early information for parents about college as students progress through school, including information related to college readiness, course preparation and requirements, and college costs.

CONCLUSION

Many developed nations have functional and affordable systems of higher education, where emphasis on global understanding and awareness is a key feature of undergraduate and graduate education. The question for the United States is essentially: How do we increase access to higher education given that many future industries, fields, and employment opportunities will demand a higher level of education? How do we prioritize higher education to ensure that the United States will have a workforce in place to sustain and position the nation to be not only competitive but an international leader in innovation? What can we learn from other developed nations that choose to invest in their citizenry at higher proportions than the current U.S. post-secondary model?

Finland and the Netherlands are perhaps the best examples of developed nations with higher education systems that are both accessible and affordable. "Both have large student bodies, high attainment rates, extensive grant programs, and student bodies that are reasonably reflective of broader society" (Usher & Cervenan, 2005, p. 4). Higher education in Sweden was also classified as highly accessible because its cost remained low or affordable for residents and generous grant programs existed for students who could not afford college costs (Usher & Cervenan, 2005). In a study that compared 16 developed nations, Usher and Cervenan (2005) explored level of affordability and access to higher education by using an index that calculates the cost of higher education as a percentage of a nation's gross domestic product (GDP). In Finland, for example, the country that has the most affordable higher education system, higher education costs represent only 1% of the GDP per capita income. Finland is particularly unique because two tracks of higher education exist for students, and both are free. There are universities, which focus on research and scholarly teaching, and there are polytechnics, which focus on vocational or professional training for a specific field. While students have to pay for aspects of their schooling, such as health care services, the education system remains accessible to all residents.

The United States, however, is the second most costly nation in terms of higher education costs, with education costs making up 26% of GDP per capita income (Usher & Cervenan, 2005). The international examples provided here are merely context for what is possible among developed nations committed to an educated populace.

Financial assistance for students represents a viable policy approach to increase Latino and underrepresented student access to and persistence in higher education. Past and current trends suggest that college costs will likely continue to rise. While loans have become a viable option to account for grant shortfalls or decreases at state and federal levels, they contribute to higher levels of debt for students from low-income backgrounds and serve as a deterrent for students who are averse to borrowing. The discourse and debate around financial aid policy therefore calls for reframing—from a discussion of cost to a discussion of national investment. Providing financial aid to college students, particularly low-income students, is an investment in the future U.S. workforce. We have seen states and the federal government at distinct points in history develop financial aid initiatives. This period requires increased domestic attention and investment if the United States is to successfully rebuild a strong national economic infrastructure.

There are also students—undocumented students—who do not qualify for any type of financial aid or loans. While representing a very small proportion of the Latino students in higher education (Passel, 2005), this segment is made up of high achievers who have overcome personal adversity to overcome challenges of being in a country that refuses to invest in their human capital. The next chapter discusses the implications of the DREAM Act on undocumented students, a policy adopted by some states to allow them to pay in-state tuition prices. Chapter 5 presents a detailed discussion of the individual challenges facing these students and their tenacity as they attempt to overcome financial, personal, and institutional challenges to remain in higher education and work to better their lives, their family status, and their communities.

Undocumented Latino Students
and the DREAM
of Pursuing College

I think that every person has the right to go to school regardless of who they are. I just want to go to school, be a citizen, and not worry about how I am going to be perceived. I am spending money trying to go to school, and this is going to benefit the state because I [would have] already gone to school and will go to work. The economic advantage is that now I am going to be a productive citizen.

—Nina, a premedical undergraduate student attending a flagship institution

Latino students who successfully persist through higher education represent a very small proportion of the Latino students enrolled in college, particularly when compared to their enrollment in the K–12 sector. This imbalance is most evident among undocumented[1] immigrants, students for whom college seems unattainable, especially if they are required to pay out-of-state or international tuition to attend college. In addition, unauthorized students are far less likely to know the requirements necessary or the process of applying to college. The undocumented students who are savvy enough to navigate high school and complete the requirements for college are still left with the considerable challenge of financing their higher education. DREAM (Development, Relief and Education for Alien Minors) Acts, or in-state tuition bills, have been one policy approach to ensure a level of affordability for undocumented students. Passel (2003) estimates that approximately 65,000 unauthorized students graduate from high school each year, many of whom have been in this country for more than 5 years, and that approximately 13,000 are enrolled in U.S. colleges.

Even with the promise of in-state tuition in 10 states, the hurdles remain considerable because a strong anti-immigrant climate is pervasive in many communities across the nation, and the fear of deportation looms over these students and their families. As seen in the case of Arizona in the three anti-immigrant policies initiated in 2010 and described earlier, a blatant discriminatory approach exists toward Latino immigrants. Their accounts represent sacrifice, selflessness, and the *ganas* (the will) to persist despite the uncertainty of their ability to work legally once they complete their degrees. This chapter explores the experiences and challenges of undocumented Latino students in select colleges and universities in Washington State and the institutional and public policy opportunities that exist for implementing functional DREAM Act policies in the United States. These research findings are unique because all of the study participants are not only persisting through college—they are succeeding academically. Their accounts represent rich perspectives and examples of the distinct hurdles that exist for students pursuing postsecondary education under the DREAM Act.

NATIONAL CONTEXT FOR UNAUTHORIZED STUDENTS IN HIGHER EDUCATION

In 1982, the Supreme Court ruled in *Plyler v. Doe* that undocumented children have the right to attend public schools. *Plyler* was a critical case that provided equal protection for undocumented children under the Fourteenth Amendment of the Constitution (Chapa, 2008; Olivas, 2004; Valencia, 2008). Few laws, however, address the needs of undocumented youth as they move from the K–12 sector into postsecondary institutions. Nationally, 10 states have passed laws to allow undocumented students to pay in-state tuition: California, Texas, Washington, Kansas, Utah, New York, Oklahoma, Illinois, Kansas, New Mexico, and Nebraska (Table 5.1).

Many of these state DREAM Acts, however, remain in peril in the courts and in legislative arenas (Olivas, 2004). For example, in Oklahoma, the Oklahoma Taxpayer and Citizen Protection Act of 2007 (HB 1804) rescinded SB 596. In addition, other states, such as Arizona (Proposition 300 in 2006), Colorado (HB 1023 in 2006), and South Carolina (HB 4400 in 2008), have further banned immigrant students from eligibility for in-state tuition rates.

The most recent challenge to the legality of in-state tuition was *Martinez v. Regents* in California, in which plaintiffs argued that in-state tuition violates federal law [Title 8 of the United States Code (U.S.C.) section 1623] by providing a "benefit" to unauthorized students.[2] In 2006, Judge Warriner upheld the decision made by higher education institutions to grant undocumented students eligibility for in-state tuition. However, in 2008, a California appeals court agreed to hear the lawsuit in the Yolo County Superior Court. And on December 23, 2008, the California Supreme Court agreed to hear *Martinez v. Regents*. The California Supreme Court voted to uphold

TABLE 5.1. States with DREAM Act Policies as of 2010

State	Legislation	Year Passed	In-State Financial Aid
California	AB 540	2001	Yes, via Top 4% Plan
Illinois	HB 60	2003	No
Kansas	KSA-76-731A	2004	No
Nebraska	Legislative Bill 239	July 2006	No
New Mexico	SB 582	March 2005	No
New York	SB 7784	2002	No
Oklahoma	SB 596 Oklahoma Taxpayer and Citizen Protection Act of 2007 (HB 1804) nullified this legislation	2003 2007	Yes, while DREAM Act was in place (prior to 2007)
Texas	HB 1403	2001	Yes, via Top 10% Plan
Utah	HB 144	2002	No
Washington	HB 1079	2003	No, HB 1706 attempted in 2009 session

AB540 on November 15, 2010, negating the plaintiffs' claim that this statute violated state and federal law. Specifically, the California Supreme Court found that AB540 "does not violate the privileges and immunities clause of the Fourteenth Amendment to the United States Constitution" (Martinez v. Regents Summary, November 15, 2010). The court further upheld the right for states to determine the criteria for in-state tuition status, such as the requirement to attend high school for the three years that currently exists in California.

This legal win in California on behalf of undocumented students represents a significant step towards securing the rights of undocumented student residents who are attempting to earn postsecondary degrees.

While state DREAM Act legislation has been a positive step toward ensuring access for undocumented students to higher education, we do not know the extent to which these laws have provided equitable access to services and whether schools and colleges are adhering to the intent of the law. The actual implementation and oversight of DREAM Act laws, particularly those involving civil rights, rely on the interpretation and implementation efforts of higher education officials and staff. This research provides a case study of undocumented students in college in Washington, a state with a DREAM Act Policy (HB 1079) that was enacted in 2003. We know very little about the experiences of undocumented Latino students as they attempt to navigate higher education institutions in states with DREAM Act policies.

THE POLICY CONTEXT IN WASHINGTON STATE

The state of Washington, like many in this nation, has witnessed dramatic growth in the Latino adult and K–12 population. From 1986 to 2007, for example, the K–12 population grew by 372%. Latinos represented approximately 15% of the K–12 population in 2008, and nearly 20% of kindergartners in the state are Latino. By 2030, the Latino population is expected to increase by 150% (Contreras et al., 2008; Office of Financial Management, 2008). Part of this growth is due to migration patterns, largely among individuals of Mexican descent, who contribute to the agricultural economy by providing the farming industry with low-wage labor in various industries, such as apples, asparagus, and cherries. These labor patterns, in addition to high birth rates among the U.S.-born Latino population, account for the rapid demographic growth among Latinos.

The state legislature passed House Bill 1079 in 2003, allowing unauthorized students who have been in the state for 3 years and have graduated from high school to pay in-state tuition to attend colleges and universities in the state. In April 2008, the Washington legislature commissioned studies on the achievement gap, where one of the key recommendations was to expand financial aid opportunities for undocumented students who, through no fault of their own, came to this country and have been part of the U.S. education system. The report recommended that 1079 students be eligible to compete for state financial assistance (Contreras et al., 2008). In February 2009, HB 1706 was introduced, which would "expand resident student eligibility for purposes of the state need grant program," allowing unauthorized students to be eligible for state need grant programs. HB 1706 was referred to the higher education committee for review and died in committee but marked an important milestone in Washington legislative history, where the lives of immigrant college students received targeted and positive consideration.

LITERATURE ON UNDOCUMENTED STUDENTS AND PERSISTENCE

An emerging body of literature on unauthorized students transitioning to or attending institutions of higher education in the fields of law, sociology, public policy, and education provides a foundation for this study (Abrego, 2008; Alfred, 2003; Chapa, 2008; Gonzales, 2008; Olivas, 2004; Perez,

Espinoza, Ramos, Coronado, & Cortes, 2009; Ruge & Iza, 2005). A great deal of attention in the literature on undocumented students relates to legal status, legislative developments, and emerging student activism in states with large concentrations of undocumented students, such as California and Texas.

Olivas (2004) thoroughly documents the legal development of college residency laws and policies, and addresses the core issues related to immigrant status both before and under the Illegal Immigration Reform and Immigrant Responsibility Act (IIRIRA) in 1996, as well the status of unauthorized immigrant students in a post-9/11 framework via Patriot Act and the DREAM Act policies. This legal discussion addresses precedents related to immigrant students, including *Plyler*, Proposition 187, and features of the DREAM Act that would repeal Section 505 under IIRIRA, a provision that gave states autonomy to determine state residency (Olivas, 2004). The most recent version of the DREAM Act (2009) would also repeal Section 505 under IIRIRA.

Ruge and Iza (2005) similarly discuss precedent decisions related to undocumented students as well as select state policy developments. They further make the case for in-state tuition for undocumented students as federally permissible and a "socially responsible" approach to immigrant youth, claiming that the economic benefits outweigh the perceived harm and that concerns that undocumented students displace U.S. students and workers are ill-founded.

In addition to legal scholarship that has emerged related to unauthorized students, activism among AB 540 (California) students has emerged as a research focus. Gonzales (2008) conducted a case study in which he explored student activism in California among student leaders in college and found that many students in his sample considered activism to be their vehicle to impact their current status in the policy arena and inform the community about their rights. He also found that undocumented students experienced a great deal of misinformation in the high school, community college, and university contexts. Many institutional officials were unaware of the AB 540 law in California and, as a result, did not know that undocumented students could attend college.

Similarly, Abrego (2008) documents student activism among AB 540 college students and the role that the law has played in providing a mechanism for student legitimacy, a sense of confidence, and a rallying point for student mobilization efforts on campus and in the community. Abrego claims that AB 540 has had "transformative effects" in the daily lives of unauthorized students because the label serves as a disguise.

Finally, Perez and colleagues (2009), using a cluster analysis, examined academic resilience among undocumented students; they found that students with supportive parents and peers who were involved in extracurricular activities experienced higher levels of academic success when compared to the control group, despite greater levels of adversity related to their legal and socioeconomic status.

This chapter focuses on understanding persistence by revealing the experiences of undocumented students as they navigate through higher education institutions in a state with a DREAM Act policy in place. While the state of Washington has a growing Latino population (Contreras et al., 2008), limited research has been conducted on the experiences of Latino students, and very little attention has been placed on unauthorized Latino college students across all institutional sectors.

This research also draws from literature on the persistence of underrepresented students pursuing higher education (Arbona & Nora, 2007; Cabrera, Nora, & Castaneda, 1992; Haro, 2004; Hurtado, 1994; Hurtado & Ponjuan, 2005), specifically the factors that contribute to retention and perseverance among low-income first-generation Latino college students, such as financial concerns, academic preparation, social integration, and family background (Nora, Barlow, & Crisp, 2006; Swail, Redd, & Perna, 2003). Very few studies have explored the challenges facing unauthorized students in higher education and how these students navigate college. In addition, few studies have explored campus resources that have been most helpful to Latino students and the factors that contribute to their persistence. Mendoza (2008), using a small sample of undocumented students at one university, found that unauthorized students were more likely to use diversity offices and select staff to help them navigate college. This chapter, which uses a more broad and gender-balanced sample, provides a unique account of individual student experiences and tales of resilience among students who have thrived despite continued adversity that stems from their legal status and explores the following questions:

(1) How does 1079 status impact the experiences of Latino students as they transition to and navigate through higher education institutions?

(2) Do these undocumented student experiences differ by institutional type?

(3) What are the institutional and policy implications of these student experiences for more effective approaches to addressing the needs and concerns of these high achievers?

The data in this chapter stem from a qualitative case study of 1079 students, specifically the experiences and challenges facing unauthorized Latino students in higher education in Washington State. My personal experience with attempting to hire research assistants to work on a statewide study on Latino educational opportunity provided an inside view of the challenges facing 1079 students in seeking meaningful research opportunities, a factor known to contribute to student success and persistence in higher education (Contreras & Gándara, 2006; Haro, 2004; Hurtado & Kamimura, 2003; Swail et al., 2003). I began to hear of the difficulties facing these students in securing employment to help them pay for college and enable them to earn their respective degrees.

The research protocol asked students a range of questions relating to their background characteristics, competing demands with school, work, community engagement, support networks, and the navigational processes they employed in their respective colleges and universities, given their un-authorized status. Using a snowball sample across higher education institutions in Washington State, 20 semistructured in-depth interviews were conducted in the Fall of 2008 and in January 2009 with Latino college students who attended various postsecondary institutions, including a Research I institution (a selective state flagship),[3] a regional comprehensive 4-year institution, and six community colleges.

Data from the semistructured interviews were coded for emergent themes (Creswell, 2008; Maxwell, 2005). This chapter explores how having unauthorized status impacts Latino student experiences in higher education. This chapter also presents the challenges that these undocumented Latino students encounter in multiple contexts as they work toward earning their college degree, as well as the implications of these findings for practice and improving the implementation of DREAM Act policies in the United States.

Meet the Students

The student sample was diverse in age, gender, and parent education levels. Eight women and twelve men responded to the request for participation. Table 5.2 provides an overview of select characteristics of the interview participants. The majority of the respondents were from Mexico, had come to the United States with their parents (or a parent), and had incomes less than $15,000 in 2008. Thirteen students reported that they worked on average more than 20 hours per week while attending college full time. The students who did not work while in college had received private scholarships.[4] Thirteen of the respondents had at least one parent with an education level of high school or less.

Seven of the students began their postsecondary education at a community college, and six of them successfully transferred to a Research I institution in the state. All of the students in the sample were high achievers, with high grade point averages in college and involved in some form of community activity (e.g., school organization, nonprofit, church). Finally, almost all of the students (with the exception of one) aspired to earn a graduate or professional degree.

TABLE 5.2. Select Background Characteristics of Interview Participants

Pseudonym	Age	Institutional Type Attending	Income in 2008	Country of Origin	Years in U. S.	Occupation	Hours per Week Working	Major	GPA	Highest Level of Education Sought	Parent Education
Eden	23	CC Transfer student, now at Research I	<$10,000	Mexico	13	Nanny	20	Communication	3.3	Grad/prof. degree—Law	Grade school or less (both)
Lorenzo	21	Research I	$15,000-$19,999	Mexico	7.5	Construction	30	Economics/political science	3.0	Grad/prof. degree	Dad, PhD; Mom, BA
Alejandro	23	Research I	<$10,000	Mexico	9	None—Gates Scholarship	NA	Ethnic studies	3.0	Grad/prof. degree—Law	Grade school or less (both)
Ricardo	18	Research I	$10,000-$14,999	Bolivia	7	Community college administrator	10	Undecided	3.5	Grad/prof. degree	Dad, high school; Mom, BA
Nadia	19	Research I	$10,000-$14,999	Mexico	17	None—Gates Scholarship	NA	Sociology	3.2	Grad/prof. degree	Dad, no formal ed.; Mom, high school
Jaime	23	CC transfer, now at Research I	$20,000-$29,000	Mexico	16	Network administrator	20	Business	3.2	BA degree	Dad, BA; Mom, high school
Saul	21	Research I	<$10,000	Mexico	8	NA	NA	Biology	3.0	Medical school	Dad, grad degree; Mom, BA
Monique	20	Community college	<$10,000	Mexico	11	Prep cook	17–30	Political science	3.5	Grad degree	Grade school or less (both)
Patricio	21	Regional 4-year (rural)	<$10,000	Mexico	20	Debt collector	40–45	Education	3.3	Grad degree	High school (both)
Nina	18	Research I	<$15,000	Mexico	6s	NA—Costco scholarship	NA	Public health	3.5	Medical school	Dad, grad degree; Mom, some college

TABLE 5.2. Select Background Characteristics of Interview Participants

Name	Age	Institution	Income	Origin	Years in U.S.	Work	Hours	Major	GPA	Aspiration	Parents' Education
Lydia	29	CC transfer student, now at Research I	<$39,000 (husband)	Mexico	8 yrs	Cleaning offices, waitress	40 (in past)	Business	3.5	Grad/prof. degree	Dad, grade school; Mom, middle school
Jesus	23	Research I	<$10,000	Colombia	8 yrs	Cleaning offices custodial	26–30	Chemical engineering	3.3	Grad/prof. degree	Dad, BA; Mom, high school
John	24	CC transfer, now at Research I	<$10,000	Nicaragua	20 yrs	3 campus jobs	30	Sociology	2.7	Grad/prof. degree	Dad, BA; Mom, grade school or less
Julio	18	Research I	$15,000–$19,000	Mexico	7 yrs	Barbecue restaurant	40–50	Political science	3.3	Grad/prof. degree	Dad, grade school; Mom, ninth grade
Ray	22	CC transfer, now at Research I	<$15,000	El Salvador	8 yrs	Restaurant	15	Electrical engineering	3.5	Medical school	Dad, technical degree; Mom, grade school
Amalia	20	Regional 4-year (rural) WA	<$10,000	Mexico	9 yrs	None—Gates Scholarship	NA	Children's studies	3.0	Grad/prof. degree	Dad, no formal ed; Mom, middle school
Samuel	20	Research I	<$10,000	Mexico	7 yrs	Restaurant	30	Political science	3.1	Grad/prof. degree	Dad, some college; Mom, middle school
Jordon	21	CC transfer, now at Research I	<$29,000	Argentina	8 yrs	Nonprofit youth counselor	15–20	Latin American studies	3.7	Grad/prof. degree	Dad, some college; Mom, BA
Juana	28	Doctoral student at Research I	$65,000	El Salvador	18 yrs	K-12 administrator	45	Education	3.8	Grad/prof. degree	Middle school (both)
Karina	22	Master's student at regional 4-year (rural)	<$10,000	Mexico	16 yrs	Graduate researcher	20	Social work	3.4	Grad/prof. degree	Some college (both)

A LOOK AT THE EXPERIENCES OF UNDOCUMENTED STUDENTS ATTEMPTING TO FINISH COLLEGE

Several themes emerged from the interviews with students that reveal a unique set of experiences for undocumented Latino students in higher education in Washington. Their stories are not uniform by any means, however. These students arrived in the state with different migration experiences, family education backgrounds, and personal histories. The one common reason that their parents gave them for migrating to the United States was the desire to provide their children with the educational opportunities and economic mobility that did not exist for them in their home countries due to challenging economies, corruption, or limited social and economic mobility.

The key themes that emerge from the semistructured interview responses include (1) the tenuous road to higher education fueled by discrimination and blatant racism in the K–12 sector; (2) the pervasive presence of fear in their lives, for themselves and their families, especially the prospect of separation; (3) financial difficulty paying for college with limited access to financial aid; (4) campus experiences, often discriminatory, as well as exposure to resources and supportive individuals they could trust to help them navigate college; and (5) the *ganas*, or will to persist, as seen through the determination to overcome challenges in their personal or academic lives and give back to their communities in the process. The following discussion elaborates on these key findings.

The Road to the Doors of Higher Education

Experiences with teachers and school counselors were mixed among interview participants. Students had both positive and negative experiences with school staff as they attempted to transition to higher education. In the case of Lorenzo, a student at a Research I institution, his experience with a school counselor was helpful at first, in placing him on the path to graduate and enroll in rigorous classes (Advanced Placement curriculum) before she learned of his undocumented status. Lorenzo started school as a sophomore and had to make up 2 years of coursework in 1 year to be eligible to graduate on time from high school. His counselor explained all the work he would have to do to make up for missing his freshman year, and he worked to meet this challenge:

> I would stay after school, do all this work at home just to make up
> for all the credits from freshman year, and she was a skeptic about it,
> but after sophomore year I had a 4.0 and I finished all the work from
> freshman year and sophomore year. She was very impressed.

Lorenzo continues to describe his interaction with the counselor as changing dramatically the following year, when the counselor learned more about his immigration status:

> Junior year she was very excited with me, and she really wanted to help me out; she helped me to take the PSAT. She followed up with me; we planned the rest of my classes. Then she [says], "Well, it's time for you to start thinking about college; I want you to look at these applications." I have tons of questions . . . what am I going to do? I exposed my situation to her and after I told her, she completely changed. I remember her telling me "Well, this changes things—I don't know if you're going to go to college now." Her face changed, her eyes changed, everything changed. And I would say, "Well, I was hoping you could help me to find out what can I do. Are there scholarships?" And she [said], "You know what, I really don't know, I have to get back to you." I tried scheduling appointments with her; she never saw me again after that day. She referred me to another counselor. She just never talked to me again.

Lorenzo, who could have been discouraged from enrolling in college based on his experience with his high school counselor, was fortunate to have a cousin who helped him navigate the college application process. His cousin, who was an alumnus of the state's flagship institution, intervened and motivated him to consider applying to the flagship:

> I really didn't feel like telling any other counselor about my situation. I made the decision of going to community college instead of [the flagship]. Out of nowhere my cousin from DC, [who] was visiting for the holiday season, heard about my decision of going to community college through my aunt and she just went ballistic on me—and said "How can you do this? You have the grades, I know you have the attitude, the initiative—don't go to a community college, you should be at [the flagship]." . . . My cousin slapped me around and said "I'm going to take you to meet some people. I'm going to come back in about a week." She went back to her work, asked for a couple of days off, and flew back from DC and took me to meet all these different people from [the flagship]. She was telling them what a great student I was. That's when they brought up for the first time to me information about 1079.

Lorenzo's experience with his counselor was a typical one for Latino students in general, who are discouraged from attending a competitive univer-

sity—or college altogether (Valencia, 2002). His cousin countered this negative influence, emerged as an influential role model in his life, and helped to
shape his college path as a result.

A small handful of the students had positive experiences in secondary
education as they attempted to transition to higher education; they were
exposed to supportive teachers and staff who encouraged them to consider
college. Samuel, a student who recently transferred to a flagship institution
from a community college, recalled how his ESL teacher would not only ver-
bally encourage him to go to college but would also talk to his mom about
his progress. This teacher understood the financial challenges Samuel would
face. He describes her efforts:

> My ESL teacher really encouraged me to go to college. She literally
> went around to the other teachers in the school to help raise money
> for me for the first year. She knew about my status and how hard it
> would be for me to get any financial assistance. So she ended up writ-
> ing me a personal check to help me with college.

Information about HB 1079 at the secondary level was mixed among
the student participants. Few school counselors or teachers were aware of
the process or form needed to be eligible for in-state tuition under the 2003
law. In our study on middle and high school experiences and opportunities
to learn in urban, rural, and urban ring school districts in Washington State,
we found that information at the school sites was lacking; students were often given misinformation and told either that they could not go to a university because of their unauthorized status or that they would be considered
international students (and required to pay out-of-state tuition) (Contreras
et al., 2008).

Living in Fear

Patricio is a hardworking student from rural eastern Washington. He has
lived in this country for 20 years. While he very much considers the United
States home, he is also keenly aware of the fact that he and his family are
technically "visitors." His father, a hardworking supervisor of farm workers
in eastern Washington, had an accident during the winter storms that left
him stranded and in need of emergency assistance. Patricio describes how
this experience led to his father's deportation:

> He was driving and somehow his car got out of control and the police
> just took him to jail. They asked him for legal documents. Of course,
> my father did not have that and they put him into the ICE Depart-

ment [Immigration, Customs and Enforcement]. They decided that he needed to get out of the country. He's been here for 10 years and no criminal record whatsoever, but it's just one of those circumstances and the rule of the judge. Pretty sad news.

Patricio's case represents the worst fear of undocumented students and families—to be separated from family members after living and working here for years.

Many of the students felt pressure to not get noticed or "discovered," and they never discuss their status with their peers. Unlike the findings from Abrego's (2008) study, where AB 540 students were empowered, active, and vocal within the campus community, in Washington, this level of activism has not occurred despite the passage of HB 1079. This is likely related to the smaller proportional critical mass of undocumented students on college campuses in the state. For example, Lydia, a business school student attending a flagship institution, who has been in the United States for 8 years, stated, "I never talk about my status." The majority of students who participated in this case study did not consider the 1079 label as having a "transformative effect" and continued to live in the shadows, fearful that others would discover their undocumented status. Jesus, a chemical engineering student also at the flagship institution, described his hesitancy with letting people know about his 1079 status: "I know a lot of people in my situation, but I also was afraid to mention my status—not afraid but embarrassed mostly." Jesus went on to explain the difficulty with reconciling the fact that he is here illegally even though he came to the country with his parents.

There was a general consensus of fear and mistrust among the student participants with sharing information about their 1079 status with their peers and school officials. Nina, an 18-year-old first-year student at a flagship institution and a Costco scholarship recipient, explained her dilemma of trying to find work to pay for additional living expenses, such as clothing and school supplies, that her stipend does not fully cover, depending on the cost of her books. She describes her cautious search process and how her father discourages her from working at all:

> I am trying to ask people I trust if they know of a job that I can do that would be OK with my status. I have gone to my adviser to ask her. My dad just worries. He works long hours, cleans carpets, and he does repair work, like a handyman. He says that "I worked really hard just to get us here for you to then get deported back."

Nina's father, who works at a cleaning company, was an architect in Mexico, but as she recalls, "Due to corruption, he could not find a job. I remember it was really hard on us because there were times when we didn't have money to eat [in Mexico]; it was really hard." Her father is fearful of being separated from his daughter. But Nina is not a stranger to hard physical labor. She cleaned offices with her parents while in middle school and for part of high school. Her dad however, really wants her to be able to study and do well in school. He saves as much as he can to help offset Nina's living costs so she doesn't have to work and can focus on her dream of going to medical school and becoming a doctor.

The climate in Washington is unlike that in states with larger, active undocumented student populations, as in California and Texas. There are few coordinated efforts to address the needs of 1079 students. One organization, however, the Latino Educational Achievement Project (LEAP), has been instrumental in raising this issue with the legislature and promoting community awareness; it was largely responsible for advocacy efforts to ensure that a DREAM Act passed in 2003. However, despite such efforts, the students who participated in this study perceive the climate to be hostile at times, with the presence of Minutemen active in rural communities, legislative attempts to "crack down" on illegal immigration by requiring residents to prove their legal status to obtain a driver's license, and ongoing ICE raids in both rural and urban settings.

Financial Barriers

The biggest challenge facing all of the Latino students who participated in this study was concern about their finances. Many Latino students struggle with the challenge of financing college and require ongoing support to successfully persist (De La Rosa & Tierney, 2006). For undocumented students, the problem with financing college is exacerbated because they do not qualify for state or federal financial aid. Many scholarship organizations also require proof of legal status for eligibility. Even the private scholarship recipients, who for the most part did not work during the academic year, spent their summers working in the fields back home or in construction to help with the cost of living for the following academic year. While their scholarships provided for tuition and living expenses, they did not fully cover additional costs associated with attending college (e.g., books, clothing, food). These students had to plan wisely to offset these costs. However, the majority of students interviewed were not private scholarship recipients.

Latino students largely responded to their financial needs by working. More than half worked more than 20 hours per week while going to school full time. The jobs that the students possessed ranged from being a nanny, cleaning offices, construction worker, debt collector, and restaurant worker to being a network administrator for a small business (see Table 5.1).

Patricio, a student from a regional 4-year university in eastern Washington works 40–45 hours a week as a debt collector, making it difficult for him to engage with professors and peers on campus. He describes his challenges related to financing his education:

> A challenge that I face of course is financial aid, with not qualifying for money, and work–study. I mean, I would have so much free time to do activities with a job on campus. Since I don't have that, I have to go to Spokane every day and work. Then, by the time I get out of work, the school offices are closed and my professors are gone. I never have the time to go to a club meeting or just wander around campus [and] talk to people.

Patricio describes the trade-off for working long hours, which leaves him somewhat isolated from the college campus and ultimately affects his level of engagement at his college.

Community college students were most likely to experience isolation due to work and were least likely to have access to scholarships. While four undocumented students in the sample received private scholarships to attend their university, there were no such funding mechanisms for community college students. Ray, an electrical engineering student who transferred from a community college to a flagship institution, describes his financial concerns:

> The biggest challenge is money. At Highline Community College I was able to support myself, but I didn't have enough time to study because I needed to work about 4 days a week.

Many students, like Ray, work a great deal to be able to afford the cost of college. As Ray describes, the hours spent working take a toll on studying and school performance and are likely to be a factor in persistence for unauthorized community college students. Monique, a community college student, discussed the possibilities that would likely result from having in-state aid:

> If we could have in-state financial aid, that would make the life of many undocumented students, including myself, to not be afraid of getting an AA because of the money. If the government did that we would see more business [and] Latino leaders.

Monique considers financial aid as a legitimizing political act and an investment in the future that would have sizable returns. She, like her peers who attended community colleges before transferring, has work as her only option for financing college.

The Role of Campus Experiences and Supportive Individuals

Campus experiences included isolation, challenging experiences with school officials, and interaction with supportive individuals in specific campus offices with a reputation of having a "welcome environment" for 1079 students. These experiences are common among underrepresented students in higher education generally, particularly at large selective public institutions (Hurtado & Ponjuan, 2005). Perceptions of prejudice or discrimination on campus have been found to negatively affect the educational aspirations and withdrawal behavior among Latino students in college, ultimately harming degree attainment (Cabrera, Nora, & Castañeda, 1993; Nora et al., 2006; Nora & Cabrera, 1996). For undocumented students, their legal status has the potential to elevate levels of isolation and discouragement as well as incidents of discrimination by individuals with anti-immigrant sentiments.

Latino students who began higher education in a community college were more likely to work longer hours and had less awareness of campus resources and offices. Many of them did not confide in university staff largely due to a lack of a connection and, similar to their peers in 4-year institutions, fear of individuals learning about their undocumented status. Jaime, a transfer student who now attends a Research I institution, recalls how he found the information he needed about college eligibility and courses for his major by researching online:

> I spent hours online just going to like different websites figuring out what I needed to do, and I found out I just need to fill out a little piece of paper [an affidavit] saying that I qualified for HB 1079. I remember I was driving by [the CC], I was like, I'm just going to stop by and fill out the application and see what happens. I remember it was just a $35 application fee and I was a student. If I hadn't done that research, I know that I wouldn't have been able to—make myself ask for an application. Then navigating through entire programs . . . the first years I was there, I just went to class and left. They have everything online; I never actually talked to anybody.

Jaime's experience was most common for undocumented Latino community college students, who were more likely to be commuter students and spent less time at the institution than their peers attending 4-year universities. Using online information was also considered to provide a layer of safety for students. Nadia, a student attending the flagship institution, was from a rural community and felt intimidated about approaching university staff. She also relied heavily on the Internet to access campus information: "Usually people are not aware of 1079 or they don't know. There is no specific place where you could go and find out information unless you do it yourself on the Internet."

Community college students, in particular, also may not have access to large diversity offices with their own set of advisers. The Internet was their portal to information about classes, policies, requirements, and transfer. While Jaime is the exception, a highly motivated and persistent student who sought out information about his classes and majors with very little assistance from campus entities, the lack of a personal connection to college campuses has also been found to contribute to isolation and dropping out of college altogether, particularly for first-generation students (Castellanos, Gloria, & Kamimura, 2006; Hurtado & Kamimura, 2003; Hurtado & Ponjuan, 2005).

Other community college students found out about opportunities and shared information through their participation in Latino campus organizations such as the MeChA (Moviemiento Estudiantil Chicano de Aztlan) club on their campus. This was also true for students in 4-year institutions. Peer networks—through Latino, community service, or campus clubs—were important avenues for accessing information and for giving back to the Latino community.

Because of their own limited knowledge of HB 1079 in high school, students also made it a point to give back to students like themselves, by doing student workshops for Latino high school students and parents in Spanish and informing community members about the process of applying for college for students with 1079 status. Many students found information online as a first step. As they built friendships and relationships on campus, their comfort level in seeking information and advice grew. However, the students who sought information from professional staff explained that these interactions were not always productive, unless they knew the person was sensitive to unauthorized students.

At the regional 4-year institution, Amalia is an undergraduate who wants to pursue a master's degree in social work. She decided to find out what she needed to qualify for admission to the graduate program. The head of the program attempted to discourage her from applying because of her status:

> She was the head of the program. She [asked], "So what are you going to do if you don't fix your status? What are you going to do if you're not going to be able to work in your field? Grad school is really expensive, especially if you don't qualify for federal aid." Then she tells me, "If I were you, I would not be talking about your status in school because people might get offended."

Amalia was fortunate to have other university staff to counter these negative experiences, but it left her discouraged about the prospect of graduate school. Thankfully, in addition to her undergraduate adviser, Amalia also had a roommate who encouraged her to move forward. She recalls her reaction to this experience:

> I said [to her] "Thank you for your time; I will figure out another way to go to grad school." I went to talk to my [undergraduate] adviser and she told me, "Don't even bother—don't listen to that." I also talked to my roommate, telling [her] "What's the whole point of me going to school? She has a point—why, if I don't have a Social Security number?" Then my roommate said, "You know what, never listen to those things, just keep going, whatever happens is going to happen, so keep going with school." And that's pretty much what I did.

Amalia was fortunate to have supportive individuals to reassure her and help her to ignore these negative comments. Stanton-Salazar and Spina (2003) see the nature of such networks as fortuitous relationships, where peers, role models, or relatives play a significant motivational role in students' lives. For a moment, however, this director was successful in causing Amalia to second-guess herself and question the benefit of pursing college and graduate degrees if she would be unable to legally work in this country after reaching her goal. Amalia's experience suggests that messages from staff have the ability to derail undocumented students from their pathway of achievement.

Alejandro, like Amalia, had select negative interactions with staff at his university. In Alejandro's case, it was the financial aid office. Alejandro was trying to secure employment authorization, which he had been granted before, to be able to continue to work on campus. As he approached financial aid staff to clarify the situation, he experienced discriminatory and threatening remarks:

> I went to see about my employment authorization card because at first I was given the card, which allowed me to work. So I went to financial aid after it was denied to ask them; they said it was a mistake. The person ended up telling me, "That was just pure luck. You are lucky that you have not been deported." I wish I were able to stop this discrimination for immigrants.

At the flagship institution, even those who had negative experiences with a handful of staff members repeatedly named the same set of advisers, in the Office of Diversity on campus, who they felt they could trust and who provided them with assistance in their classes and with financial issues. These academic advisers served to counter the negative, discriminatory messages students received in other campus offices. These advisers took extra care in walking 1079 students through their options, realizing that many of them were balancing jobs and helping their families. Jesus, a chemical engineering major who works 26–30 hours a week doing custodial work in an office complex in between demanding classes, discussed how at first he was hesitant to disclose his 1079 status but found a counselor in the process who has been very supportive of him educationally and personally:

> I was talking to my Chem E [chemical engineering] counselor, and he mentioned that I should fill out a FAFSA, because I wasn't doing good in one of my Chem E classes. I had no other choice but tell him that I couldn't. He's trying to find private scholarships for me. But before that, I've never told anyone.

Jesus also described how he also found support in the diversity office at the flagship institution, where counselors were open to discussing his concerns about his status.

The role of adults in the lives of these undocumented Latino students appears to be a contributing factor to their persistence in college thus far. The student experiences varied widely in higher education institutions, regardless of institutional type. Given the range of experiences and information provided to 1079 students, there appears to be a void in knowledge of this legislation and limited professional development among college and university staff. Participants repeatedly said that staff members who were either Latino or worked for diversity offices appeared to be the most aware of HB 1079 and willing to assist Latino students in navigating every aspect of college. These staff members provided undocumented Latino students with scholarship information as well as access to community resources and potential job leads; they served as a bridge to the academic world for many of these students. Possessing a higher education and (in many cases) graduate degrees themselves, they also served as role models for 1079 students.

Possessing the *Ganas* to Persist

The undocumented students who were interviewed had one word in common which describes them—*ganas,* which means the will or determination to achieve. One example of *ganas* exhibited by many of the study participants was their work ethic, since many worked to earn money for school and help with family expenses. They worked tireless hours in restaurants, cleaning offices, and doing construction work to pursue their dream of earning a college degree. Lydia, a business student who began her higher education at an urban community college before transferring to a flagship institution, recalls how she and her husband worked long hours 7 days a week so they could afford to pay for her tuition.

> The first years in college, I slept 4 hours every day for 2 years. We would work—I had classes from 8 to 12, then I came back home, took a shower, and I went to work from 2–11 P.M. in the restaurant. Then I would go with my husband to clean offices at night until 2 in the morning. It was here in Bellevue we worked until 2:30–3 in the morning, and would do it every day all over again . . . to save money for school. Four hours for 2 years.

Ganas can also be seen in the students' passion for succeeding in this country and their determination to give back to their communities and families. It was not uncommon for students not only to work and study but also be very active in the community.

Julio, a student attending the flagship institution, described how he is passionate about going back to his urban high school to work with parents and students. He describes the student club's efforts:

> We do activities, especially for parents—we are really focused on parents because our parents don't really get involved in our school. So we made conferences for them—all in Spanish. We [had] a barbecue on the lake. Sent invitations, called every parent, told them it was going to be in Spanish, had food. We [had] three workshops for them about an hour long each. We talked to them about the DREAM Act, community college, and about gang problems. So we decided to make this an annual conference. We broke the record of Latino parents attending the school for the first time for a school-related event.

Ganas was evident in student attitudes and behaviors toward their education, community, and life. This overwhelming desire to succeed was a common characteristic of the undocumented Latino student participants. Alejandro, now in his third year at the flagship institution, wants to become an attorney "to help others overcome injustice." He describes the drive that has helped him to navigate higher education:

> I don't want to be a failure, I want to succeed. And when people try to step on me or try to treat me like crap, I show them—it just gives me more energy, more courage, more anger to fight for what I want. I don't let people bring me down. I am very persistent and I don't settle for less.

Alejandro's approach to school and life is also seen in the accounts from many of the students interviewed for this study, regardless of the type of institution they were attending. Their past and current struggles, combined with their will to succeed, set them apart as a highly resilient group.

LOOKING BEYOND THE COLLEGE DEGREE: POLICY CONSIDERATIONS

Many U.S. residents question the motivation behind unauthorized immigration and why these families take such risks in coming to the United States. The overwhelming answer among study participants was that their parents wanted a better life for their children—a life they believe can be achieved through the economic and educational opportunities that exist in this country. The majority of these students considered themselves part of this country. Students also described the incredible sacrifices their parents made to come to the United States, to expose their children to educational opportunities. The DREAM Act in Washington does not dispel student fears and concerns about working or living in this country after they earn their college degree. State DREAM Acts, as they stand, do not provide permanent residency for unauthorized students, nor do they provide a seamless pathway to citizenship. As a result, many unauthorized students who would otherwise be capable of going to college believe that a college degree may not be worth it. Even those already in college worry about the future.

Patricio's case exemplifies how undocumented students worry about their future. He wants to be a bilingual teacher in a rural community. Having been in the United States for over 20 years, after coming as a 1-year-old, he has limited ties to Mexico. He worries that he will be unable to enter the field of education that he has been trained for:

> I am concerned about not being able to get my legal documents in time, able to use that knowledge I learned, that I strived for, and not being able to teach in the U.S. . . . that all of this time is just a waste. I am hopeful that something is going to happen and that I will have my legal status so I can become a high school teacher. I'm a good person, I contribute to this country a lot, I love this country—why can I not have papers that will allow me to be a teacher? Washington needs bilingual teachers. I am the person to do that job, but I can't.

The majority of students considered working and contributing to their families and communities as a priority. Students were very concerned about economic stability. Their commitment to education was largely intertwined with an optimistic belief in the American Dream and is consistent with pre-

vious research on immigrant students that describes the concept of immigrant optimism as the driving force behind student persistence and sacrifice
(Orozco, Orozco, & Todorova, 2008). Undocumented students believed
that they could achieve success, assist their families financially, and provide
leadership in their communities.

The experiences of unauthorized Latino students in higher education
convey stories of hard work, perseverance, and a commitment to establishing a productive and meaningful life in this country. For undocumented
students who started at a community college in particular, their hurdles are
even more disconcerting, with all of them working, having less access to
campus resources, and having limited or no access to private scholarships.
The findings presented here, through student accounts of their personal
experiences and struggles, provide a basis for policy recommendations for
state and national leaders to consider as they continue to be educated on
the complexity of immigration, particularly the challenges facing immigrant
children. The core areas that would facilitate more positive college experiences among undocumented students include (1) a federal DREAM Act,
(2) access to federal and state financial aid, (3) conducing formal audits of
the implementation of the DREAM Act within states, and (4) professional
development for staff who interact with unauthorized students.

The Need for a Federal DREAM Act

A federal DREAM Act would allow students to qualify for permanent
residency upon completion of high school (or equivalency). It would provide a level of security for unauthorized students and a pathway toward
citizenship. In addition, previous DREAM Act legislation has not addressed
the need for federal financial aid opportunities for undocumented students.
One important consideration for future drafts of a federal DREAM Act, in
order to allow students to realize their full academic potential, is to provide
undocumented students with the ability to compete for and be eligible to
receive federal financial aid. All of the students interviewed were hopeful
about a national DREAM Act and even more hopeful about permanent
residency status and a road to citizenship, which would allow them to work
legally while in school, qualify for financial aid, and remain here to work in
the United States upon degree completion.

Allow DREAM Act Students to Compete for
In-State Financial Aid

States that already have a DREAM Act do not need to wait for a federal
DREAM Act to provide in-state financial aid to these high achievers. Un-

documented youth are not only highly capable, they are also likely to give back to their local communities and foster economic growth. Monique, the community college student, reminds us how in-state financial aid "would make the life of many undocumented students, including myself, to not be afraid of getting an AA [degree]." Allowing undocumented students to compete for state aid is not only equitable; it is morally right to provide students who came to this country as minors educational opportunities comparable to those of their peers.

Formally Audit the Implementation of State DREAM Acts

One approach to addressing institutional adherence to state laws in states with DREAM Acts is to conduct formal audits of their implementation in higher education systems and institutions. In Washington, many secondary schools as well as institutional officials are not fully aware of the 1079 law, and there is no oversight to ensure accurate information is communicated to parents and students. As a result, misinformation is often communicated to prospective applicants and their families. Contreras and colleagues (2008) found that unauthorized prospective college students had access to varying levels of information and misinformation from higher education officials as well as school officials. A formal auditing process by state entities or routine monitoring from state Offices for Civil Rights would help to ensure that DREAM Act laws are implemented. As seen in the case of Alejandro, a financial aid officer at the flagship he attended threatened his status as a 1079 student. While Alejandro was inquiring about obtaining an employment card after being granted one previously by the university, the financial aid staff member commented, "That was just pure luck. You are lucky that you have not been deported." Such statements are threatening to 1079 students and are counter to the intent of the policy—it is not the responsibility of university staff members to "report" or "police" students who are well within their right to attend higher education institutions.

The Need for Greater Professional Development

Professional development is needed for college and university staff in states that have DREAM Act policies. Institutional staff members are responsible for conveying the most up-to-date and accurate information to their students. Advisers, college counselors, financial aid staff, and outreach personnel are all on the front line of interaction with college students, where a critical element of their position is to assist students in navigating college. However, as this study has revealed, not all college staff are willing to provide information to undocumented students and either behave in a discriminatory manner or discourage undocumented students from obtaining the answers they need regarding financial aid, programs, or courses. Consider Amalia's experience, for example, where she recounted her interaction with the graduate program director and heard the following comments: "Grad school is really expensive, especially if you don't qualify for federal aid," and "If I were you, I would not be talking about your status in school because people might get offended." Professional development relating to DREAM Act policies is necessary for college officials who routinely conduct outreach, engage in recruitment, and work in critical offices dealing directly with students in order to prevent staff from discouraging unauthorized students by giving them inaccurate information.

CONCLUSION

Undocumented Latino students in higher education are the most vulnerable student population within the Latino college population because their statuses as a resident and student are constantly influx and at the mercy of policy and legal communities. This level of instability, coupled with a pervasive anti-immigrant climate in the nation today, has fueled varying levels of implementation of the DREAM Act in Washington among higher education officials—hindering the experiences for undocumented Latino students in college. The findings from this study illustrate the need for greater oversight and professional development in all types of institutions and for a commitment to educating students and parents in K–12 and postsecondary sectors on the options that undocumented Latino students have for pursuing higher education.

As this chapter illustrates, undocumented Latino students are determined, hardworking, engaged, and optimistic, despite the fear and anxiety they experience due to their legal status. Their stories are part of the American story, with a shared history of immigration, persistence, optimism, initiative, and hard work—this nation would be ill served if it continues to turn its back on these deserving students who positively contribute to the place they consider to be their home.

CHAPTER 6

Anti-Affirmative Action Policies and Latino Student Access to Public Higher Education

The public policy arena in the past 15 years has been the battleground for what has now become a continuous rollback of civil rights legislation. Bans on affirmative action have not only threatened access to flagship public institutions but sent clear messages from state electorates to underrepresented students and communities about the value of a diverse student body and population. These bans come at a time when major demographic shifts are taking place across the country. Such bans further convey a disconnect between the electorate and a growing multicultural student base throughout many states in the nation. Furthermore, anti-affirmative action bans are misguided and negate existing inequities in schooling, uneven socioeconomic profiles between White and underrepresented students, and the fact that forms of affirmative action exist in the form of legacy admits (Kahlenberg et al., Golden, 2006) wealth, fame or prestige (Golden, 2006). The fact is, that historically and presently, the children of alumni, particularly large donors, receive special consideration for admission to elite universitieis. At Harvard for example, more than half of children of large donors, who constitute COUR (Harvard's Committee on University Resources), had at least one child who had been admitted to Harvard (Golden, 2006). In the *Price of Admission*, Golden chronicles the pattern of admissions consideration based on legacy, wealth, fame or being a child of a faculty member. He argues that these groups, who constitute the ruling class or elite in America are essentially buying their way into selective, elite institutions, thereby reinforcing social reproduction. In addition, he calls these preferential processes wealth blind admissions, and lays out the challenges that universities face as they are consistently working to secure donors and raise endowments. Both Kahlenberg and Golden suggest recommendations for ending such preferences, but the political will remains difficult to sustain. The concepts of *equity* and *merit*, when applied to children of wealthy donors, take on much broader definition versus when these terms are applied to low-income, first generation, underrepresented students. Affirmative action for historically underrepresented and underprivileged students has long been characterized by opponents as a government "handout"—an unfair advantage that somehow impedes on the opportunities afforded to whites and other privileged students. Thus, an ongoing struggle over affirmative action, to retain a level of underrepresented student access to selective institutions, remains highly contested in the policy arena and continues to influence the practices within the halls of flagship and elite institutions of higher education.

In the wake of several propositions that ban affirmative action in states like California, Texas, and Washington, higher education administrators, policy makers, and students alike continue to grapple with understanding the nature of access to public institutions. More than a decade after such bans have been implemented, what impact have bans on affirmative action had on admission to public institutions of higher education? Furthermore, have state policy responses, such as percent plans, widened accessibility for Latino and underrepresented students?

State contexts and responses are critically important, because every state that has anti-affirmative action policies in place is left with the challenge of ensuring access to public higher education institutions while abiding by laws that remove the single most important tool designed to help university officials and staff achieve diversity goals. This story is therefore still in the process of being written, with the short-term impact of anti-affirmative action policies apparent but the larger impact on the educational infrastructure of localities and states still unknown. As the nation becomes increasingly diverse, with over 42% of the K–12 population belonging to an underrepresented ethnic group (NCES, 2010), state responses to the population that funds their respective systems of higher education are critical (see Heller, 2005; St. John, 2003). The economic vitality and sustainability of states rests upon the ongoing investment of its residents. If entire segments are largely excluded from selective institutions of higher education and systems, this talent may go unrealized and underutilized. It has been well documented that students who attend selective institutions are more likely to graduate from college, enroll in postgraduate study, and have higher earnings than their peers who attended less selective institutions (Bowen & Bok, 1998; Carnevale & Rose, 2003). Access to flagship institutions is therefore a significant and necessary avenue to raising the social capital and life options among underrepresented students and their communities.

This chapter explores the impact of anti-affirmative action bans on Latino and underrepresented student access in California and Washington specifically, given their varying political contexts. In addition, additional state responses such as those that have occurred in Texas, Florida, and Michigan are discussed. Data used for this chapter pertain to undergraduate admissions largely because medical and law school data are not readily available despite the fact that the greatest impact is seen in these professional schools and colleges, with dramatically diminishing underrepresented student access to elite medical and law schools. However, understanding undergraduate access and equity post–affirmative action is equally important because these students become the pool that graduate and professional schools draw upon for their programs. The data used in this chapter therefore include systemwide undergraduate data from the University of California; qualitative data from a study I conducted in 2002 on University of California access post–Proposition 209; 10 years of individual-level data on applicants, admits, and enrollees at the University of Washington campus; secondary data from the University of California Office of the President; and relevant literature and studies that have been conducted by leading scholars examining states with bans on affirmative action.

POLICY CONTEXT

The Civil Rights Act of 1964 was intended to provide opportunities to communities that have historically been excluded from public and social institutions in this country in practice. The landmark *Bakke* case in 1978 further set the precedent for allowing race as a consideration in university admissions for the purpose of achieving diversity on a college campus. This case reaffirmed the intent of the Civil Rights Act of 1964 and served as an avenue for using race as one of several factors for admissions, financial aid decisions and scholarships, program participation, and faculty employment at colleges and universities.

During the 1990s we witnessed the beginning of what has become a systematic attack on affirmative action policies in the higher education sector, with a focus almost exclusively on the issue of admission to flagship institutions. Beginning with the passage of SP-1 by the UC Regents and led by then-regent Ward Connerly, the UC Regents voted to ban the use of race as a consideration in college admissions at all levels in 1995. Proposition 209 followed 1 year later, with 54% of California voters passing Proposition 209. Coinciding with the passage of Proposition 209 was the *Hopwood* decision in Texas (1996), where the Fifth Circuit Court ruled that race could not be used as a consideration in admissions because it violated the equal protection clause of the Fourteenth Amendment for four White plaintiffs. Washington followed closely behind California with I-200 in 1998, and on November 9, 1999, Florida Governor Jeb Bush signed Executive Order 99-281, otherwise known as The One Florida Initiative. This order mandated that affirmative action practices end in all government employment, contracting, and education.

In 2001, realizing the damage that this policy had done to UC applications and admissions to the University of California, the UC Regents rescinded SP-1. The UC Regents had hoped to alter the declines in underrepresented student applicants and send a message that the UC system "welcomed" students from all ethnic backgrounds. However, with Proposition 209 in place, this vote was more symbolic than impactful.

The Supreme Court decision in *Grutter v. Bollinger* left a window of opportunity for race to be considered as a "compelling interest" for institutions of higher education as they attempt to shape a class representative of the state and nation. The Supreme Court held that race could be used as a consideration in university admissions but that quotas were illegal. Yet Michigan remained a battleground for this issue following the Supreme Court decision. Three years following *Grutter*, the state of Michigan passed Proposal 2 in 2006, The Michigan Civil Rights Initiative, with 58% of the voters in favor of ending affirmative action. And in 2008, Nebraska voters passed Initiative 424, with 58% of voters approving of banning affirmative action. However, in 2009, the Texas federal court through the decision by Justice Sparks strongly upheld UT–Austin's admissions policies as consistent with the Supreme Court's *Grutter* decision. And so the battle over affirmative action and the debates surrounding racial equity continue in higher education through the courts and initiative processes.

Figure 6.1 illustrates the policy context for the ban on affirmative action in higher education in the United States since 1995.

Thirty years after the 1978 *Bakke* decision, the challenges to this landmark case continue—most recently with the *Parents Involved in Community Schools vs. Seattle School District* case. Parents filed suit against the Seattle School District's practice of using race as a consideration in school assignment. The Supreme Court ruled in 2007 that the school board did not adequately convey how school assignment to achieve racial integration in the district was a "compelling state interest."

As Figure 6.1 illustrates, there are several state policy and legal responses that emerged in response to bans on affirmative action. The UC system responded by investing in outreach. The UC Regents under the leadership of President Atkinson following the passage of Proposition 209 in 1996 allocated $100 million for outreach efforts and programs to be spread across the UC campuses (from 1997 to 2001) and to invest in K–12 partnerships as well as support the development of new programs. In 2007 the outreach budget was $83.3 million and continues to be threatened annually. Further, increases to the outreach budget have not kept pace with inflation in California. At the same time, undergraduate fees at UC increased by 7% and 10% at the CSU

FIGURE 6.1. Policy Context of Anti-Affirmative Action Policies and Responses in the United States

1995	UC Passes SP-1
1996	Proposition 209 Passed in CA
	Hopwood decision in TX
1997	10% Plan in TX
1998	I-200 passes in WA
	Smith v. University of Washington Law School filed
1999	One Florida Initiative
2001	UC Passes Holistic Review & Top 4% in CA
	UC Rescinds SP-1
2002	Smith v. University of Washington Law School decision
2003	Grutter and Gratz in MI
2005	UW implements Holistic Review
2006	Proposal 2 passes in MI
2007	Seattle Supreme Court Decision
2008	Nebraska Initiative 424 Passed
2009	Federal Court upholds *Grutter*

campuses in 2007. And the recent budget shortfalls and crisis in California have led to greater tuition increases across public institutions.

California, Texas, and Florida also responded with percent plans following the bans on affirmative action. In 1997, the Texas legislature adopted a Top 10% Plan, whereby the top 10% of each high school's graduates would be guaranteed admission to any of the 35 public universities in the state. As for Florida, at the same time Governor Bush implemented the "One Florida" initiative he implemented the Talented 20 policy. The Talented 20 program guarantees the top quintile of each high school admission to the Florida State University system, comprised of 11 public universities.

Following the example of Texas and Florida, in 2001 the UC Regents in California passed the Eligibility in a Local Context (ELC), or the Top 4% Plan, along with holistic review in admissions. These policies were a response to the persistent declines in undergraduate applicant numbers to the UC system among underrepresented students of color following the passage of Proposition 209. Like the Texas and Florida plans, California's plan was designed to recruit the top achievers from each local high school context.

The Top 4% Plan, however, does not guarantee access to any institution a student wants to attend but rather to a public university in the state. In addition, the Top 4% Plan in California has been the least successful of all policy responses to bans on affirmative action in raising the percentage of underrepresented students admitted to the University of California, particularly the flagship campuses.

The state of Washington has not had a series of policy responses to the passage of I-200, in part because the flagship institution already admits over 50% of its applicants. Prior to the implementation of I-200, *Smith v. the University of Washington Law School* was filed by applicants who were denied admission to the UW Law School in 1994, 1995, and 1996. The court ruled that the UW law school practices at the time of admission (prior to I-200) were consistent with *Bakke* and that a diverse student body was a compelling institutional interest. Now, however, with the passage of I-200, it is not permissible for Washington public institutions to use race as a consideration for university admission. In 2005, Senate Bill 5575 was introduced in an attempt to reinstate race as a consideration in university admissions. The Higher Education Coordinating Board and the Senate P-16 Committee supported the bill limiting affirmative action practices to admission practices in public colleges, but the bill failed to pass.

EXPLORING THE CONCEPTS OF ACCESS AND EQUITY IN HIGHER EDUCATION

Following the passage of Proposition 209 and the *Hopwood* decision in Texas, researchers began examining the role that the ban on race played on university admissions, particularly on higher education access and equity for underrepresented students (Contreras, 2005a; Gándara, 2000; Geiser & Caspary, 2005; Kane, 1998b; Karabel, 1998; Orfield, 1997). Researchers also sought to understand whether proxies for race, such as socioeconomic status, might achieve comparable levels of underrepresented student diversity attained under affirmative action. Kane (1998a), for example, using the High School and Beyond database, assessed the likelihood of admission under a race-neutral approach but taking into account family income, parental education, and high school characteristics. Kane found that class-based admissions models do not produce the same levels of diversity compared to a model in which race is a factor in admissions decisions. In fact, to achieve the level of diversity among underrepresented students under a race-conscious approach would require that the class-based policy assign a negative weight for student SAT scores and applicants with higher incomes and parent education levels (Kane, 1998a). So using socioeconomic status as an added value for students would mean assigning negative values not only to socioeconomic status but also to test scores for students with higher-income backgrounds in order to try to offset their competitive advantage.

Karabel (1998), using College Board data, also found that a class-conscious policy would have only a limited effect on UC admissions because even after controlling for income, racial and ethnic differences remain large in the cognitive indicators used for admission, such as SAT scores. Karabel found that class is an important predictor of performance on the SAT and noted that there were large distinctions in the performance of underrepresented students compared to their White and Asian American peers, where class alone cannot mitigate school and cultural capital effects entirely.

Saenz, Oséguera, and Hurtado (2007) also examined the issue of access via college enrollment patterns at selective institutions to explore whether underrepresented students were losing ground at selective universities relative to their peers in this post–affirmative action era in admissions. Using data from the Integrated Postsecondary Education Data System (IPEDS), the Census, and Cooperative Institutional Research Program (CIRP) administered by HERI (the Higher Education Research Institute at UCLA) for 3 years—1994, 1999, and 2004—they found that White students have experienced a slight advantage in representation relative to the high school graduating population, Asian/Pacific Islanders have gained an advantage in access to selective universities and are more likely to attend these institutions, and affluent families (with high levels of parental education) across all racial/ethnic groups were able to increase their representation at selective institutions. These findings suggest that in the years following bans on affirmative action, a considerable reduction in access to selective institutions has occurred, particularly among low-income students of color, with students from higher socioeconomic backgrounds gaining an advantage over their peers. These findings suggest that equitable access to institutions of higher education post–affirmative action, particularly public flagships, has been adversely affected. It is therefore even more critical to examine the responses taken by states and institutions to ensure a greater level of accessibility in light of existing policy constraints.

CALIFORNIA POST–PROPOSITION 209

California post–Proposition 209 has been at the center of political discourse and ongoing evaluation. The fact remains that even with affirmative action in place, prior to 209, admission rates among underrepresented students to the UC system were far lower than those of their White and Asian American peers (Contreras, 2005a). Proposition 209 further exacerbated a long history of limited access and representation among minority student populations. In 2003, I studied the impact of Proposition 209 at three California UC Campuses (UCLA, UC–Riverside, and UC–Davis), where I found considerable differences in the applicant and admit pools pre- and post-209. Among the noteworthy results, GPA was a highly significant predictor of admission, with increasing salience post-209; SAT II Writing and SAT II Math scores increased an applicant's likelihood of admission post-209 ($p < .001$); Advanced Placement (AP) course enrollment improved the likelihood of admission post-209; and fathers' education and parental income had a more positive effect on determining admissions for African American students at UCLA. This study found merit to be a "moving target," with the standards for admission based on the quality of the applicant pool. Merit was and continues to be a central concept for determining admission to flagships and moderately selective campuses, and emerged as a theme among the senior administrators I interviewed. A senior administrator at UCLA framed how the concept of merit was operationalized post-209:

> Defining what constitutes merit at a particular campus, and what enough merit is to warrant admission, is going to change depending on how competitive you are and on how many applications you have. (quoted in Contreras, 2005b, p. 1)

The problem with this approach to admissions is that it does not fully take into account the persistent inequities throughout the education system for underrepresented students and redefines the notion of UC eligibility to "competitive eligibility"—that is, students must not only be eligible and be in the top 12.5% of their class but must be *competitively eligible* for admission to the highly selective and moderately selective UC campuses (Contreras, 2005b). Thus, underrepresented students seeking admission to selective UC campuses should possess profiles comparable to those of their White and Asian peers with respect to coursework, GPA, and test scores, even under the holistic review (comprehensive review) framework and despite disparities in school contexts.

When interviewed in 2002, a senior administrator at UCLA foreshadowed the nature of profiles that Proposition 209 would lead to in admissions:

> We are going to see students on average having a 4.0 or higher, students with SAT scores averaging somewhere around 1300 or higher, students with extensive course background above and beyond what we require minimally. And by that design alone, we know that there will not be a lot of students of color in that group because historically,

FIGURE 6.2. Admit Rate for UC Berkeley by Race/Ethnicity, 1994–2009

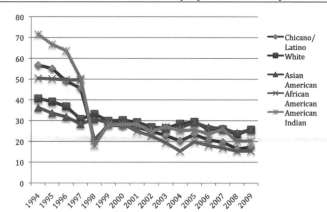

when you deal with the environment, the school, the few families that have college graduates in it, you know who those students are typically going to be. (quoted in Contreras, 2003)

The concern among university leaders I interviewed at UCLA was the issue of access for underrepresented students post-209, especially those students who attended schools with fewer human and physical resources. These students would be unlikely to have comparable profiles to their more affluent peers and thus not as competitively eligible for the flagship UCLA and UC–Berkeley campuses.

Based on the admit rates over time for the flagship campuses, it appears that the prediction expressed by the senior administrator, which suggested that overall declines in access for students of color would occur, has come to fruition. Figures 6.2 and 6.3 illustrate the admit rates for the two flagship campuses in the UC system. As predicted by many, access to the most competitive UC campuses for underrepresented students declined sharply post–Proposition 209 despite continued increases in applicants from all ethnic groups in the past 16 years. In addition, Figure 6.2 shows a more competitive admissions cycle at UC–Berkeley across racial/ethnic groups, with declining admit rates for all groups. However, the biggest losers post-209 in admission, as slots for UC–Berkeley have become increasingly competitive, are underrepresented Latino, African American, and American Indian applicants even under comprehensive review policy.

In addition to declining admit rates to the two flagship institutions, moderately selective campuses also witnessed changes in admit rates for underrepresented students, as seen in the case of UC–Davis. Figure 6.4 illustrates

FIGURE 6.3. Admit Rate for UCLA by Race/Ethnicity, 1994–2009

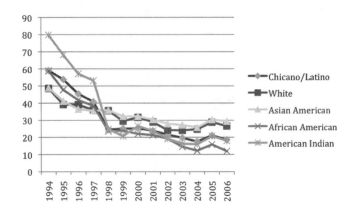

the declines in admit rates across ethnic groups, with the lowest admit rates among African American, American Indian, and Chicano Latino students post-209. These data further suggest that what were once considered moderately selective campuses, such as UC–Davis, have now become more selective universities, with competition rising for admission across pools of student applicants.

Following the passage of Proposition 209, institutional processes had to change, affecting various programs that targeted underrepresented students. Thus, outreach efforts or limitations on such efforts also could have influenced the applicant pool. According to a senior administrator in charge of outreach programs and efforts at UC–Davis, Proposition 209 inhibited their ability to target specific groups and stalled the progress of their outreach efforts.

> A major tool was taken away. And it was taken away at a time when people were really feeling they were seeing a difference. The numbers were changing, the campus environment, the diversity of the campus was changing . . . and so to have that tool . . . because it's not only in the admissions process. There were also some pre-enrollment programs like our summer bridge programs that targeted underrepresented students so they could get good solid footing; most of those programs now focus on disadvantaged students but not specifically underrepresented ethnic group students. It [Proposition 209] certainly changed those efforts. And then there is the continuing dialogue about what can you do? (quoted in Contreras, 2003)

FIGURE 6.4. Admit Rate for UC Davis by Race/Ethnicity, 1994–2009

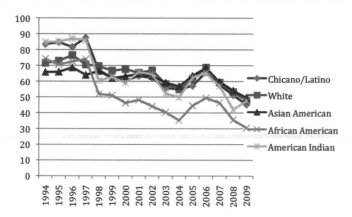

This senior administrator at UC–Davis echoed some of the frustration experienced across the three campuses I studied post-209. These select university leaders all expressed concern about their ability to attract a similar applicant pool compared to the students they were able to target when they were able to practice affirmative action. Administrators believed that these students were attracted to UC campuses as a result of direct outreach, follow-up, and program supports (Contreras, 2003). Further, a level of frustration with the electorate was clearly evident, because Proposition 209 not only stalled the progress that had been made, but the legislation made it clear that fostering diversity in public higher education was not a strong priority among the electorate. The privilege that White and affluent students possess in socioeconomic standing or perhaps as legacy students has been absent from the political discourse on equity in university admissions (Kahlenberg, 2010; Golden, 2006). The outcomes that result from this preferential standing in society, which leads to greater school resources and access to a college-going culture and network, are deemed merit and achievement rather than privilege. A senior administrator from UC–Davis characterized the climate and dilemma post-209:

> As the more conservative elements began to gain more acceptance in challenging affirmative action, then people came out of the woodwork. A lot of it is just basic bigotry and prejudice and just a lack of understanding about the dynamics that opportunity has been given to some people because of their race—the actual advantages that groups of people have had over time, over lots and lots of time, because of their race. How do you correct that without some form of affirmative action?

The direct and open attacks on affirmative action left some administrators frustrated because, as mentioned in Chapter 1, the original intent of affirmative action had been legislatively turned on its head, thus ignoring the current inequities that remain prevalent for Latino, African American, and American Indian students.

Winners Post-209

The campuses that did win in the post–affirmative action framework were the least selective campuses, a phenomenon that has cemented the tiered system that exists within the University of California. At UC–Riverside, applicants have risen steadily since 1994, and the yield rate is the highest among African American and Latino student admits. Figure 6.5 illustrates a steady admit rate at UC–Riverside for all students, including underrepresented students.

Following the passage of Proposition 209, UC–Riverside experienced an increase in applicants among underrepresented students. This phenomenon, called a "cascading effect" (Gándara, 2000), created tiers within the UC system so that campuses became highly stratified and resulted in Latinos and African Americans attending the least selective UC institutions. At UC–Riverside, the administration optimized their efforts to recruit underrepresented students who would be shut out of the more selective UC campuses. A senior administrator at UC–Riverside commented on the changes in UC–Riverside admissions:

> We have had very dramatic increases in both the number of applicants and total enrollees from underrepresented groups. There are multiple factors, the notion of cascading, and the reality . . . especially the minority students in the post SP-1 and 209 era are looking to other UC campuses for options. And that has affected the pool that has looked into the Riverside campus.

This same senior administrator at UC–Riverside attributes the increases in part to the policy climate but also due to their increased efforts to pursue underrepresented students and present a welcoming climate to potential applicants by establishing strategic partnerships in diverse communities.

> We realized after SP-1 that we had to very aggressively pursue some community-based organizations that work with UC-eligible students. We established very strong relationships with local organizations. Combined with the fact that we are working very closely with local churches . . . that has been a defining factor in our ability to recruit

FIGURE 6.5. UC Riverside Admit Rate 1994–2009

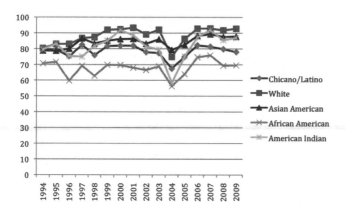

African Americans. And we are going right to the parents [because] it is literally the parents who have to be convinced.

UC–Riverside is also one of the most diverse campuses in the UC system. For example, in 2009 Chicano/Latino students made up 29% of the student population. Further, UC–Riverside was one of the first research institutions to qualify for HSI (Hispanic-serving institution) status with the federal government. While UC–Riverside has taken advantage of this status and the policy climate post-209 to diversify its student body, the systemic question regarding increased stratification remains at the forefront of discourse about equity across the UC system.

Private Institutions

In addition to the less selective UC campuses increasing their underrepresented student enrollment, private institutions successfully acquired top Latino, African American, and American Indian students. Geiser and Caspary (2005) explored attendance patterns among students who elected not to attend a UC campus using data from the National Student Loan Clearinghouse (NSLC). They examined the college choices of first-time freshman from 1997 to 2002 and found that 59% of the top underrepresented minorities who were denied admission to UCLA or UC–Berkeley decided to exit the UC system altogether (Geiser & Caspary, 2005). This varies tremendously from nonunderrepresented students in their sample, with 57% of the top applicants choosing to attend another UC campus if denied admission to the two flagships. Their findings suggest that the top underrepresented Latino, African American, and American Indian students were likely to "have comparable options within highly selective private institutions where affirmative action and recruitment efforts are likely to differ from a UC campus" (Geiser & Caspary, 2005, p. 398).

THE CASE OF WASHINGTON STATE POST–I-200

In the aftermath of the passage of Initiative 200 (I-200) on November 3, 1998, the state of Washington has yet to fully understand the impact that this policy has had on university access for underrepresented students at the state's flagship institution. Framed as a "civil rights" initiative for Washington voters, the policy followed the passage of Proposition 209 in California (1996). Initiative 200, like Proposition 209, prohibited the use of racial preferences in university admissions and in hiring processes at public institutions and was passed by 58% of Washington voters. Ten years after the passage of I-200, we know very little about the role this policy has played in access to the state's flagship university, the University of Washington, with respect to underrepresented student applications, admission, and enrollment at the undergraduate and graduate levels.

Few researchers have examined the impact of I-200 on university admissions in Washington. Brown and Hirschman (2006) studied the trends in application and transition rates in Washington and found sizable declines from 1998 to 1999 for African American, Chicano/Latino, and American Indian students applying to and enrolling in the University of Washington. Brown and Hirschman (2006) attribute the decrease in enrollment to the drop in applications among minority students to UW–Seattle and categorized these declines as temporary. They recommended increasing the application rates in order to raise the number of underrepresented students enrolling in the University of Washington. However, after I examined the applicant, admission, and enrollment rates to the University of Washington from 1997 to 2007, an issue that has not been widely addressed became apparent: the yield rate following the passage of I-200 and over time. That is, the question of access post I-200 is not merely an issue of increasing the applicant pool; the yield rate is also an important context in understanding what occurred at the flagship institution. For example, close to half of Latino admits did not accept offers of admission to the University of Washington (50.3%) in 1998; in 2007, this percentage declined to approximately 44%. (See Table 6.4.) Thus, a student's decision to accept their admission offer to the flagship plays an equally important role in assessing university admissions (Long, 2010).

Following the passage of I-200 in Washington, a "chilling effect" on applications emerged among underrepresented applicants, which is a pattern of student behavior seen in California and Texas (Orfield & Miller, 1998). Students and families reacted with their feet and decided to apply to other institutions of higher education or self-elect themselves out of 4-year institutions altogether due to the perceived climate in higher education. The University of Washington witnessed a dramatic decline in freshmen applications from underrepresented students of color following the passage of I-200. Specifically, there was a 33.2% decline from 1998 to 1999 in Chicano/Latino freshmen applicants, a 22.6% decline for American Indian applicants, and a 31.2% decline for African American student applicants (Office of Educational Assessment, see www.washington.edu/oea/). This decline in applications undoubtedly affected both admissions to and enrollment at the University of Washington campus among students of color immediately following the passage of Initiative 200, narrowing an already modest pool of students even further.

In the wake of the Supreme Court decision in *Parents Involved in Community Schools v. Seattle School District* in June 2007, which further banned the use of race as a consideration in school assignment in Seattle public schools, the issue of affirmative action and the movement to remove such policies in the education sector remains at the forefront of public discourse. In 2009, for example, federal judge Sam Sparks in Texas upheld the *Grutter* decision, allowing race to be one of several factors used in admission decisions at the University of Texas. Challenges to affirmative action are therefore likely to continue as the public policy arena continues to be the forum where the policies enacted during the civil rights movement are being challenged within individual states. Thus, understanding the role that these public policies have played in access to and enrollment in the University of Washington–Seattle in the past decade provides an important context and case study for higher education policy and practice.

The concept of access pre– and post–I-200 and the variables that contributed to admission to and enrollment in the University of Washington campus in 1998, 1999, 2004, and 2007 are examined in this section to determine whether I-200 has adversely impacted admission to the flagship institution. Access to the flagship is critical to assess because the University of Washington is below parity in enrolling the proportion of Latino students that make up the K–12 population. Parity rates are one way to measure progress toward access to higher education (Contreras, 2003, 2005b). Bensimon and colleagues (2005) termed this phenomenon an equity index ratio, where an indicator such as high school graduates is measured against their share of the total population. For example, Latino students represented over 14% of the K–12 population in 2007 and approximately 11% of the high school graduates in the state. Yet they represented 5.6% of the students admitted to the University of Washington in 2007. Forty-one percent of Latino applicants were denied admission to UW. And African American students represented 5.6% of the K–12 system and 2.9% of admits to UW–Seattle, with over a third of applicants denied admission in 2007.

The University of Washington–Seattle

Trends in admission data are examined to assess changes in applicant, admit, and yield rates prior to and after the passage of I-200 at the University of Washington among freshmen applicants in 1997, 1999, 2004, and 2007. These years were selected purposely because they represent four policy regimes:

1. 1998 is the year prior to the passage and implementation
2. The 1999 data refers to the year immediately following the initiative
3. 2004 is right before the holistic review policy passed by the UW Board of Regents in 2005
4. 2007 is post–holistic review

Together, the data for these years allow for analyses of applicant, admit, and enrollment changes for select years over the span of a decade.

Context for Undergraduate Admissions at the University of Washington

The University of Washington (UW) operates under the Higher Education Coordinating Board's guidelines, a body that oversees the requirements for admission to all 4-year public institutions of higher education. A minimum index score of 28 was required for university admission to any public 4-year institution in the state. Under this index, several factors were part of a formulaic scoring and ranking system based on the completion of a college preparatory high school program (Table 6.1), cumulative grade point averages, and scores on the SAT or ACT college entrance exams (Higher Education Coordinating Board, 2005). This statewide college admission index was largely the basis for admission decisions at the University of Washington prior to I-200 and the change in standards to holistic review in 2005.

In 2005, the Board of Regents at the University of Washington implemented a holistic review of freshmen applicants, which, in addition to the academic index, includes a range of variables from personal characteristics to school context, as seen in Table 6.1. The holistic review process requires at least two reviewers per application using an expanded admissions framework from the academic or formulaic framework used prior to 2005. The first full year of implementation of comprehensive review was in 2006 after the Board of Regents approved the new admissions framework and faculty

TABLE 6.1. UW Standards for College Admission Under Holistic Review

Complete Higher Education Coordinating Board HECB college admissions standards (coursework) and relevant scores (used 1997–2004)	Academics/school assessment area (holistic review)	Personal characteristics/achievements Assessment area (holistic review) Race removed as factor
English (4 years)	Strong level of academic record?	Noted tenacity and persistence?
Math (algebra, geometry, adv. math) (3 years)	Taken advantage of AP curriculum?	Record of community service?
Social studies (2 years)	Does high school have "verified" rigorous grading practices?	Personal adversity or disability overcome?
Science (1 lab) (2 years)		
Foreign language (3 years)		Unique background or perspective based on life experiences?
Fine, visual, or performing arts or elective (1 year)	Participated in UW sponsored program? (e.g., GEAR up)?	
Scholastic record (GPA) that demonstrates preparation	Senior year performance?	Is high school low-performing?
SAT scores or ACT scores		

Note: The Academics/School Assessment Area and Personal Characteristics columns are a sample of questions/considerations that admissions reviewers use in admissions decisions and not a comprehensive or verbatim list of the exact questions used.
Source: Office of the Registrar, University of Washington.

reviewed the new process (Ballinger, 2007).

Post–I-200 Story

Concurring with state growth trends, the number of applicants to the University of Washington has been growing steadily over the past decade. An average of 54% of the applicants to the University of Washington were females from 1997 to 2007. What is most alarming is the persistent divide between men from underrepresented groups and their female counterparts who are applying to UW. It appears that fewer African American, Latino, and American Indian men are applying to the flagship and more are self-selecting themselves out of the applicant pool.

The gap has widened post–I-200, particularly among American Indian and Latino applicants to UW, with females representing approximately 60% and males 40% in 2007. For Latinos, this same gap between male and female applicants can be seen following I-200 in 1999. While there are consistent gaps across all ethnic groups in the applications between men and women, the gender gap between application rates appears to be greatest among underrepresented students. This gap, of course, is present in the profiles of students admitted from 1998 to 2007, with more women being admitted than men across ethnic groups.

The University of Washington has seen increases in the overall number of applications post–I-200 from all ethnic groups, with the greatest increases seen in the percentage of Asian American students applying, from 18.8% in 1998 to 23.1% in 2007. The percentage of Latino students who applied to UW increased from 3.6% of applicants to 6.25%, as seen in Table 6.2.

Admit rates for Latino and African American students to the University of Washington after I-200 had greater declines than those of other ethnic groups (Table 6.3). In addition, of the African American, Latino, and American Indian students admitted to the University of Washington in the years examined, a considerable dropoff exists among those who chose to enroll in the university. In particular, there was a decline in the percentage of Latino students who were admitted and then enrolled in UW (Table 6.4). In 2007, for example, 44.2% of the admitted students chose to enroll, while in 1998 50.8% enrolled. The overall enrollment rates for Latinos suggest that they are selecting institutions other than the flagship.

The University of Washington's yield rates for Latino students present both a challenge and opportunity for the campus leadership to place greater emphasis on creating a hospitable climate for Latino students as well as reaching out to Latino parents. The declining yield rates among Latino admits illustrate that greater efforts and attention is necessary to ensure higher levels of representation for the state's fastest-growing segment of high school graduates and K–12 population in the state. While the data show declining yield rates immediately following the passage of I-200 for Latino and American Indian students, they also show steady rates of African American undergraduate applicants accepting offers of admission to UW. Finally, the post–holistic review data do not show sizable percentage gains in the admit rates among underrepresented student groups. In fact, the admit rates for American Indian, Latino, and African American students declined from 2004 levels in 2007, when holistic review was in place in admissions. These data suggest that holistic review has not resolved the dilemma that I-200 presents: the inability to focus outreach specifically to recruit students from underrepresented backgrounds. As a result, although application rates have increased, admit rates among underrepresented students have not. These findings, compounded by declining yield rates among American Indian and Latino students in particular, show adverse affects of I-200 on admit and yield rates to the flagship institution in the state of Washington. Thus, the story for the flagship University of Washington post–I-200 is one of missed opportunity to optimally recruit and enroll a more diverse student body.

TABLE 6.2. Applications to UW–Seattle Among First-Time Freshmen by Ethnicity, Select Years (percent)

Race/Ethnicity	1998	1999	2004	2007
African American	2.7 (373)	2.3 (301)	3.0 (469)	3.2 (582)
American Indian	1.2 (159)	1.0 (133)	.01 (161)	1.1 (203)
Asian American	18.8 (2561)	18.8 (2457)	21.5 (3400)	23.1 (4182)
White	57.2 (7797)	56.7 (7402)	55.0 (8679)	51.1 (9247)
Hawaiian/ Pacific Islander	.009 (118)	.004 (50)	.008 (121)	.006 (112)
Latino	3.6 (495)	3.4 (438)	4.6 (737)	6.2 (1125)
Not identified	11.3 (1536)	13.3 (1741)	7.2 (1133)	5.8 (1050)
Foreign	4.3 (587)	4.1 (532)	6.9 (1083)	8.7 (1582)
N	13626	13054	15783	18083

TABLE 6.3. Admit Rate to the University of Washington, First-Time Freshmen by Ethnicity, Select Years (percent)

Race/Ethnicity	1998	1999	2004	2007
African American	68.9	59.5	55.2	52.6
American Indian	67.3	69.9	70.2	67.0
Asian American	66.7	80.3	74.4	69.0
White	66.3	78.6	69.5	68.2
Hawaiian/ Pacific Islander	89.0	68.0	58.7	60.7
Latino	77.2	71.7	66.5	58.6
Not identified	66.1	80.2	67.9	63.8

TABLE 6.4. Yield Rates: Admitted Students Who Enrolled at the University of Washington, First-Time Freshmen by Ethnicity, Select Years (percent)

Race/Ethnicity	1998	1999	2004	2007
African American	48.2	48.0	55.6	52.3
American Indian	51.4	44.1	56.6	53.7
Asian American	58.1	55.1	54.7	55.0
White	44.3	41.7	43.6	44.1
Hawaiian/ Pacific Islander	36.2	32.4	46.5	51.5
Latino	50.3	42.0	43.7	44.2
Not identified	43.0	46.3	34.1	27.9

PERCENT PLANS—MIXED REVIEWS?

Percent plans have been a response by states to anti-affirmative action policies in an attempt to ensure a level of diversity in university admissions to selective institutions. Tienda, Cortes, and Niu (2003) examined the role of percent plans in Texas based on a survey conducted among high school seniors while they were making their college decisions and after their first year of college through Texas Higher Education Opportunity Project (THEOP). The research project, which began in 2000, explored the extent to which the Top 10% Plan influenced college decisions among high school students and found that student knowledge of the Top 10% policy predicts college intentions and also influences student choices to seek admission and enroll in 4-year institutions.

In another study, Long, Saenz, and Tienda (2010), using 18 years of longitudinal data from THEOP, examined whether the Top 10% Plan in Texas broadened access to the state's flagship institutions, UT–Austin and Texas A&M University. Long and colleagues (2010) found that the Top 10% Plan has positively influenced student diversity across the UT system by expanding the applicant pools among underrepresented students who attend high schools in rural areas, small towns, and midsize cities. They attribute the transparency of the law for taking the guesswork out of defining merit, particularly for schools not traditionally considered to be feeder schools to the flagship institutions.

Although the Top 10% law shows promise for having lasting effects on expanding access to higher education in light of the *Hopwood* decision, the policy has not fully solved the dilemma of equitable access among underrepresented students to the flagship public institutions. Harris and Tienda (2010), using both the changes in the cohorts of graduating seniors and application rates to UT–Austin and Texas A&M, found that shares of Latino and African American applicants to the flagship institutions declined post–*Hopwood*, ultimately influencing the number of underrepresented student admits to the flagships.

Horn and Flores (2003) also examined the impact of percent plans in California, Texas, and Florida and found that such plans rely on the assumption that schools are racially segregated. Among the key findings, Horn and Flores found that the proportion of underrepresented students who enrolled in flagship schools has not kept pace with their relative proportions in the college-age population and population of high school graduates.

Similar to the results of studies conducted in other anti–affirmative action states, Marin and Lee (2003), who examined the Talented 20 plan in Florida, concluded that the students admitted under such plans would have been admitted to a public institution without the assistance of such a plan. They further note how the Talented 20 plan, like the other percent plans, does not guarantee admission to the two most highly selective campuses in the system, Florida State and the University of Florida.

Chavez (2006), who examined the 4% Plan in California, found that only 22% of schools met their estimated ELC student number eligible for

admission to a UC campus. Chavez further explored the application rates
to the University of California among students who had completed the A-G
requirements, a known barrier for UC eligibility for Latino and underrepresented students. Examining the percentage of applicants from select schools
is relevant to understanding educational equity in California because the
California Master Plan of 1960 determined that the UC system would admit
the top 12.5% of the state's high school graduating classes. Chavez found
that at approximately 24% of California high schools, the number of underrepresented students applying to UC was comparable to their proportion of
A-G graduates within their high schools. Her findings suggest that the 4%
Plan is in fact too low of a percentage to have a significant impact on UC
diversity. These findings further illuminate the school inequities that exist
at the high school level in California, which ultimately influence a student's
likelihood of applying to and enrolling in college.

MOVING FORWARD:
THE CONCEPT OF EQUITY AS A CONSIDERATION

We saw that admit rates declined in California and Washington among underrepresented students post–209 and I-200 at the flagship institutions. And
in California, admission rates also declined at moderately selective campuses like UC–Davis. In addition to declines in admit rates at the flagship
institution in Washington, enrollment rates diminished post–I-200. Higher education access post–affirmative action for underrepresented students
therefore remains limited despite several policy plans such as percent plans
and holistic review in admissions practices. There simply is no substitute for
utilizing race as a factor in admissions. And given the *Grutter* decision by
the U.S. Supreme Court and the recent decision in *Abigail Noel Fisher and
Rachel Multer Michalewicz vs. University of Texas at Austin; et. al.* (2009),
in Texas by Judge Sparks concurring with *Grutter*, a window of opportunity remains open to consider race and ethnicity as one of many factors that
deem a student "merit-worthy" of admission to an institution.

In 2005, I outlined five recommendations for the UC system to consider.
I revisit three of them here, including: clarifying the concept of merit at
flagship institutions and how it is operationalized in admissions processes;
establishing equity indexes or an equity-in-opportunity policy for higher
education systems; and assessing and considering the status of parity among
graduating pools of students by ethnicity, the K–12 population, and admitted classes to flagship public institutions (Contreras, 2005). In California,
the concept of merit was called a "moving target" by a senior university
official post–Proposition 209. This classification and practice make it difficult for outreach and admissions staff to convey transparent admission

guidelines to prospective students and parents. If merit is a "moving target," then which student groups are most likely to set the baseline for merit? Are flagship institutions merely a reflection of highly stratified schools, largely segregated by race and class? How do legacy admits factor into conceptualizations of merit and is this practice justifiable, beyond the obvious financial incentives to cultivate donors? These are questions for higher education systems, institutions, and leaders to consider as slots for the public flagship institutions become even more competitive. Given the competing slots for admission, a more expansive approach to merit, one rooted in social justice and equity, is critical to ensuring that public higher education is accountable to the tax base that funds their very existence. Merit as a "moving target" is inherently inequitable. Thus, taking the mystery out of merit would provide a framework for understanding how eligibility is determined. Finally, a closer look at preferences for the wealthy is long overdue. How can institutions legally continue to justify one form of affirmative action, legacy preferences, while racial and ethnic diversity falls short of the multicultural high school graduate population? Banning these practices that are based on wealth and ancestry would help to ensure a greater level of equity for students who do not come from privilege.

An equity-in-opportunity policy or equity index is a second recommendation that proposes considering students' school, family, economic, and linguistic context when measuring their aptitude for undergraduate success. This recommendation stems from the work of the indicators project at UCLA (Oakes, 2002), which identifies the inputs that students have access to within their school and community contexts to successfully prepare and transition to college. This policy construct goes beyond holistic review practices because it formalizes the approach to measuring opportunity, using a broad set of indicators of access, within high school contexts.

Finally, I raise the issue of parity with multiple student population characteristics to understand and measure progress toward a more inclusive and accessible higher education context within states (Contreras, 2003, 2005a). Bensimon and colleagues (2005) describe this same phenomenon as an equity index ratio, which is a formula that also measures the representation of a particular group in a category (such as access) against their representation in a larger population. Measuring parity rates between applicants to flagship institutions and cohorts of high school graduates by race/ethnicity (Harris & Tienda, 2010) is one approach to assessing underrepresented student access. In addition, a parity standard would provide a direct return to taxpayers, who essentially support the public higher education system that exists in respective states (Contreras, 2005a; St. John, 2003). In a time when states are fast becoming multicultural and bilingual, it is important to measure the degree to which a state is serving all residents by cultivating talent from all ethnic groups to attend postsecondary institutions.

The "Sleeping Giant" Is Awake: Raising Latino Student Achievement and Success Through Education Policy

The "Sleeping Giant" was a term applied to Latinos throughout the 1980s and 1990s to depict a community that had not yet realized its political potential, given the tremendous demographic growth trends, particularly throughout the Southwest. Now that the long-predicted Latino population boom is here and extends beyond southwestern states, the national political arena and business sector are starting to take notice of this growing voting block and emerging market. We have seen presidential candidates trying to speak Spanish on the stump, marketing campaigns on Spanish-language television, and the growing presence of Latino images in television and film, all attempting to reach out to Latino voters, consumers, and audiences. At the same time, we are witnessing elected officials targeting Latino immigrants through attempts to alter the Fourteenth Amendment; a state law in Arizona requiring proof of residency; and an attempt by Congress in 2006 to pass a "Secure Fence Act," which called for constructing a 700-mile fence across the southern border of the United States. This paradoxical relationship is not new to the Latino population. From 1942 to 1964, the United States implemented the *bracero* program, which brought over 4 million workers into the United States to provide low-cost labor to the agricultural sector (Menchaca, 1995). This labor block at different periods in U.S. history has shouldered the wave of frustration resulting from local and national economic downturns. This frustration has made its way into the policy arena and everyday discriminatory practices across institutional sectors. Presently, undocumented Latino workers continue to fill a void in various economic sectors, and, like the *braceros*, they are taken advantage of, exposed to long hours and poor working conditions, and their children are subjected to inequities in the school system. In addition, in an attempt to dehumanize their existence, undocumented immigrants have and continue to be referred to as "illegal aliens," reflecting the federal government's long-standing classification and usage of the term in immigration law. This characterization feeds the already blatant disregard for the rights of undocumented individuals residing in the United States.

In addition to the continuous wave of Latino immigrants to the United States, there are also long-standing communities of Latinos that are third-, fourth-, or fifth-generation and beyond in many states. However, their fates are similar to that of Latino immigrants, with limited gains in social and economic mobility across generations (Grogger & Trejo, 2002; Telles & Ortiz, 2008). Their treatment in the United States is therefore intertwined with the discriminatory climate that exists toward Latinos. And now that Latinos are fast becoming a significant proportion of the U.S. population and have a voting presence, a culture of fear, propagated by groups that have traditionally dominated all social and economic structures, has emerged full force.

This chapter proposes policy recommendations that will alter the current path and stagnant progress among Latinos in the United States. National, state, and local political participation is key to influencing educational policies that affect Latinos and poor children. This chapter is also a wake-up call to the Latino community to serve as partners in the solutions proposed—to be active agents of change, leadership, and inspiration to the children in our midst who are longing for advocates and role models. No longer can the Latino community rely solely on "the system" to recognize its needs or concerns. Actively engaging in the change process requires the commitment and tenacity to engage the policy arena at multiple levels to address the shortcomings of existing policies that directly impact Latino, underrepresented, and low-income children. The paradox of limited investment in Latinos may be altered, in part, through greater levels of Latino community involvement in helping to determine which investments are made, how to address current levels of inequity, and what levels of government share in the responsibility of providing students with an education that prepares them to be productive residents, neighbors, and leaders.

EFFECTIVELY UTILIZING THE LEGAL ARENA
TO PROMOTE EDUCATIONAL EQUITY

Using the legal arena to promote educational equity is not new in the field of education. Beginning in the 1930s, the Latino and African American communities launched battles for educational equality in the courts. Organizations like the NAACP, MALDEF, and the ACLU have also been at the forefront of advocating for student and civil rights in the education sector. In addition, landmark Supreme Court cases such as *Brown v. Board of Edu-*

cation in 1954 helped to pave the way for a more integrated educational system, where the practices of "separate but equal" services in schools, ruled as legal by the Supreme Court in *Plessy v. Ferguson* (1896), were no longer legally permissible. For Mexican Americans and Chicanos in the Southwest, the legal battles began almost three decades earlier than *Brown* in 1925 with *Romo v. Laird* case, where Adolfo Romo from Arizona sued Tempe Elementary School District No. 3 on behalf of his four children, who were required to attend the Eighth Street School, the school designated for Spanish or Mexican children (Valencia, 2008). Romo sought admission for his children to other schools in the district that had better teachers and resources. Although the ruling was favorable to Romo, it applied only to his children, who were allowed to seek admission to other schools in the district. While the case affected only an individual family, it marked the first in a long series of segregation cases where language and pedagogy have been used as the rationale for separating Latino children from their peers (Valencia, 2008). Two subsequent cases, *Independent School District v. Salvatierra* (1930) in Texas and *Alvarez v. the Lemon Grove Incident in California*, involved Mexican American students who were segregated on the basis of not being White and/or speaking Spanish, when only Black children, who were legally considered to be of another race, were segregated. Neither ruling, however, addressed the premise of segregation and equality.[1] In 1946, in *Mendez v. Westminister School District* in California, The League of United Latin American Citizens (LULAC) filed a complaint on behalf of five families to challenge the placement of their children in separate Mexican schools in Los Angeles. This judge for the U.S. district court of Los Angeles found that the practice of school segregation was unconstitutional and violated the equal protection of these students. This case was a notable step toward ending the practices of "separate but equal." However, children subjected to segregated schools would have to wait until the *Brown* decision in 1954 for the Supreme Court to rule on the unlawful practices of "separate" schools.

Despite the *Brown* decision, the issue of school segregation remains a pervasive issue for the Latino community. The Keyes decision (1973) in Denver by the U.S. Supreme Court recognized the rights of Latino students as eligible for desegregation remedies, due to the discrimination they faced in schools. In addition, the court paid special attention to the linguistic needs of Latino children.

In the current context, the issue of segregation has been expanded to include "within-school segregation," whereby Latino students are isolated or underserved in a school context that is racially diverse on the basis of language proficiency. In the case of *Santamaria v. Dallas Independent School District* (2006), The Mexican American Legal Defense Fund (MALDEF) filed a complaint on behalf of the Santamaria family, whose children were placed into English as a Second Language (ESL) classes even though they had not been classified as English Learner (EL) students. The argument successfully presented to the courts by MALDEF contended that their segregation limited their opportunity to learn, labeled and treated Latino students as inferior, and violated the Equal Protection Clause of the Fourteenth Amendment and the 1964 Civil Rights Act (Valencia, 2008).

School placement on the basis of residency and neighborhood boundaries also fosters Latino student segregation. Latino students attend largely segregated schools because they tend to live in ethnically isolated communities (Gándara & Contreras, 2009). Housing segregation in several types of districts (rural, urban, urban ring) and gentrification patterns in large urban settings are therefore closely intertwined with the problem of school segregation (Gándara & Contreras, 2009).

A hopeful glimpse toward integration can be seen in the case of Jefferson County in Louisville, Kentucky. After the Supreme Court decision in *Meredith v. Jefferson County School Board* (2007) ruled against race as a consideration in school placement, the district implemented a multifaceted approach to student placement that included a broader conception of diversity based on racial composition, family income, and parent educational attainment levels. According to recent research by Orfield and Frankenberg (2004), over 90% of parents believe that diversity has an important educational benefit for their children, and 89% believed that their child should learn among children from different economic and racial backgrounds. The district's approach in Jefferson County therefore, by more broadly defining student diversity in its placement decisions, serves as a potential model for integration despite the legal limitations that ended their previous integration plan.

Seattle is on the spectrum opposite Jefferson County, as their response to the Supreme Court decision and efforts to ensure a level of diversity across schools has been minmal. On November 18, 2009, the Seattle School Board passed a plan based on neighborhood boundaries for student placement in high schools and middle schools throughout the district. Due to the Supreme Court's 5–4 ruling in *Parents Involved in Community Schools v. Seattle School District 1* (2007), schools may no longer use race/ethnicity as a sole factor in assigning students to schools. The response in Seattle, therefore, represents a return to student placement based on geographical location within the district. Gary Orfield is critical of school placement efforts tied to home ownership and residential patterns because they inherently produce ethnic segregation and isolation (Orfield, 1997; Orfield & Eaton, 1996; Orfield & Lee, 2005). Historically, such efforts based on housing patterns have put Blacks and other low-income students at a disadvantage (Gándara & Orfield, 2010; Orfield, 1981, 1996; Orfield & Frankenburg, 2004).The district plan represents a step toward rolling back the clock on racial integration of public schools. The school placement plan based on residency is likely to further exacerbate the inequities already affecting underrepresented students across schools within the district. Seattle provides an important oppositional test case to Jefferson County Public Schools in Kentucky as to how legal rulings are implemented and shape the approaches to addressing racial isolation in the education sector. While the issue of school segregation has become far more complex, the legal arena has been and remains a viable tool for addressing the inequitable access to comparable infrastructures and educational services.

Now more than ever, the legal system is relevant to the rights of Latinos. As seen in the case of Arizona, where undocumented immigrants have been targeted through legislation, civil rights organizations such as the ACLU and MALDEF have fought to halt the implementation of various aspects of SB 1070. On July 28, 2010, Judge Susan Bolton put on hold provisions of the law that would require police to check immigration status while enforcing other law violations. Because 26 other states have initiated legislation similar to Arizona's, this law is likely to be challenged further in the courts. The battleground to challenge such discriminatory laws largely exists in the courts.

More important and alarming is the recent attempt in August 2010 to revise Section 1 of the Fourteenth Amendment, an effort by members of the Republican Party that targets the children of undocumented immigrants by challenging their right to citizenship if born on U.S. soil. They have called for Senate hearings to modify the citizenship clause, claiming that undocumented "anchor babies" are essentially using their children to petition for legal residency status (Kahn, 2010). Such claims by leading Republicans serve to dehumanize undocumented immigrants and unjustly characterize them and their children as criminals. As immigration reform continues to enter the national debate and the economic downturn continues nationally, the Latino community are likely to continue to serve as a scapegoat and target of hostility.

FINANCES AND RESOURCES

As a result of the inequitable distribution of financial resources in the public education system, landmark cases have also emerged to address uneven investment and serve as proof of the differential opportunities to learn that Latino, low-income, and underrepresented students experience in schools. The legal arena has been at the forefront of challenging educational inequity, particularly cases that address the issue of school resources and the necessary components for funding an equitable education. Over 35 states have witnessed school finance lawsuits to address the issue of school finance reform and resource allocation across schools.

Serrano v. Priest (1971), (*Serrano* I) in California was the first school finance case that successfully challenged the disparities in school expenditures produced through property wealth variations and the ability of select districts to generate revenues for schools (Rodriguez, 2007). The *Serrano* cases lasted for over two decades and ultimately led to equalizing basic education funding across California school districts in the *Serrano* II (1976) and *Serrano* III (1977) decisions (Rodriguez, 2007). The *San Antonio School District v. Rodriguez* (1971) and *San Antonio Independent School District v. Rodriguez* (1973) (*Rodriguez* II) cases, occurring around the same time as the *Serrano* cases in California, established the foundation for the 1973 Texas Supreme Court decision in *Edgewood v. Kirby* (1987) by challenging the funding disparities between districts with high and low property wealth. In the *Edgewood* decision, the judge sided with the plaintiffs and mandated that all students, whether they were enrolled in school districts with high or low property wealth, be afforded equal educational opportunities and access to school funds (Valencia, 2008). Despite these victories, the issue of school finance equity remains a topic for the courts, as many states have followed the path of challenging state and district school funding structures. Table 7.1 outlines key contemporary education finance cases in the United States. Recent school finance litigation rulings in Washington— *Federal Way School District v. State of Washington* (2009) and *McCleary v. State of Washington* (2010)—addressed the legality of school funding in the state. The *Federal Way School District* case successfully argued that school districts were denied funds to provide educational opportunities to students, which is required by the state constitution. *McCleary* was an adequacy case, challenging the state's funding for basic education services across districts. On February 19, 2010, Judge Erlick found that the state had failed to adhere to the state's constitutional requirement and fulfill its "paramount duty" to fund basic education services to all students "within its border." His ruling is considered among the strongest adequacy rulings that deemed the state's funding system unconstitutional.

A third legal case tied to school funding that has been recently decided and directly applies to Latino students deals with funding allocated to English Learners in Arizona to provide them with equal educational opportunities. *Horne vs. Flores* was filed in 1992 and, after a series of decisions, was decided by the Supreme Court in a 5 to 4 decision on June 25, 2009. The Court overturned the state court's decision in favor of State Superintendent of Public Instruction Horne, which now allows the state of Arizona to determine its approach and requirement for educating English Learners. The dissenting opinion, written by Justice Breyer (with Justices, Ginsburg, Souter, and Stevens), argued that the majority decision was wrongly based on a "procedural framework," rather than one that focuses on compliance with state and federal laws of EL students, which grants them equal protection. He further reminded the Court that EL students need for schools to provide them with the "tools" to succeed:

TABLE 7.1. Key Contemporary Education Finance Cases in United States

Case	Year Filed	Decision
McCleary v. State of Washington	2007	2010; Favor of Plaintiffs. State of WA fails to provide basic educational opportunity and fulfill its "paramount duty" in educating all residents
Federal Way School District, No. 210 v. State of Washington	2006	2009; Favor of Plaintiffs. State Supreme Court rules that funding for school salaries do not require districts to uniformly fund staff salaries.
Pendelton School District v. State of Oregon	2006	2009; Favor of Plaintiff. State has failed to fund the Oregon Public School System "to meet the quality education goals established by law."
Nebraska Coalition for Educational Equity and Adequacy (NCEEA) v. Heineman.	2007	2007; Favors Defendant; Supreme Court affirmed district court decision: "The district court determined the Coalition's allegations that the Legislature had failed to provide sufficient funds to provide for an adequate education posed a non-justiciable political question" (p. 3).
DeRolf v. State of Ohio	1991	2002; Favored Plaintiff: Ohio Supreme Court ruled that the state "fails to provide for a thorough and efficient system of common schools" which is required by the Ohio Constitution.
Montoy v. State, No. 99-C-1738 (Shawnee County) (November 21, 2001)	2001	2006; Favor of Defendant after the state adhered to 2003 ruling (which favored plaintiff) and required state to remedy funding inequity by allocating resources for at risk students.
Williams v. State of California	2000	2004; Favor of Plaintiff and led to $138 million in state allocations for instructional materials and $800 will be allocated toward capital projects (facilities repair).
Zuni School District v. State, CV-98-14-II (Dist. Ct., McKinley County) (October 14, 1999)	1999	2007; New Mexico Supreme Court Ruled in favor of state, allowing the state to utilize federal impact aid in the calculations for state appropriations.
Abbeville County School District v. State, 515 S.E.2d 535 (S.C. 1999)	1999	2007; "The students in the Plaintiff Districts are denied the opportunity to receive a minimally adequate education because of the lack of effective and adequately funded early childhood intervention programs designed to address the impact of poverty on their educational abilities and achievements." (p. 1).
Tennessee Small School Systems v. McWherter, 851 S.W.2d 139 (Small Schools I)	1993	2009; State Supreme argues against funding disparities across schools and asserts that local control does not justify inequality in resource distribution.
Horne, Arizona Superintendent of Public Instruction v. Flores, et. al.	1992	2009; Favor of State (Horne).

Source: http://www.schoolfunding.info

The case concerns the rights of Spanish-speaking students, attending public school near the Mexican border, to learn English in order to live their lives in a country where English is the predominant language. In a Nation where nearly 47 million people (18% of the population) speak a language other than English at home, U. S. Dept. of Commerce, Economics and Statistics Admin., Census Bureau, Census 2000 Brief: Language Use and English-Speaking Ability 2 (Oct. 2003), it is important to ensure that those children, without losing the cultural heritage embodied in the language of their birth, nonetheless receive the English language tools they need to participate in a society where that second language "serves as the fundamental medium of social interaction" and democratic participation. Rodríguez, Language and Participation, 94 Cal. L. Rev. 687, 693 (2006). In that way linguistic diversity can complement and support, rather than undermine, our democratic institutions. *Id.*, at 688. (*Horne, Arizona Superintendent of Public Instruction v. Flores, et. al.* p. 45.)

Justice Breyer's dissenting opinion opens up the larger issue of language as a democratizing tool. To deny EL students the opportunity and tools they need within schools to learn English and become biliterate, is to deny them skills that complement and support a healthy democracy, which education fosters.

MOVING AN EDUCATION POLICY AGENDA FORWARD

In *The Latino Education Crisis* (2009), Patricia Gándara and I issued a call to action for the nation to address the serious crisis among Latino students and the implications for the United States if the current path is not altered. That call to action included a policy agenda with a set of seven recommendations for all stakeholders to consider addressing to meet the unmet needs of Latino students in the United States today. These central issues provide a complementary policy framework for this chapter, as I discuss how the educational policy arena and various actors, including the Latino community, may work to change the current policy framework to address the needs of Latino students throughout the education system. These seven components of a policy agenda are considered a necessary step in what we called "Rescuing the American Dream" for Latinos and all children who experience inequities in their educational contexts. The recommendations include the following:

1. Better health care and access to social services
2. Subsidized preschool programs
3. Housing desegregation and stabilizations initiatives
4. Target recruitment and better preparation for teachers
5. Immigration policy reform, including passage of the DREAM Act

6. Support for dual-language education
7. Dropout prevention and college access programs. (Gándara & Contreras, 2009, pp. 330–332)

In this book, I have laid out additional areas within the larger educational policy arena that complement and expand upon the recommendations listed above, including the following:

1. Addressing the cracks in the pipeline that inhibit the successful transition to college for Latinos
2. The need for a college for all policy
3. Reframing the discussion around testing and accountability
4. The need for accurate state longitudinal data systems that informs practice
5. Addressing college affordability
6. Increasing financial aid availability
7. Revisiting the need to pass the DREAM Act
8. Realizing the unfinished business of the stated objectives of affirmative action policy
9. Utiling P-20 Councils to Address Educational Inequity and Uneven Postsecondary Access

Increase the Number of Latinos Transitioning to and Graduating from College

Raising college transition rates and the percentages of Latinos who earn college degrees is a policy agenda intertwined with the need to address the dropout crisis among communities of color (Gándara & Contreras, 2009; Orfield, 2004). The data presented in Chapter 2 present an alarming story where approximately half of all Latinos, male and female, graduate from high school. The work of Levin, Belfield, Muennig, and Rouse (2007) further describes the economic sense it makes for the public to invest in raising high school graduation rates, with long-term public savings and increased tax benefits from the workforce. Prioritizing high school graduation in the education policy arena is a first step, but not nearly enough. Of the 55% that do graduate high school, less than half will go onto college, 60% of whom enroll first in community colleges. And of this already shrunken pool, only 42% will graduate from college within 6 years. The pattern of falling off the educational path continues at every stage in the education pipeline. A P-20 approach, one that connects the various aspects of the educational pipeline, is a necessary infrastructural change. States and the federal government should prioritize efforts that connect successes along the educational continuum rather than focusing only on specific age groups for short-term outcomes. In addition, assessing student progress from preschool through college should also be a priority across states and mandated by the federal government. We are unable to assess student achievement progress and equity if faulty data continue to inform policy decisions and educational investments. Furthermore, creating a college-going culture early (Gándara & Contreras, 2009; McDonough, 2004; McDonough & Gildersleeve; 2005) is critical to increasing the number of Latinos and students that transition successfully to postsecondary education. Raising college preparedness and postsecondary graduation rates are necessary steps toward ensuring the economic vitality of this country and a citizenry that is poised for global competitiveness.

A College-for-All Policy

In addition to the need to prepare and transition more Latino students to college, a college-for-all policy at the federal level would send a strong signal across the P-20 continuum that college or a form of postsecondary training is expected of all students. Such a policy would implement a more skilled work force and equip individual students with the additional skills and training necessary to compete in a global marketplace. Imagine a society where students had either a college degree or specific training that enabled them to sustain their families and communities (Gándara and Contreras, 2009). While not all colleges or training programs are equal, the benefits of additional years in college and professional certification beyond high school has been found to provide economic returns to states, communities, and the federal government in the form of greater tax revenues for public infrastructures and personal disposable income (Baum & Payea, 2004). If there is one take away from this current and extended economic recession, it is the importance of education.

In the present economic recession, individuals without a college degree have higher levels of unemployment. In January 2011, according to the Bureau of Labor Statistics, the unemployment rate for individuals with less than a high school diploma was 14.2%, for high school graduates 9.4%, and 4.2% for individuals with a college degree. In addition, Latinos were also more likely to have a higher unemployment rate than Whites: 11.9% compared to 8% (based on data from the Bureau of Labor Statistics, 2011). One could argue that in addition to inherent employer biases that minorities experience from potential employers (Kirschenman & Neckerman, 1991; Neckerman & Kirschenman, 1991; Wilson, 1990), the lower Latino educational attainment levels confine them to a more limited set of job options, thus accounting for higher unemployment rates. The ongoing recession illustrates that higher educated individuals are better prepared for market uncertainty. Those without a college degree (2-year and 4-year) are more likely to experience a longer period of unemployment versus those with college degrees.

A college-for-all policy would ensure that individuals possess a higher level of training that affords greater employment options. This additional training and education would come from a diverse base of postsecondary institutions that currently exist—from 2-year to technical colleges to traditional 4-year institutions and highly selective institutions for example. Individuals have a multitude of choices to engage in postsecondary training that ultimately benefits both the individual and our society with a highly trained workforce to adhere to the demands of diverse sectors. Regardless of institutional type, college completion does lead to long-term social and economic benefits for multiple entities (Baum & Payea, 2004). Raising college completion rates will therefore expand the workforce and contribute to national economic development (Hanushek & Kimko, 2000; Lee & Rawls, 2010).

For the Latino community, expanding the base of educated workers is critical to the nation's economic health (Gándara & Contreras, 2009). Thus, a college-for-all policy would provide a mandate for postsecondary training and degree attainment for all students aspiring and alter the culture of high schools to prepare students for a successful transition to higher education.

Reframe Approaches to Testing and Accountability

Reframing the current accountability framework is long overdue. Many scholars have critiqued the current framework for the emphasis that is placed on testing and the influence that high-stakes tests have had on pedagogical approaches, evaluating teacher effectiveness, and the overall morale among teachers, students, and staff attempting to raise achievement levels among students to pass exams (Amrein & Berliner, 2002; Nichols, Glass, & Berliner, 2006; Valenzuela, 2004). Further, for most states, gaps in achievement place the onus of passing such exit exams on the student, rather than the school or district that fails to provide appropriate opportunities to learn and achieve across schools (Contreras et al., 2008). Chapter 3 highlighted the differences in achievement between Latinos and their peers, particularly the lowest levels of achievement occurring among EL students. The test score patterns, regardless of the state context, have remained consistent over the past 50 years, with underrepresented, low-income students scoring lower than their White peers. These data suggest that an uneven set of inputs exist for disadvantaged students. Thus, test scores are not likely to change unless educational practices change. Placing the responsibility for passing exit exams largely on students who have the most to lose has turned out to be bad public policy. We also have very little evidence from the 28 states that have them in place that exit exams have raised student achievement levels or preparation, or have dramatically reduced high school dropout rates (Reardon, Atteberry, Arshan, & Kurlaender, 2009). While we need good assessment tools that measure student progress, testing has the potential to represent more than measures that tell us about the same gaps in achievement that have existed since the inception of testing. Instead, assessment tools should actually be used to inform practice and education service delivery.

Developing and Utilizing State Longitudinal Data Systems to Inform Practice

NCLB and state policies related to student testing and accountability fall short of utilizing analyses of testing data to inform practices for raising student achievement and education service delivery. While test scores are largely summative, that is, used to assess student achievement in particular content areas, data from these assessments are rarely transmitted to teachers and parents on an individual level and thus do not play a formative role.

Currently, approximately 48 states claim to have longitudinal data systems in place. However, when rated by the Data Quality Campaign (DQC), a national collaboration that encourages states and policy makers to establish and utilize high quality data systems to raise achievement, only one state, Texas, had completed nine of its 10 essential state actions that the DQC considers essential to creating a high quality longitudinal data system. In addition, only nine states had linked their data systems across sectors (DQC, 2009). These essential actions as outlined by the Data Quality Campaign are good benchmarks for states to measure their progress towards ensuring the accuracy of statewide data systems and the usage of these data across the P-20 continuum to inform achievement and long-term outcomes.

For Latino and EL students, these longitudinal data play a critical role in understanding access (or inequitable access) to relevant and rigorous curriculum, tracking, informing pedagogical practices at the school level, understanding the efficacy of EL instruction and approaches, and tracing patterns of school leavers and their academic standing at the point of departure. Unfortunately, many state data systems are not easily accessible to the public. Having linked data does not translate into effective use—states must work towards making data transparent, easily accessible to the public, and accurate in its content to ensure valid analysis.

Accuracy in data collection and coding are therefore critical for optimal utility to states. While many states have created or are in the process of creating P-20 data systems, many states have just begun to enact what DQC calls "action ten": state audits to assess data quality, and it is unclear whether such audits include auditing the reporting practices by school districts.

Address College Affordability

The response to budget downturns recently seen across the United States by higher education systems and institutions has been to raise tuition rates for students. This approach has students borrowing in unprecedented amounts and rates, and it is an unsustainable avenue for ensuring a promising economic future for our nation's youth. Students graduating from college in 2010, for example, have high debt and are entering the workforce while salaries are at an all-time low—that is, if they are able to secure employment. According to a report by the College Board, the median debt amount for students who graduated from a public university in 2008 was $17,700, a 4% increase from 2004 (Steele & Baum, 2009). Thus, consistently raising tuition rates will likely set the next generation up for financial difficulty and contribute to a growing debt problem. Furthermore, because Latino students are more likely to be debt-averse (Cunningham & Santiago, 2008), these students are more likely to enter community colleges, where transfer rates and degree attainment rates are lower. Addressing college affordability in the policy sector is therefore critical, particularly during economic downturns, when employment opportunities are limited.

According to President Obama's plan for expanding access to college, his American Opportunity Tax Credit, part of the 2009 Recovery Act, provides a fully refundable tax credit worth $2,500 for tuition and fees for the 2009 and 2010 tax years. While this act sends a positive message from the administration about the importance of making college affordable, this legislation essentially modified the HOPE Credit program instituted under the Clinton administration in 1997. Obama's original campaign promise of a $4,000 tax credit is a much more progressive and bold attempt to make a 4-year college affordable, particularly for low-income students and families. The policy sector is therefore a tangible arena where communities can assert their concerns about college affordability and access, and expand upon the precedents that exist at federal and state levels in providing tax credits to families.

Increase Financial Aid Availability

Cost controls for education are one important approach to ensuring that higher education remains affordable. Tax credits from the federal government are another approach to addressing rising college costs for families. However, neither approach to affordability fully addresses the financial needs students experience to attend college. Increasing the availability of financial aid for students is also one of the best policy approaches and investments in human capital that we as a society can make in our own economic future. These students are already in the doors of higher education, and with degrees, their productivity is likely to be greater over the long term (Baum & Payea, 2005). The trend in higher education to increase loans rather than provide financial aid or scholarships places economically disadvantaged students in the difficult position of accruing levels of debt that are unprecedented in higher education. No longer is the college graduate able to afford the lifestyle of his or her parents a generation ago. Rather, the high levels of debt are creating a foundation for a youthful "debtor generation" whose job choices are based on their ability to pay back sizable student loans while trying to enjoy the fruits of their individual educational investment to earn a college degree. As states increasingly choose to raise student tuition for public higher education institutions, increased financial aid opportunities are an important part of the equation to ensure postsecondary access for high-achieving Latino and underrepresented students. As Chapter 4 points out, state merit aid programs have relatively narrow conceptions of merit, disproportionately placing low income and underrepresented students at a comparative disadvantage to their White peers from higher income families (Heller & Marin, 2004; Marin, 2002). One approach for states to consider as they administer their merit aid programs is expanding the criteria to include more expansive background characteristics such as first-generation status; immigration background (e.g., if they came to the United States in high school); or received EL services while in K–12—factors that indicate a greater likelihood of having socioeconomic barriers or experiencing systemic inequities in school. Another criterion for merit aid that some private foundations have implemented is specific scholarships for students who plan to enter into the teaching profession. Expanding access to state, federal, and institutional merit aid, especially programs funded by state lotteries that all consumers fund, and by examining who they currently benefit, is one viable approach to addressing Latino student access to aid.

Financial aid helps to buffer the rising costs of tuition and living expenses and conveys to students an appreciation for their personal investment and dedication to their educational advancement. Students must not bear the responsibility for the economic shortfalls of systems, institutions, and states while they are trying to become more productive citizens. Their role as taxpayers, educated and skilled workers, and engaged citizens will have greater returns to society if they have a college degree in hand.

Pass a Federal DREAM Act

While we are in need of comprehensive immigration reform (Gándara & Contreras, 2009; Gonzales, 2007), a federal DREAM Act for the most deserving students is one policy that could be enacted separately and ahead of comprehensive immigration reform. The DREAM Act is a win-win situation for this country. Chapter 5 illustrated the lives of hardworking, high-achieving Latino students who want nothing more than to be able to be productive citizens and revealed the struggles that undocumented students experience in trying to obtain the right to work and attend school that many people take for granted. And yet these students from community colleges and 4-year institutions still remain optimistic about their place in a country that rejects their right to be here—even if this is the only home they have known. These students provide a wonderful example of individuals who choose to give back to their families and broader communities, across racial and ethnic lines. They are profiles of leadership, compassion, and dedication. Finally, the educational success achieved by undocumented students in the sample is earned, not given. Without a federal DREAM Act in place, we as a nation are losing out on our ability to capitalize on the talents of some of the brightest, most disciplined young minds with a strong work ethic that is consistent with the principles this country was founded upon.

Realize the Unfinished Objectives of Affirmative Action Policy

As Chapter 6 notes, admit rates in California and Washington declined at the flagship institutions and, in California, also declined at moderately selective UC campuses such as UC–Davis. This example sheds light on an important fact that remains relevant to policy discourse on affirmative action: that banning the use of race in admissions, despite policy alternatives like holistic review and percent plans, has diminished access to flagship institutions (Contreras, 2005b; Harris & Tienda, 2010; Orfield & Miller, 1998; Horn & Flores, 2003). Admission rates among underrepresented students at selective institutions have always been a challenge and nowhere near parity with the composition of students that exist in the K–12 population and graduating classes (Contreras, 2005b). However, as seen in the data from Washington and California, and as a senior UC administrator described, "A major tool was taken away."

Race was never the sole factor for college admission in any of the major higher education systems or Research I institutions where legal cases have emerged. The debate has become conflated with concepts of merit, fairness, and reverse discrimination—concepts that do not fully acknowledge the current system of inequity that low-income, first-generation, underrepresented students continue to experience in schools. The multidecade discussions centered around gaps in student achievement and opportunities to learn throughout the United States indicate that inequities in service delivery have been and remain real and pervasive for underrepresented students, particularly students from low-income backgrounds.

Perhaps reframing the goals of affirmative action policy is a necessary first step. When I examined access to the University of California following Proposition 209, one of my key recommendations called for clarifying the concept of merit. In California admissions, merit was a "moving target" defined by an ever-changing applicant pool. Students who had the financial resources to take SAT preparation courses, lived in areas where abundant Advanced Placement (AP) course offerings existed at their school, had minimal worries about school violence, or were not required to contribute to their household finances were measured against students with very different social and economic contexts. Even under holistic review policies, we have yet to see a return to pre-209 levels, which never represented optimal representation or reflected a level close to parity with the ethnic representation in K–12 schools. One of the recommendations of this study (Contreras, 2005b) was to establish an equity index that staff would use in admissions decisions. The index would more systematically validate school context in admissions considerations (Contreras, 2005b). The equity index, modeled after the work of the Indicators Project at UCLA (Oakes, 2002), would identify the inputs that schools have to provide an infrastructure for learning, achievement, and college transition. The reality remains that, even under holistic review, students who have taken a more rigorous high school curriculum or participated in dual-enrollment programs get a boost in admissions consideration. These students are also less likely to be Latino or from underrepresented groups because socioeconomic status is closely intertwined with access to a college-going culture and a rigorous high school curriculum. Reframing the concept of affirmative action to one that proposes an equity-in-opportunity policy is an important paradigm shift that removes the perceived notion that students are given a greater competitive advantage than their White or more economically advantaged peers. Under an equity framework, students would be more heavily measured by achievement in their school context rather than being unfairly measured for the socioeconomic limitations of their background. Finally, the proposed shift to an equity framework would also challenge the current practice of legacy admits, which unfairly advantages wealthy students from elite backgrounds and further contributes to social stratification in this country.

Utilizing P-20 Councils as Vehicles for Addressing Inequity and Uneven Postsecondary Access

Currently at least 38 states have P-16/P-20 councils. Efforts among these councils have ranged from examining statewide standards and assessments to supporting the creation of systemic P-20 data systems. P-20 councils in 31 states play an advisory role to the Governor in their respective states, while three states (North Carolina, Oregon, and Tennessee) have administrative authority over select state programs (Education Commission of the States, 2010).

P-20 councils have the potential to play an important role within states, with their ability to push Governors' agendas to address systemic inequities and opportunity gaps across sectors, as well as the opportunity to increase collaborative efforts across institutional and policy-making bodies. They also have the potential to push states to more effectively use longitudinal data to inform policies and practices related to EL instruction, exit exam performance, dropouts, curricular offerings and equity, teacher quality and transition to college rates among students.

THE PATHWAY TO SHAPING EDUCATIONAL POLICY

Latinos can no longer expect leaders to develop educational policies to address their needs and concerns if they are not part of the political process at national, state, and local levels. Being part of these key processes is one way of ensuring that the needs and concerns of their children, particularly as it relates to English Language Learners and the neglect these students encounter in schools, do not remain inequitable. There are various ways to ensure Latino student needs are met in schools. The first is for parents to be engaged in the educational process of their children, and the second is to become politically involved. First, parent involvement is critical to ensuring students' positive self-concept, modeling education as a priority within the home, and influencing the direction of student experiences (e.g., course placement) throughout the education system. Parents who are involved in their child's education are more likely to see positive achievement in school and positive attitudes toward school (Hoover-Dempsey et al., 2001). Thus, there is no replacement for advocating for the educational experiences and rights of one's own child.

The second recommendation applies to civic engagement and the need for Latinos to become active politically at multiple levels. Figure 7.1 illustrates the percent of eligible Latinos who are registered to vote and the percentage in which they turn out in elections across select years compared to White registered voters. Overall, Latinos represented approximately 8% of the voter population in the United States compared to 83% of Whites and 12% of African Americans. Recall, however, from Chapter 1, that Latinos represent 15% of the national population. These data could also reflect the youthful age distribution of Latinos. In addition, 92% of Latinos under the age of 18 are American born, while 42% over the age of 18 were born in the U.S. (U.S. Census Bureau, 2009). However, as Figure 7.1 shows, only 60% of the Latino population are registered to vote, which translates into unrealized potential for shaping policies that are relevant to the economic, health, social, and educational concerns among Latinos in the United States. In addition, the lower percentage of registered voters inhibits the Latino community from having a strong voice in electing officials that are responsive to the needs of Latinos. What is promising, however, is the fact that higher percentages of eligible registered Latinos have been voting in recent years and the levels are returning to the levels witnessed from 1984 to 1992, with the highest level of representation occurring in 1992, with 91% of Latino registered voters participating in elections. In 2008, the voter turnout for Latino registered voters was 89.4% (U.S. Census Bureau, 2008).

Another ray of hope is seen through the national mobilization efforts among Latinos on May 1, 2006 to protest anti-immigration attacks by the Bush administration that criminalized undocumented immigrants (Fraga et al., 2010). The marches represented an unprecedented level of unity across Latin American, immigrant communities and supporters, and signaled to policy makers that Latinos have become a viable force in the political landscape (Fraga et. al., 2010). The elections that have taken place in subsequent years, national elections in particular, have witnessed steady growth in both the number of Latinos registering to vote and voting (Barreto, 2005; Fraga, 2010).

In addition to turning out to vote and becoming civically engaged, it is equally important for Latinos to become active in the political arena by seeking elected office. Representation at multiple levels of government would ensure that the linguistic, cultural, and economic needs of Latino students are raised in public settings.

This remains a challenge for the Latino community. While there have been increasing numbers of Latinos elected to office, the majority of such representation has occurred in states with high concentrations of Latinos, and less so in states with growing Latino communities. The latter states are therefore grappling with problems of representation and acknowledgment in the education and policy sectors. The number of Latinos in elected federal positions has also been limited, with only 26 elected officials. However, one promising statistic is the number of school board officials that have been elected to office, as seen in Table 7.2. Local school boards play a vital role in setting education policy for districts, and parents are likely to have more influence on their community by focusing at this local level.

The Importance of Multicultural Unity

The potential for the Latino community to utilize the policy arena to influence changes in the education sector is considerable. Moreover, creating cross-ethnic coalitions around core equity issues is likely to be the most effective approach to change the poor state of education service delivery. Thus, in addition to maximizing voting potential at multiple levels, multicultural alliance building with groups that suffer similar school contexts is increasingly important for developing an education policy agenda that also

FIGURE 7.1. Percent of Latino Registered Voters and the Turnout Percentage, Whites vs. Latinos, Select Election Years, 1984–2008

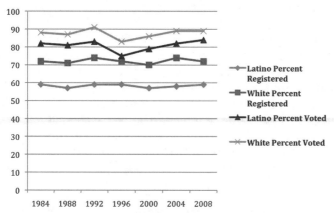

Source: US Census Bureau, 2008, Current Population Reports: Voting and Registration in the Election of November 1992, 1994, 1996, 1998, 2000, 2002, 2004, 2006 and 2008.

TABLE 7.2. Latino Elected Officials by Level of Office, 2007

Level of Office	Number
Federal	26
Statewide officials (including governor)	6
State legislators	238
County officials	512
Municipal officials	1640
Judicial/law enforcement officials	685
School board/education officials	1847
Special district officials	175
Total	5129

Source: *A Profile of Latino Elected Officials in the United States and their Progress Since 1996* (2007). A Publication of the National Association of Latino Elected Officials. Downloaded, October 1, 2009 at: http://www.naleo.org/pr071207.html

reframes the old deficit paradigms that are continuously applied to students of color. Such unity may occur at various levels, including:

- School level—PTA participation or the creation of bilingual/multicultural parent groups
- School board level
- City level—mayor's office; city commissions
- State level–elected officials and state commissions

- Federal/congressional level
- Senators
- Cabinet level

Recognizing the interdependence across disenfranchised and underserved communities is an important step toward raising educational standards for all children across racial and ethnic lines. Such efforts also reinforce the importance of equity and challenge hegemonic approaches to communities that continue to lack a voice in the education practices that directly impact their children. As the nation continues to become increasingly multicultural, with approximately 40% of the U.S. population comprised of underrepresented ethnic groups by 2020 (KewalRamani, Gilbertson, Fox, & Provasnik, 2007), the need for multicultural unity and awareness is timely.

CONCLUSION

The Brown Paradox is essentially America's paradox for failing to invest in the human capital of Latinos in the United States. Various public policies have and continue to jeopardize the very future of this nation. And now that Latinos are a significant proportion of public school students, we are beginning to consider the economic consequences of creating a permanent underclass that is unlikely to be able to sustain public services, Social Security, and a national infrastructure based on tax revenues that stem from income, homeownership, and productivity.

In a time of constrained and competing demands for improving the levels of resources allocated to education, the direction of our nation is in our hands. We can choose to establish the goal of educating America's children as a top priority, or we may continue on the current path of neglect that many of our students experience, despite major advances in technology and our status as a world leader among developed nations. I return to the quote in Chapter 1 where my niece described to me all of the inequities in her school that signaled she was attending what she called a "poor school." This image presents a vivid picture of the stark disparities that exist for Latino and low-income students in schools today. Multiple actors at various levels have the potential to alter a path that some say has already been predetermined. A Latino underclass is not a viable option for a nation that was established as a "melting pot" and encouraged citizen participation and ownership in democratic principles. Now it is our turn to ensure that the images of dilapidated schools, children without textbooks, lack of sports equipment at recess, or lack of access to extracurricular activities (like the school band) that positively influence student engagement and achievement do not represent the promise that this generation leaves for its children.

Notes

Chapter 1

1. The term English Language Learners (ELLs) is used interchangeably with English Learners (ELs) and Limited English Proficient (LEP) in this test and applies to students classified as needing linguistic instruction and services in schools and are enrolled in specific programs to assist them in learning English.

2. For an in-depth analysis of federal and state pre-K initiatives as well as estimated appropriations, see the Pre[k]now website at www.preknow.org.

Chapter 2

1. See, for example the College Board reports by Baum and Ma (2007) and Baum and Payea (2004), which describe the positive social and economic returns to higher education.

2. Four years represents the on-time graduation rate.

3. The definition of a dropout in the CCD file is based on school district reporting of an event dropout. The CCD provides an event dropout number through the U.S. Department of Education's Edfacts system. An event dropout number represents the proportion of students dropping out each year by October 1 of that year. The limited reporting of event dropouts therefore leaves out students who drop out after the October 1 collection date. However, for states that follow a July to June calendar, the dropout totals are calculated at the end of the academic year and are included in the CCD files.

4. For detailed information on the ACT benchmark score calculation index, see ACT Profile Report-National: Graduating Class 2009, www.act.org.

Chapter 3

1. Each state determines the passing rates for exit exams. For example, in California, students are required to pass the English component with 60% or higher, while the math section of the exam requires a score of 55% or higher. The state of Washington will, for example, phase in end of course exams in 2012 and these will serve as exit exams for graduation.

2. The National Defense Education Act of 1958 (NDEA) led to the creation of the National Defense Education Program under the Department of Education, administered from 1949 to 1966.

3. For a detailed discussion of NCLB and its impact in the state of Texas, see Valenzuela (2004). See also the work of Nichols, Glass, & Berliner (2006).

4. For a detailed account and critique of SB 4, see Valencia & Villarreal (2003).

Chapter 4

1. For a detailed discussion of the social context for Latino education, see Gándara and Contreras (2009).

Chapter 5

1. The term *undocumented* is used interchangeably with *unauthorized* in this chapter to describe students that are not legal residents of the United States.

2. For a detailed discussion on the legal cases pertaining to in-state tuition, see Olivas (2008).

3. The "Research I" label is used to describe a state flagship university, which grants doctoral degrees and is based on the Carnegie classifications for higher education institutions.

4. Students were awarded either an Achievers scholarship from the Bill and Melinda Gates Foundation or a Costco scholarship, both of which provide both tuition and living expenses.

Chapter 7

1. For a detailed discussion of legal cases on the issue of segregation, see Valencia (2008).

References

Abigail Noel Fisher and Rachel Multer Michalewicz vs. University of Texas at Austin et. al. (2009). No. 1:08-cv-00263-SS

Abrego, L. (2008). Legitimacy, social identity, and the mobilization of the law: The effects of AB540 on undocumented students in California. *Law & Social Inquiry, 33*(3), 709–734.

Abedi, J., & Gándara, P. (2006). Performance of English language learners as a subgroup in large-scale assessment: Interaction of research and policy. *Educational Measurement: Issues and Practice, 25*(4), 36–46.

Adelman, C. (1999). *Answers in the tool box: Academic intensity, attendance patterns, and bachelor's degree attainment.* Washington, DC: U.S. Department of Education.

Alexander, M. (2010). *The new Jim Crow.* New York: The New Press.

Alfred, J. (2003). Denial of the American Dream: The plight of undocumented high school students within the U.S. educational system. *New York Law School Journal of Human Rights, 19*, 615–650.

Ali, R., & Jenkins, G. (2002). *The high school diploma: Making it more than an empty promise.* Oakland, CA: Education Trust West.

Alonso-Zaldivar, R., & Tompson, T. (2010, July 30). 87% of Hispanics value higher education, 13% have college degree. *USA Today.* Retrieved February 11, 2011, from http://www.usatoday.com/news/education/2010-07-30-poll-hispanic-college_N.htm

America's high school graduates. Results from the 2005 high school transcript study. The Nation's Report Card. National Center for Education Statistics, U.S. Department of Education (NCES 2007-467). Washington D. C.

American Federation of Teachers. (2004). *Closing the achievement gap: Focus on Latino students* (AFT Educational Issues Policy Brief No.).

American Federation of Teachers. (AFT). (2006). *Smart testing: Let's get it right.* Retrieved April 22, 2011 from http://www.aft.org/pdfs/teachers/pb_testing0706.pdf

American Federation of Teachers. (2007, June). AFT on Highly Qualified Teachers. Publication of the American Federation of Teachers, Washington, DC. Retrieved February 11, 2011, from http://www.aft.org/pdfs/teachers/nclb_highlyqualteachers0607.pdf

Amrein, A. L., & Berliner, D. C. (2002). High-stakes testing, uncertainty, and student learning. *Education Policy Analysis Archives, 10*(18). Retrieved November 11, 2007, from http://epaa.asu.edu/epaa/v10n18/

Arbona, C., & Nora, A. (2007). The influence of academic and environmental factors on Hispanic college degree attainment. *The Review of Higher Education, 30*(3), 247–269. DOI: 10.1353/rhe.2007.0001

Arizona Department of Education (2011). *AIMS results.* Retrieved March 16, 2011, from http://www .ade.az.gov/profile/publicview/

Aud, S., Fox, M., & KewalRamani, A. (2010). *Status and trends in the education of racial and ethnic groups* (NCES 2010-015). Washington, DC: U.S. Department of Education, National Center for Education Statistics.

Aud, S., Hussar, W., Planty, M., Snyder, T., Bianco, K., Fox, M., Frohlich, L., Kemp, J., & Drake, L. (2010). The condition of education 2010 (NCES 2010-028). National Center for Education Statistics, Institute of Education Sciences, U.S. Department of Education. Washington, DC.

Ballinger, P. (2007). Why and how socioeconomic factors should be used in selective college admissions. *New Directions for Student Services, 3–15.*

Bangser, M. (2008). *Preparing high school students for successful transitions to postsecondary education and employment.* New York, NY: MDRC.

Banks, J. (1993). Multicultural education: Development, dimensions and challenges. *Phi Delta Kappan, 75*(1), 22–28.

Banks, J. (2006). Multicultural education: Development, dimensions and challenges. In *Race Culture and Education.* New York: Routledge.

Barreto, M. A. (2005). Latino immigrants at the polls: Foreign-born voter turnout in the 2002 election. *Political Research Quarterly, 58,* 79–86

Baum, S., & Ma, J. (2010). *Trends in college pricing.* New York: College Board.

Baum, S., Ma, J., & Payea, K. (2010). Education pays 2010: The benefits of higher education for individuals and society. New York: College Board.

Baum, S., & Payea, K. (2004). Education pays 2004: The benefits of higher education for individuals and society. New York: College Board.

Baum, S., & Payea, K. (2005). *Trends in college pricing 2005* (College Board Trends in Higher Education Series). Retrieved from http://www.collegeboard.com/trends

Baum, S., & Schwartz, S. (2006). *How much debt is too much: Defining benchmarks for manageable student debt.* New York: College Board.

Baum, S., & Steele, P. (2007). *Trends in college pricing.* Retrieved March 16, 2011, from http://www.collegeboard.com/prod_downloads/about/news_info/trends/trends_aid_07.pdf

Beadie, N. (2004). Moral errors and strategic mistakes: Lessons from the history of student accountability. In K. A. Sirotnik (Ed.), *Holding accountability accountable: Toward responsible concepts and practices* (pp. 35–50). New York: Teachers College Press.

Belfield, C., & Levin, H. (2007a). *The price we pay.* Washington, DC: Brookings Institution Press.

Belfield, C., & Levin, H. (2007b). *The return on investment for improving California's high school graduation rate.* Retrieved February 22, 2011, from http://www.lmri.ucsb.edu/ dropouts /pubs.htm

Bennett, M. (1996). *When dreams came true: The GI Bill and the making of modern America.* Washington, DC: Brassey's.

Bensimon, E. M., Hao, L., & Bustillos, L. T. (2005). Measuring the state of equity in higher education. In P. Gandara, G. Orfield, & C. Horn (Eds)., *Leveraging promise and expanding opportunity in higher education.* Albany: SUNY Press.

Betts, R., Rueben, K., & Danenberg, A., (2000). *Equal resources, equal outcomes? The distribution of school resources and student chievement in California.* San Francisco: Public Policy Institute of California.

Bialystok, E., & Hakuta, K. (1994). *In other words: The science and psychology of second-language acquisition.* New York: Basic Books.

Bourdieu, P., & Passeron, J. C. (1977). *Reproduction in education, society, and culture.* London: Sage.

Bowen, W., & Bok, D. (1998). *The shape of the river: Long-term consequences of considering race in college and university admissions.* Princeton, NJ: Princeton University Press.

Brooks-Gunn, J., Guo, G., & Furstenberg, F. (1993). Who drops out of and who continues beyond high school? A 20-year follow up of Black youth. *Journal of Adolescent Research, 3,* 271–294.

Brown v. Board of Education, 347 U.S. 483 (1954).

Brown, S., & Hirschman, C. (2006). The end of affirmative action in Washington State and its impact on the transition from high school to college. *Sociology of Education, 79,* 106–130.

Cabrera, A., Amaury, N., & Castañeda, M. (1993). College persistence: Structural equations modeling test of an integrated model of student retention. *Journal of Higher Education, 64*(2), 123–139.

Cabrera, A., Nora, A., & Castañeda, M. (1992). The role of finances in the persistence process: A structural model. *Research in Higher Education, 33*(5), 571–593. DOI 10.1007/BF0097375.

Cabrera, A. F., Nora, A., & Castañeda, M. B. (1993). College persistence: Structural equations modeling test of an integrated model of student retention. *Journal of Higher Education, 64*(2), 123–139.

Cabrera, A., Stampen, J., & Hansen, W. (1990). Exploring the effects of ability to pay on persistence in college. *Review of Higher Education, 13,* 303–336.

California Department of Education, (2010). *Standardized testing and reporting (STAR) results.* Retrieved March 16, 2011, from http://star.cde.ca.gov/star2010/

Camarillo, A. (1979). *Chicanos in a changing society: From Mexican pueblos to American barrios in Santa Barbara and Southern California, 1848–1930.* Cambridge, MA: Harvard University Press.

Cammarota, J. (2004). The gendered and racialized pathways of Latina and Latino youth: Different struggles, different resistances in the urban context. *Anthropology & Education Quarterly, 35*(1), 53–74.

Carnevale, A., & Rose, S. (2003). *Socioeconomic status, race/ethnicity, and selective college admissions.* New York: The Century Foundation. Retrieved April 22, 2011, from http://tcf.org/publications/pdfs/pb252/carnevale_rose.pdf

Castellanos, J., Gloria, A., & Kamimura, M. (2006). *The Latino/a pathway to the Ph.D.* Virginia: Stylus Publishing.

Cataldi, E. F., Laird, J., & KewalRamani, A. (2009). *High school dropout and completion rates in the United States: 2007* (NCES 2009-064). National Center for Education Statistics, Institute of Education Sciences, U.S. Department of Education. Washington, DC. Retrieved [date] from http://nces.ed.gov/pubsearch/pubsinfo.asp?pubid = 2009064

Center on Education Policy. (2010). *State high school tests: Exit exams and other assessments.* Retrieved March 16, 2011, from http://www.google.com/cse?cx=001382591 411870128679%3Ail0cupb_8ya&ie=UTF-8&q=State+High+School+Tests&sa=Se arch&siteurl=www.cep-dc.org%2F

Chambers, J. W. (2000). The G.I. Bill. In *The Oxford companion to American military history.* Oxford University Press. 2000. Retrieved September 10, 2009, from Encyclopedia.com: http://www.encyclopedia.com/doc/1O126-TheGIBill.html

Chapa, J. (2008). A demographic and sociological perspective on Plyler's children, 1980–2005. *Northwestern Journal of Law and Social Policy, 3.*

Chavez, L. (2006, October 27). *Eligibility in the local context and applications to the university of California.* Paper presented at the Earl Warren Institute on Race, Ethnicity, and Diversity's Conference on Equal Opportunity in Higher Education: The Past and Future of Proposition 209. Berkeley, California.

Chrispeels, J. H., & Rivero, E. (2001). Engaging Latino families for student success: How parent education can reshape parents' sense of place in the education of their children. *Peabody Journal of Education, 76*(2), 119–169.

Christle, C., Jolivette, K., & Nelson, C. (2005). Breaking the school to prison pipeline: Identifying school risk and protective factors for youth delinquency. *Exceptionality, 13*(2), 69–88.

Cimbricz, S. (2002). State-mandated testing and teachers' beliefs and practice. *Education Policy Analysis Archives, 10*(2). Retrieved November 2, 2007, from http://epaa.asu.edu/epaa/v10n2.html

Colasanti, M. (2007, July). Sanctions on driving privileges. Publicaiton of Education Commission of The States. Retrieved September 2, 2011, from http://www.ecs.org/html/IssueSection.asp?issueid=222&s=What+States+Are+Doing

Coleman, J. (1988). Social capital in the creation of human capital. *American Journal of Sociology, 94*(S1), 95–120.

College Board. (2009, February 4). The 5th annual AP report to the nation, national profile. Publication of the College Board, New York.

College Board. (2010a). Trends in college pricing. Publication of the College Board, New York.

College Board. (2010b). Trends in student aid. Publication of the College Board, New York.

Conchas, G. (2006). *The color of success.* New York: Teachers College Press.

Contreras, F. (2003). College admissions in the affirmative action era & post Proposition 209: Assessing the impact of public policy on college access in California. Unpublished doctoral dissertation, Stanford University.

Contreras, F. (2005a). Access, achievement & social capital: Standardized exams & the Latino college bound population. *Journal of Hispanics in Higher Education.* Thousand Oaks, CA: Sage.

Contreras, F. (2005b). The reconstruction of merit post Proposition 209. *Educational Policy.* Thousand Oaks, CA: Sage.

Contreras, F., & Gándara, P. (2006). Latinas/os in the Ph.D. pipeline: A case of historical and contemporary exclusion. In J. Castellanos & A. Gloria (Eds.), Journey to a Ph.D.: The Latina/o Experience in Higher Education (pp. 91–111). Virginia: Stylus Publishing.

Contreras, F., Stritikus, T., O'Reilly-Diaz, K., Torres, K., Sanchez, I., Esqueda, M., Ortega, L., Sepulveda, A., & Guzman, B. (2008). *Understanding opportunities to learn for Latinos in Washington* (Report prepared for the Washington State Commission on Hispanic Affairs and Washington State Legislature under HB 2687).

Cosentino de Cohen, C., & Clewell, B. (2007). *Putting English Language Learners on the educational map* (Education in Focus, Urban Institute Policy Brief).

Creswell, J. (2008). *Research design: Qualitative, quantitative, and mixed methods approaches.* Thousand Oaks, CA: Sage.

Crosnoe, R. (2006). *Mexican roots American schools.* Stanford, CA: Stanford University Press.

Crosnoe, R. (2007). *The high school as a context of adolescent development.* Presented at the Society for Research in Child Development, Boston, MA.

Cunningham, A., & Santiago, D. (2008). Student aversion to borrowing: Who borrows and who doesn't (Report prepared by the Institute for Higher Education Policy and Excelencia in Education).

Darling-Hammond, L. (1997). *Doing what matters most: Investing in quality teaching.* New York: National Commission on Teaching and America's Future.

Darling-Hammond, L. (2000). Teacher quality and student achievement. *Educational Policy Analysis Archives, 8*(1). Retrieved [DATE] from http://epaa.asu.edu/epaa/v8n1

Darling-Hammond, L. (2010). *The flat world and education: How America's commitment to equity will determine our future.* New York: Teachers College Press.

Data Quality Campaign (2009, March). *The next step: Using longitudinal data systems to improve student success.* Publication of the Data Quality Campaign, Washington, DC.

Day, J. C., & Newburger, E. C. (2002). The Big Payoff: Educational Attainment and Synthetic Estimates of Work-Life Earnings. (Current Population Reports, Special Studies, P23-210). Washington, DC: Commerce Dept., Economics and Statistics Administration, Census Bureau. Available at http://www.census.gov/prod/2002pubs/p23-210.pdf

Debra P. v. Turlington, 644 F. 2d 397 (5th Cir. 1981). Retrieved February 22, 2011, from http://www.fldoe.org/asp/hsap/hsap1983.asp

Debra P. v. Turlington, 474 F.Supp. 244 (M.D. FL 1979).

Debra P. v. Turlington, 730 F.2d 1405 (11th Cir. 1984)

Delgado-Gaitán, C. (1990). *Literacy for empowerment: The role of parents in children's education.* London: Falmer Press.

Delgado-Gaitán, C. (1994). Spanish-Speaking families' involvement in schools. In C. Fagnano & B. Weber (Eds.), *School, family and community interaction: A view from the firing lines* (pp. 85–98). San Francisco: Westview Press.

Delgado-Gaitán, C. (2001). *Involving Latino families in schools: Raising student achievement through home-school partnerships.* Thousand Oaks, CA: Corwin.

Deli-Amen, R., & Lopez-Turley, R. (2007). A Review of the Transition to College Literature in Sociology. *Teachers College Record, 109*(10), 2324–2366.

De La Rosa, M. L., & Tierney, W. G. (2006). Breaking through the barriers to college: Empowering low-income communities, schools, and families for college opportunity and student financial aid. Center for Higher Education and Policy Analysis, University of Southern California. Retrieved December 10, 2009 from http://www.pathwaystocollege.net/pcnlibrary/ViewBiblio.aspx?aid = 1803

de los Santos, A. G., & de los Santos, G. E. (2005). Latina/os and community colleges. In J. Castellanos, A. M. Gloria, & M. Kaminura (Eds.), *The Latina/o pathway to the Ph.D* (pp. 37-53). Sterling, VA: Stylus.

de los Santos, Jr., A., Alfredo, G., Keller, G., Nettles, M., Payán, R., & Magallan, R. (2006). Latino achievement in the sciences, technology, engineering, and mathematics. *Journal of Hispanic Higher Education, 5*(3), 288.

de los Santos, Jr., A. & de los Santos, G. (2003). Hispanic-serving institutions in the 21st Century: Overview, challenges, and opportunities. *Journal of Hispanic Higher Education, 10*(2), 377–391.

de los Santos, G., Asgary, N., Nazemzadeh, A. & DeShields, O. (2005). The agony and the ecstasy: Current status of Hispanic individuals' achievement in higher education and earnings—with a glimpse to the future. *Journal of Hispanic Higher Education, 4*(2), 149.

Delpit, L. (1995). *Other people's children: Cultural confrontation in the classroom.* New York: The New Press.

Delpit, L. (2001). The politics of teaching literate discourse. In E. Cushman, E. Kintgen, B. Kroll & M. Rose (Eds.), *Literacy: A critical sourcebook* (pp. 545–554). Boston: Bedford/St. Martin's.

DeShano da Silva, C., Huguley, J., & Kakli, Z. (2007). The opportunity gap. *Harvard Educational Review*.

DiMaggio, P. (1982). Cultural capital and school success: The impact of status culture participation on the grades of U.S. high school students. *American Sociological Review, 47,* 189–201.

Donato, R. (1997). *The other struggle for equal schools*. Albany: State University of New York Press.

Dougherty, C., Mellor, L., & Jian, S. (2006). *The relationship between Advanced Placement and college graduation* (National Center for Educational Accountability, 2005 AP Study Series, Report 1).

Dowd, A. C., & Coury, T. (2006). The effect of loans on the persistence and attainment of community college students. *Research in Higher Education, 47*(1), 33–62.

Duran, R. (2008). Assessing English-language learners' achievement. *Review of Research in Education, 32,* 292–327.

Durand, J., Telles, E., & Flashman, J. (2006). *Hispanics and the future of America*. Washington, DC: National Academies Press.

Educational Testing Service (ETS). (2003). *Parsing the achievement gap: Baselines for tracking progress*. Princeton, NJ: Author.

Education Week (2010). *Quality counts 2010* [Data File]. Retrieved March 16, 2011, from http://www.edweek.org/rc/2007/06/07/edcounts.html?intc=thed

Federal Way School District, No. 210 v. State of Washington (2009).

Ferguson, R. (1998). Can schools narrow the Black-White test score gap? In C. Jencks & M. Phillips (Eds.), *The Black-White test score gap* (ED 423 765) (pp. 318–374). Washington, DC: Brookings Institution.

Ferguson, R. F., & Ladd, H. F. (1996). How and why money matters: An analysis of Alabama schools. In H. F. Ladd (Ed.), *Holding schools accountable: Performance based reform in education* (pp. 265–298). Washington, DC: Brookings Institution Press.

Figueroa, J. L. (2002). *Out of the neighborhood and into the ivory tower: Understanding the schooling experiences of Latino male undergraduates attending an institution of higher education*. Ph.D. dissertation, University of California, Berkeley, United States, California. Retrieved February 28, 2011, from Dissertations & Theses: Full Text. (Publication No. AAT 3063358).

Fitzgerald, B. K. (2006). Lowering barriers to college access: Opportunities for more effective coordination of state and federal student aid policies. In P. C. Gándara, G. Orfield, & C. L. Horn (Eds.), *Expanding opportunity in higher education: Leveraging promise*. Albany: State University of New York Press.

Flores, A. (2007). Examining disparities in mathematics education: Achievement gap or opportunity gap? *The High School Journal, 91*(1), 29–42.

Flores, S. M., Horn, C. L., & Crisp, G. (2006). Community colleges, public policy and Latino student opportunity. *New Directions for Community Colleges, 133,* 71–77.

Fraga, L., Garcia, J., Segura, G., Jones-Correa, M., Hero, R., & Martinez-Ebers, V. (2010). *Latino lives in America: Making it home*. Philadelphia: Temple University Press.

Fraga, L. R., Meier, K., & England, R. (1986). Hispanic Americans and educational policy: Limits to equal access. *Journal of Politics, 48*(4), 850–876.

Frankenberg, E., Lee, C., & Orfield, G. (2003). *A multiracial society with segregated schools: Are we losing the dream?* (Report prepared for The Harvard Civil Rights Project).

Fry, R. (2002). *Latinos in higher education: Many enroll, too few graduate.* Washington, DC: Pew Hispanic Center.

Fry. R. (2007). *How far behind in math and reading are English Language Learners?* Washington, DC: Pew Hispanic Center.

Gándara, P. (1982). Passing through the eye of the needle: High-achieving Chicanas. *Hispanic Journal of Behavioral Sciences, 4,* 167–179.

Gándara, P. (1995). *Over the ivy walls.* Albany: State University of New York Press.

Gándara, P. (2000, February 1–2). *Latinos and higher education: A California perspective.* Paper presented to the Chicano/Latino Public Policy Seminar and Legislative Day—Proceedings, Sacramento, CA.

Gándara, P. (2010). Latino students and the curse of triple segregation. *Educational Leadership, 68*(3).

Gándara, P., & Baca, G. (2008). NCLB and California's English language learners: The perfect storm. *Language Policy, 7,* 201–216.

Gándara, P., & Bial, D. (2001). *Paving the way to postsecondary education: K-12 intervention programs for underrepresented youth* (NCES No. 2001205). Washington, DC: National Center for Education Statistics.

Gándara, P., & Contreras, F. (2009). *The Latino education crisis.* Cambridge, MA: Harvard University Press.

Gándara, P., & Hopkins, M. (Eds.). (2010). *Forbidden language: English learners and restrictive language policies.* New York: Teachers College Press.

Gándara, P., & Maxwell-Jolly, J. (2005). Critical Issues in the development of the teacher corps for English Learners. In H. Waxman & K. Tellez (Eds.), *Preparing quality teachers for English Language Learners.* Mahweh, NJ: Erlbaum.

Gándara, P., Maxwell-Jolly, J., & Driscoll, A. (2005). *Listening to the teachers of English language learners: A survey of California teachers' challenges, experiences, and professional development needs.* Sacramento, CA: The Regents of the University of California.

Gándara, P., O'Hara, S., & Gutierrez, D. (2004). The changing shape of aspirations: Peer influence on achievement behavior. In M. Gibson, P. Gandara, & J. Koyama (Eds.), *School connections: U.S. Mexican youth, peers, and school achievement* (pp. 39–62). New York: Teachers College Press.

Gándara, P., & Orfield, G. (2010). *A return to the Mexican room. The segregation of Arizona's English learners.* Los Angeles: The Civil Rights Project/Proyecto Derechos Civiles.

Gándara, P., Rumberger, R., Maxwell-Jolly, J., & Callahan, R. (2003). English Learners in California schools: Unequal resources, unequal outcomes. *Education Policy Analysis Archives, 11*(36).

Garcia, E. (2001). *Hispanics Education in the United States: Raíces y alas.* Lanham, MD: Rowan and Littlefield.

Garcia, E., & Gonzales, D. (2006). Pre-K and Latinos: The foundation for America's future. Retrieved [DATE] from www.preknow.org

Geiser, S., & Caspary, K. (2005). "No show" study: College destinations of University of California applicants and admits who did not enroll, 1997–2002. *Educational Policy, 19,* 396–417.

Geiser, S., Ferri, C., & Kowarsky, J. (2000). *Underrepresented minority admissions at UC after SP-1 and Proposition 209: Trends, issues & options* (Admissions Briefing Paper, University of California Office of the President).

Geiser, S., & Santelices, V. (2006). The role of Advanced Placement and honors courses in college admissions. In P. Gándara, G. Orfield, & C. Horn (Eds.), *Expanding opportunity in higher education: Leveraging promise* (pp 75–114). Albany: State University of New York Press.

Geiser, S., & Santelices, M. (2007). Validity of high school grades in predicting student success beyond the freshman year: High school record vs. standardized tests as indicators of four-year college outcomes (Research & Occasional Paper Series: CSHE.6.07, University of California, Berkeley). Retrieved [DATE] from http://cshe.berkeley.edu/

Geiser, S., & Studley, R. (2002). UC and the SAT: Predictive validity and differential impact of the SAT I and SAT II at the University of California. *Educational Assessment 8*(1), 1–26.

Gibson, M., Gándara, P., & Koyama, J. (2004). *School connections: U.S. Mexican youth, peers, and school achievement.* New York: Teachers College Press.

GI Forum v. Texas Education Agency. 87 F. Supp. 2d 667 (2000).

Gladieux, L. (2004). Low-income students and the affordability of higher education. In R. Kahlenberg (Ed.), *America's untapped resource* (pp. 17 – 57). New York: The Century Foundation Press.

Gladieux, L., & Perna, L. (2005). *Borrowers who drop out: A neglected aspect of the college student loan trend.* San Jose, CA: National Center for Public Policy and Higher Education.

Golden, D. (2006). *The price of admission.* New York: Crown Publishers.

Goldenberg, C., & Gallimore, R. (1995). Immigrant Latino parents' values and beliefs about their children's education: Continuities and discontinuities across cultures and generations. In P. Pintrich & M. Maehr (Eds.), *Advances in motivation and achievement* (pp. 183–227). Greenwich, CT: JAI Press.

Goldenberg, C., Gallimore, R., Reese, L., & Garnier, H. (2001). Cause or effect? A longitudinal study of immigrant Latino parents' aspirations and expectations, and their children's school performance. *American Educational Research Journal, 38*(3), 547–582.

Goldhaber, D., & Brewer, D. (1997). Evaluating the effect of teacher degree level on educational performance. In W. Fowler (Ed.), *Developments in school finance, 1996* (pp. 197–210). Washington, DC: U.S. Department of Education, National Center for Education Statistics (ED 409 634).

Gonzales, R. (2008). Left out but not shut down: Political activism and the undocumented student movement. *Northwestern Journal of Law and Social Policy, 3.*

Gonzales, R. G. (2007). Wasted talent and broken dreams: The lost potential of undocumented students. *Immigration Policy: In Focus 5*(13). Immigration Policy Center, of the American Immigration Law Foundation. Washington, DC.

Gonzalez, E., O'Connor, K., & Miles, J. (2001). How well do Advanced Placement students perform on the TIMSS advanced mathematics and physics tests? (Publication of the International Study Center, Boston College, Boston, MA).

Gould, S. J. (1995). *The mismeasure of man.* New York: Norton.

Greene, J., & Winters, M. (2004). *Pushed out or pulled up? Exit exams and dropout rates in public high schools* (Manhattan Institute, Education Working Paper No. 5).

Grodsky, E., & Jones, M. T. (2004). Real and imagined barriers to college entry: Perceptions of cost. *Social Science Research, 36,* 745–766.

Grogger, J., & Trejo, S. (2002). *Falling behind or moving up? The intergenerational progress of Mexican Americans.* San Francisco: Public Policy Institute of California.

Grutter v. Bollinger, 539 U.S. 306 (2003).

Guin, K. (2004). Chronic teacher turnover in urban elementary schools. *Education Policy Analysis Archives, 12*(42). Retrieved July 10, 2007, from http://epaa.asu.edu/epaa/v12n42/

Guiton, G., & Oakes, J. (1995). Opportunity to learn and conceptions of educational equality. *Educational Evaluation and Policy Analysis, 17*(3), 323–336. DOI: 10.3102/01623737017003323

Gurin, P., Dey, E., Sylvia Hurtado, S., & Gurin, G. (2002). Diversity and higher education: Theory and impact on educational outcomes. *Harvard Educational Review.*

Hakuta, K., & Bialystok, E. (1994). *In other words: The science and psychology of second-language acquisition.* New York: BasicBooks.

Hale-Benson, J. (1986). *Black children: Their roots, culture, and learning styles* (2nd ed.). Baltimore, MD: Johns Hopkins University Press.

Hamilton, B. E., Martin, J. A., & Ventura, S. J. (2007). Births: Preliminary data for 2006. *National Vital Statistics Reports, 56*(7). Hyattsville, MD: National Center for Health Statistics.

Hansen, W. (1983). The impact of student financial aid on access. In J. Froomkin (Ed.), *The crisis in higher education.* New York: Academy of Political Science.

Hanushek, E. A., & Kimko, D. D. (2000). Schooling, labor force quality, and the growth of nations. *American Economic Review, 90*(5), 1184–1208.

Haro, R. (2004). Programs and strategies to increase Latino students' educational attainment. *Education and Urban Society, 36*(2), 205–222.

Harris, A., & Tienda, M. (2010). Minority higher education pipeline: Consequences of changes in college admissions policy in Texas. *The Annals of the American Academy of Political and Social Science, 627,* 60–81. dOI:10.1177/0002716209348740

Harris, L., & Princiotta, D. (2009). *Reducing dropout rates through expanded learning opportunities.* Publication of the National Governors Association, Washington, DC.

Haycock, K. (1998). Good teaching matters. A lot. *Thinking K–16, 3*(2), 3–14.

Hearn, J., & Holdsworth, J. (2004). Federal student aid: The shift from grants to loans. In E. St. John & M. Parsons (Eds), *Public funding of higher education.* Baltimore: The Johns Hopkins University Press.

Heller, D. (1999). *The states and public higher education policy.* Baltimore: Johns Hopkins University Press.

Heller, D. (2001, October 5). *Standardized tests and merit scholarships, University of Michigan.* Presentation at the Michigan Council of Teachers of English Annual Conference, Lansing, MI.

Heller, D. E. (2002). The policy shift in state financial aid programs. In J. C. Smart (Ed.), *Higher education: Handbook of theory and research* (vol. 17, pp. 221–261). New York: Agathon Press.

Heller, D. (2005). Public subsidies for higher education in California: An exploratory analysis of who pays and who benefits. *Educational Policy, 19*(2), 349–370.

Heller, D. (2008, August). Institutional and State Merit Aid: implications for students. Paper Prepared for University of Southern California Center for Enrollment Research, Policy, and Practice Inaugural Conference. Los Angeles, August, 2008.

Heller, D. E., & Marin, P. (Eds.). (2002). *Who should we help? The negative social consequences of merit scholarships.* Cambridge, MA: The Civil Rights Project at Harvard University.

Heller, D., & Marin, P. (2004). State merit scholarship programs and racial inequality. Civil Rights Project, UCLA.

Heller, D. (2006). Early commitment of financial aid eligibility. *The American Behavioral Scientist, 49*(12), 1719.

Holmes, C. T. (1989). Grade-level retention effects: A meta-analysis of research studies. In L. A. Shepard & M. L. Smith (Eds.), *Flunking grades: Research and policies on retention* (pp. 16–33). London: The Falmer Press.

Hoover-Dempsey, K., Battiato, A., Walker, J., Reed, R., DeJong, J., & Jones, K. P. (2001). Parental involvement in homework. *Educational Psychologist, 36*(3),195–209.

Hopwood v. Texas, 78 F.3d 932 (5th Cir. 1996).

Horn, C. (2003). High-stakes testing and students: Stopping or perpetuating a cycle of failure? *Theory into Practice, 42*(1).

Horn, C., & Flores, S. (2003). *Percent plans in college admissions: A comparative analysis of three states' experiences*. Cambridge, MA: The Civil Rights Project at Harvard University.

Horn, L., Nevill, S., & Griffin J. (2006). Profile of undergraduates in U.S. postsecondary education institutions: 2003-04 with a special analysis of community college students: Statistical analysis report (NCES 2006-184). U.S. Department of Education. Washington, D.C.: National Center for Education Statistics.

Horne, Arizona Superintendent of Public Instruction v. Flores, et. al. (2009). (Nos. 08-289 and 08-294) 516 F. 3d 1140.

Hosmer, D., & Lemeshow, S. (1989). *Applied logistic regression analysis*. New York: Wiley.

Huebert, J., & Hauser, R. (1999). *High stakes: Testing for tracking, promotion and graduation*. Washington, DC: National Research Council.

Hurtado, S. (1994). The institutional climate for talented Latino students. *Research in Higher Education, 35*(1), 21–41.

Hurtado, S., Clayton-Pedersen, A., Allen, W., & Milem, J. (1998). Enhancing campus climates for racial/ethnic diversity: Educational policy and practice. *The Review of Higher Education, 21*(3), 279–302. DOI: 10.1353/rhe.1998.0003

Hurtado, S., & Kamimura, M. (2003). Latino/a retention in four-year institutions. In J. Castellanos & L. Jones, (Eds.), *The majority in the minority: Expanding the representation of Latina/o faculty, administrators, and students in higher education* (pp. 139–152). Sterling, VA: Stylus.

Hurtado, S., & Ponjuan, L. (2005). Latino educational outcomes and the campus climate. *Journal of Hispanic Higher Education, 4*(3), 235–251.

Jencks, C. & Phillips, M. (1998). The black-white test score gap: An introduction. In C. Jencks and M. Phillips (Eds.), *The black-white test score gap*. Washington, DC: Brookings Institution Press.

Kahlenberg, R. (Ed.). (2010). *Affirmative action for the rich: Legacy preferences in college admissions*. New York: The Century Foundation.

Kahn, C., August 5, 2010. Republicans push to revise 14th amendment. National Public Radio; Retrieved January 29, 2011, from http://www.npr.org/templates/story/story.php?storyId=129007120

Kane, T. J. (1998a). Misconceptions in the debate over affirmative action in college admissions. In G. Orfield & E. Miller (Eds.), *Chilling admissions: The affirmative action crisis and the search for alternatives* (pp. 17–32). Cambridge, MA: Harvard Education Publishing Group.

Kane, T. J. (1998b). Racial and ethnic preferences in college admissions. In C. Jencks & M. Phillips (Eds.), *The Black-White Test Score Gap* (pp. 431–456). Brookings.

Kane, T. J. & Rouse, C. E.. (1995). Labor market returns to two- and four-year college. *American Economic Review 85*(3), 600–614.

Kao, G., & Tienda, M. (1998). Educational aspirations of minority youth. *American Journal of Education, 106*(3), 349–384.

Karabel, J. (1998). No alternative: The effects of color-blind admissions in California. In G. Orfield & E. Miller (Eds.), *Chilling admissions: The affirmative action crisis and the search for alternatives* (pp. 33–50). Cambridge, MA: Harvard Education Publishing Group.

Kerr, C. (1999, August 24). Testimony to the Joint Committee to develop a master plan for education: Kindergarten through university. Retrieved January 25, 2011, from http://www.ucop.edu/acadinit/mastplan/kerr082499.htm

Kerr, C., Gade, M., Kawaoka, M., & Smelser, N. (2003). *The gold and the blue: A personal memoir of the University of California, 1949–1967: Volume Two: Political Turmoil.* Berkeley, CA: University of California Press.

KewalRamani, A., Gilbertson, L., Fox, M., & Provasnik, S. (2007). *Status and trends in the education of racial and ethnic minorities* (NCES 2007-039). Washington, DC: National Center for Education Statistics, Institute of Education Sciences, U.S. Department of Education.

Kim, C., Losen, D., & Hewitt, D. (2010). *The school-to-prison pipeline: Structuring legal reform.* New York: NYU Press.

King, J. (2006). Gender equity in higher education, 2006. American Council on Education.

Kirschenman, J., & Neckerman, K. (1991). We'd love to hire them, but . . . . The meaning of race for employers. In C. Jencks & P. Peterson (Eds.), *The urban underclass.* Washington, DC: Brookings Institution Press.

Kirst, M. (1984). The Changing Balance in State and Local Power to Control Education. *The Phi Delta Kappan, 66*(3), 189–191.

Kirst, M. (2003). Improving preparation for non-selective postsecondary education: Assessment and accountability issues. Retrieved June 20, 2011, from http://www.stanford.edu/group/bridgeproject/ETS%20Conference%20Paper%20-%20Oct%2003.pdf

Krueger, K. (2005). Merit scholarships. Publication of the education commission of the states. Retrieved January 29, 2011, from http://www.ecs.org/clearinghouse/61/40/6140.pdf

Ladson-Billings, G. (1995). Toward a theory of culturally relevant pedagogy. *American Education Research Journal, 35,* 465–491.

Ladson-Billings, G., & Gillborn, D. (2004). *The RoutledgeFalmer reader in multicultural education.* New York: Routledge Falmer Press.

Ladson-Billings, G., & Tate, W. (1995). Toward a critical race theory of education. *Teachers College Record, 97,* 47–68.

Lau v. Nichols, 414 U.S. 563 (1974). Retrieved February 11, 2011, from http://caselaw.lp.findlaw. com/scripts/getcase.pl?court=us&vol=414&invol=563

Lee, J., & Rawls, A. (2010). *The college completion agenda report.* New York: College Board.

Levin, H., Belfield, C., Muennig, P., & Rouse, C. (2007). *The costs and benefits of an excellent education for all of America's children.* Retrieved September 10, 2009 from www.cbcse.org/media/download_gallery/Leeds_Report_Final_Jan2007.pdf

Li, X. (2007). *Characteristics of minority-serving institutions and minority undergraduates enrolled in these institutions* (NCES 2008-156). National Center for Education Statistics, U.S. Department of Education, Washington, DC.

Li, X., & Carroll, D. (2008). Characteristics of minority-serving institutions and minority undergraduates enrolled in these institutions: Postsecondary Education Descriptive Analysis Report, National Center for Education Statistics (NCES 2008-156).

Lind, M. (2010). Legacy preferences in a democratic republic. In R. Kahlenberg, (Ed.), *Affirmative action for the rich. Legacy preferences in college admissions*. Washington, DC: The Century Foundation.

Long, B. T. (2010). Beyond admissions: Reflections and future considerations. *The Annals of the American Academy of Political and Social Science, 627,* 216–225.

Long, B. T., & Kurleander, M. (2009). Do community colleges provide a viable pathway to a baccalaureate degree? *Educational Evaluation and Policy Analysis 31*(1), 30–53.

Long, M., Iatarola, P., & Conger, D. (2009). *Explaining gaps in readiness for college-level math: The role of high school courses*. Retrieved from February 22, 2011, from http://www. mitpressjournals.org/doi/pdf/10.1162/edfp.2009.4.1.1

Long, M., Saenz, V., & Tienda, M. (2010). Policy transparency and college enrollment: Did the Texas Top Ten Percent Law broaden access to the public flagships? *The Annals of the American Academy of Political and Social Science, 627,* 82–105. DOI:10.1177/0002716209348741

Long, M., & Tienda, M. (2010). Beyond admissions: Lessons from Texas. *The Annals of the American Academy of Political and Social Science, 627,* 6–11. DOI:10.1177/0002716209348716

Lopez, M. (2008). *The Hispanic vote in 2008*. Washington, DC: Pew Hispanic Center.

Lopez, M. H., & Light, M. T. (2009) *A rising share: Hispanics and federal crime*. Washington, DC: Pew Hispanic Center, Washington, DC.

Maldonado, C., & Farmer, E. I. (2007). Examining Latinos involvement in the workforce and postsecondary technical education in the United States. *Journal for Career and Technical Education, 22*(2). 26–40. Retrieved May 10, 2011, from http://scholar.lib. vt.edu/ejournals/JCTE/v22n2/pdf/v22n2.pdf

Manski, C., & Wise, D. (1983). *College choice in America*. Cambridge, MA: Harvard University Press.

Marin, P. (2002). Merit scholarships and the outlook for equal opportunity in higher education. In D. E. Heller & P. Marin (Eds.), *Who should we help? The negative social consequences of merit scholarships* (pp. 109–114). Cambridge, MA: The Civil Rights Project at Harvard University.

Marin, P., & Lee, E. (2003). *Appearance and reality in the Sunshine State: The Talented 20 program in Florida*. Cambridge, MA: The Civil Rights Project at Harvard University.

Maxwell, J. (2005). *Qualitative research design*. Thousand Oaks, CA: Sage.

Mayer, D., Mullens, J., & Moore, M. (2000). Taking on the achievement gap: A stacked deck? North Central regional Educational Laboratory. Naperville, IL.

McCormick, N., & Lucas, M. (2011). Exploring mathematics college readiness in the United States. *Current Issues in Education, 14*(1). Retrieved February 22, 2011, from http://cie.asu.edu/ojs/index.php/cieatasu/article/view/680

McDonough, P. M. (2004). *The school–to college transition: Challenges and prospects*. Washington, DC: American Council on Education, Center for Policy Analysis.

McDonough, P. M., & Gildersleeve, R. E. (2005). All else is never equal: Opportunity lost and found on the P-16 path to college access. In C. Conrad & R. Serlin (Eds.), *The SAGE handbook for research in education: Engaging ideas and enriching inquiry* (pp. 191–209). Thousand Oaks, CA: Sage.

McGuinn, P. (2006). *No Child Left Behind and the transformation of federal education policy, 1965–2005.* Lawrence: University Press of Kansas.

Mears, D., & Travis, J. (2004). The dimensions, pathways, and consequences of youth reentry. Washington, DC: Urban Institute. Retrieved [Semptember 3, 2010 from http://www.urban.org/url.cfm?ID = 410927

Mehan, H., Villanueva, I., Hubbard, L., & Lintz, A. (1996). *Constructing school success: The consequences of untracking low-achieving students.* New York: Cambridge University Press.

Menchaca, M. (1995). *The Mexican outsiders: A community history of marginalization and discrimination in California.* Austin: University of Texas Press.

Mendez v. Westminster School District, 64 F.Supp. 544 (C.D. Cal. 1946), aff'd, 161 F.2d 774 (9th Cir. 1947).

Mendoza, R. (2008). *Latina/o undocumented student experiences in college.* Unpublished master's thesis, University of Washington.

Moran, R. (2000). Sorting and reforming: High-stakes testing in the public schools. *Akron Law Review, 34,* 107.

Moreno, J. (2002). The long term outcomes of Puente. *Educational Policy, 16*(4), 572–587.

Morgan, R., & Maneckshana, B. (2000). *AP students in college: An investigation of their course-taking patterns and college majors.* Ewing NJ: Educational Testing Service.

National Association of Latino Elected Officials. (2007). *A profile of Latino elected officials in the United States and their progress since 1996.* Retrieved October 1, 2009, from http://www.naleo.org/pr071207.html

National Association of Student Financial Aid Administrators. (2011). 2011 National profile of programs in Title IV of the Higher Education Act. Retrieved March 5, 2011, from http://www.nasfaa.org/research/projects/Research_Projects.aspx

National Center for Education Statistics. (2007). Table 5-2: Racial/Ethnic Distribution of Public Schools Students: Percentage distribution of the race/ethnicity of public school students enrolled in kindergarten through 12th grade, by region: Selected years, Fall 1972–2005. The Condition of Education 2007 (NCES 2007-064), Appendix 1, Supplemental Tables: p. 123. Washington, DC: U.S. Government Printing Office.

National Center for Education Statistics. (2008). The condition of education 2008. Retrieved June 14, 2011, from http://nces.ed.gov/pubsearch/pubsinfo.asp?pubid=2008031

National Center for Education Statistics. (2010). The condition of education 2010. Washington, DC: U.S. Department of Education, Institute of Education Sciences. Retrieved March 16, 2011, from http://nces.ed.gov/pubsearch/pubsinfo.asp?pubid=2010028

National Clearinghouse for English Language Acquisition (NCELA) and Language Instruction Educational Programs (2006). The Growing Numbers of Limited English Proficient Students, 1994–2005. Washington, DC: NCELA

National Commission on Excellence in Education. (1983). A Nation at Risk: The Imperative for Education Reform. Retrieved March 16, 2011, from http://www2.ed.gov/pubs/NatAtRisk/index.html

Neckerman, K., & Kirschenman, J. (1991, November). Hiring strategies, racial bias, and inner-city workers. *Social Problems, 38*(4), 433–447.

Nettles, M. T., Millett, C. M., & Ready, D. D. (2003). High schools on the front line: Attacking the African American/White achievement gap on college admissions tests. In D. Ravitch (Ed.), *Brookings papers on education policy, 2003* (pp. 215–252). Washington, DC: Brookings Institution.

Nichols, S., & Berliner, D. (2007). *Collateral damage: How high-stakes testing corrupts America's schools.* Cambridge, MA: Harvard Education Press.

Nichols, S. L., Glass, G. V., & Berliner, D. C. (2006). High-stakes testing and student achievement: Does accountability pressure increase student learning? *Education Policy Analysis Archives, 14*(1). Retrieved [date] from http://epaa.asu.edu/epaa/v14n1/

Nieto, S. (1996). *Affirming diversity: The sociopolitical context of multicultural education* (2nd ed.). White Plains, NY: Longman.

Nieto, S., & Bode, P. (2008). *Affirming diversity: The sociopolitical context of multicultural education.* Boston: Allyn & Bacon/Longman Publishing Group.

No Child Left Behind Act of 2001, Public Law 107-110, 107th Cong., 1st sess. (2002, January 8). Codified at U. S. Code Title 20 Sec. 6301 et. seq. Retrieved March 16, 2011, from http://www.ed.gov/policy/elsec/leg/esea02/index.html

Nora, A., Barlow, L., & Crisp, G. (2006). An sssessment of Hispanic students in four-year institutions of higher education. In J. Castellanos, A. Gloria, & M. Kamimura, *Journey to a Ph.D.: The Latina/o experience in higher education.* Sterling VA: Stylus Publishing.

Nora, A., & Cabrera, A. (1996). The role of perceptions of prejudice and discrimination on the adjustment of minority students to college. *Journal of Higher Education, 67*(2), 120–148.

NORC, University of Chicago (2010). Associated Press Univision Poll. (March 11-June 3, 2010). Poll Retrieved February 28, 2011, from http://surveys.ap.org/data%5CNORC%5CAP-Univision%20Topline_posting.pdf.

Oakes, J. (2002). Education inadequacy, inequality, and failed state policy: A synthesis of expert reports prepared for *Williams v. State of California.* Retrieved July 20, 2010 from http://repositories.cdlib.org/idea/wws/wws-rr016-1002

Oakes, J. W. (2006). How the Servicemen's Readjustment Act of 1944 (GI Bill) impacted women artists' career opportunities. *Visual Culture & Gender, 1.*

Oakes, J., Mendoza, J., & Silver, D. (2004). California opportunity indicators: Informing and monitoring California's progress toward equitable college access. Retrieved March 29, 2004, from http://www.ucaccord.gseis.ucla.edu/publications/pubs/Indicators2004.pdf

Office of Financial Management, Washington State. (2008). Available at http://www.ofm.wa.gov

Olivas, M. (1995). Storytelling out of school: Undocumented college residency, race, and reaction. *Hastings Constitutional Law Quarterly, 22,* 1019–1086.

Olivas, M. (2004). IIRIRA, the DREAM Act, and undocumented residency. *Journal of College & University Law, 30,* 435–464.

Olivas, M. (2008). Recent developments in undocumented college student issues (2005–present). Retrieved January 10, 2009, from http://www.law.uh.edu/ihelg/undocumented/homepage.html.

Orfield, G. (1992). Money, equity and college costs. *Harvard Educational Review, 62,* 337–373.

Orfield, G. (1997). Residential segregation: What are the causes? (Testimony of Gary Orfield, March 22, 1996.) *The Journal of Negro Education, 66*(3), 204–213.

Orfield, G. (2004). *Dropouts in America: Confronting the graduation rate crisis.* Cambridge, MA: Harvard Education Press.

Orfield, G., & Eaton, S. (1996). *Dismantling desegregation: The quiet reversal of* Brown

v. Board of Education. New York: New Press.

Orfield, G., & Frankenberg, E. (2004). Reviving *Brown v. Board of Education:* How courts and enforcement agencies can produce more integrated schools. In D. L. Rhode and C. J. Ogletree, Jr., (Eds.), *Brown at fifty: The unfinished legacy: A collection of essays* (pp. 185–211). Chicago, IL: American Bar Association.

Orfield, G., & Lee, C. (2005). *Why segregation matters: Poverty and educational inequality.* Cambridge: Civil Rights Project. Harvard University. Available at http:// www.civilrightsproject.ucla.edu/research/deseg/Why_Segreg_Matters.pdf

Orfield, G., Losen, D., Wald, J., & Swanson, C. (2004). Losing our future: How minority youth are being left behind by the graduation rate crisis. Cambridge, MA: The Civil Rights Project at Harvard University and the Urban Institute. Retrieved November 1, 2009 from http://www.urban.org/url.cfm?ID = 410936

Orfield, G., & Miller, E. (Eds.) (1998). *Chilling admissions.* Cambridge, MA: Harvard Education Publishing Group.

Orozco, C., Orozco, M., & Todorova, I. (2008). *Immigrants in a new land.* Cambridge, MA: Harvard University Press.

Parents Involved in Community Schools v. Seattle School District No. 1, 551 U.S. (2007).

Passel, J. S. (2003). *Further demographic information relating to the DREAM act.* Washington, DC: The Urban Institute. Retrieved November 5, 2009 from www.nilc.org/ immlawpolicy/DREAM/DREAM_Demographics.pdf

Passel, J. S. (2005). *Estimates of the size and characteristics of the undocumented population.* Washington, DC: Pew Hispanic Research Center.

Pérez Carreón, G., Drake, C., & Calabrese Barton, A. (2005). The importance of presence: Immigrant parents' school engagement experiences. *American Educational Research Journal, 42*(3), 465–498.

Perez, W., Espinoza, R., Ramos, K., Coronado, H., & Cortes, R. (2009). Academic resilience among undocumented Latino students. *Hispanic Journal of Behavioral Sciences, 31*(2), 149–181.

Perna, L. W. (2004). *Impact of student aid program design, operations, and marketing on the formation of family college-going plans and resulting college-going behaviors of potential students.* Boston, MA: The Education Resources Institute, Inc. (TERI).

Perna, L. W. (2006). Understanding the relationship between information about college prices and financial aid and students' college-related behaviors. *American Behavioral Scientist, 49*(12), 1620.

Peske, H., & Haycock, K. (2006). Teaching inequality: How poor and minority students are shortchanged in teacher quality. Education Trust. Washington DC.

Planty, M., Hussar, W., Snyder, T., Kena, G., KewalRamani, A., Kemp, J., Bianco, K., & Dinkes, R. (2009). *The condition of education 2009* (NCES 2009-081). Washington, DC: National Center for Education Statistics, Institute of Education Sciences, U.S. Department of Education.

Planty, M., Hussar, W., Snyder, T., Provasnik, S., Kena, G., Dinkes, R., KewalRamani, A., & Kemp, J. (2008). *The condition of education 2008* (NCES 2008-031). Washington, DC: National Center for Education Statistics, Institute of Education Sciences, U.S. Department of Education.

Planty, M., Kena, G., & Hannes, G. (Eds.) (2009). The condition of education: 2009 in brief (NCES 2009-082). National Center for Education Statistics, Institute of Education Sciences, U.S. Department of Education, Washington, DC.

Plessy v. Ferguson, 163 U.S. 537. (1896).

Plyler v. Doe, 457 U.S. 202 (1982).

Rawls, J. (1971). *A theory of justice.* Cambridge, MA: The Belknap Press.

Ream, R. K., & Rumberger, R. W. (2008). Student engagement, peer social capital, and school dropout among Mexican American and non-Latino white students. *Sociology of Education, 81*(2), 109–139.

Reardon, S., Atteberry, A., Arshan, N., & Kurlaender, M. (2009). *Effects of the California High School Exit Exam on student persistence, achievement, and graduation* (Paper prepared for the Stanford Institute for Research on Education Policy & Practice. Working Paper, 2009-12).

Regents of the University of California v. Bakke, 438 U.S. 265 (1978).

Rist, R. (2001). Students' social class and teacher expectations: The self-fulfilling prophecy in ghetto education. In J. H. Strouse (Ed.), *Exploring socio-cultural themes in education: Readings in social foundations* (pp. 117–202). Upper Saddle River, NJ: Merrill Prentice-Hall.

Rodriguez, G. (2007). Cycling on in cultural deficit thinking. In G. Rodriguez & A. Rolle (Eds.), *To what ends and by what means?* (pp. 107–143). New York: Routledge.

Rodriguez, G.M. & Rolle, R.A. (2007). *To what ends and by what means? The social justice implications of contemporary school finance theory and policy.* New York: Routledge.

Rousseau, C.. & Tate, W. (2003). No time like the present: Reflecting on equity in school mathematics. *Theory Into Practice, 42*(3), 210–216.

Ruge, T., & Iza, A. (2005). Higher education for undocumented students: The case for open admission and in-state tuition rates for students without lawful immigration status. *Indiana International and Comparative Law Review, 15*.2.

Rumberger, R. (1995). Dropping out of school; A multi-level analysis of students and schools. *American Education Research Journal, 32,* 583–625.

Rumberger, R., & Gándara, P. (2000). The schooling of English Learners (Report prepared for the Linguistic Minority Research Institute and PACE).

Rutherford, F. (1998). *Sputnik and science education.* Paper presented at the American Association for the Advancement of Science.

Sable, J., & Plotts, C. (2010). *Documentation to the NCES Common Core of Data Public Elementary/Secondary School Universe Survey: School Year 2007–08* (NCES 2010-302rev). Washington, DC: National Center for Education Statistics. Retrieved March 16, 2011, from http://nces.ed. gov/pubsearch/pubs.info.asp?pubid=2010302

Saenz, V. B. (2002). Hispanic students and community colleges: A critical point for intervention. ERIC Digest. Los Angeles, CA: ERIC Clearinghouse for Community Colleges.

Saenz, V., Oseguera, L., & Hurtado, S. (2007). Losing ground? Exploring racial/ethnic enrollment shifts in freshman access to selective institutions. In G. Orfield, P. Marin, & S. Flores (Eds.), *Charting the future of college affirmative action: Legal victories, continuing attacks, and new research* (pp. 79–104). Los Angeles: University of California at Los Angeles, The Civil Rights Project.

Saenz, V., & Ponjuan, L. (2009). The vanishing Latino male in higher education. *Journal of Hispanic Higher Education, 8*(1), 54–89.

San Antonio Independent School District v. Rodriguez, 411 U.S. 1 (1973).

Santamaria v. Dallas Independent School District opinion and order, No. 06-692 (N.D. Tex. Nov. 16, 2006)

Santiago, D.A., & Cunningham, A. F. (2005). *How Latino students pay for college: Patterns of financial aid in 2003–04.* Washington, DC: Excelencia in Education and the Institute for Higher Education Policy.

Schmidt, P. (2010). A history of legacy preferences and privilege. In R. Kahlenberg (Ed.), *Affirmative action for the rich. Legacy preferences in college admissions.* Washington, DC: The Century Foundation.

Schultz, T. W. (1961). Investment in human capital. *The American Economic Review, 51*(1), 1–17.

Serrano v. Priest, 5 Cal.3d 584 (1971) (Serrano I)

Serrano v. Priest, 18 Cal.3d 728 (1976) (Serrano II)

Serrano v. Priest, 20 Cal.3d 25 (1977) (Serrano III)

Snyder, H. N., & Sickmund, M. (2006). *Juvenile offenders and victims: 2006 national report.* Washington, DC: U.S. Department of Justice, Office of Justice Programs, Office of Juvenile Justice and Delinquency Prevention.

Solorzano, D., & Ornelas, A. (2004, February/March). A critical race analysis of Latina/o African American advanced placement enrollment in public high schools. *The High School Journal,*15–26.

Stanton-Salazar, R. (2001). *Manufacturing hope and despair.* New York: Teachers College Press.

Stanton-Salazar, R. D. (2004). Social capital among working-class minority students. In M. A. Gibson, P. Gándara, & J. P. Koyama (Eds.), *School connections: U.S. Mexican youth, peers, and school achievement.* New York: Teachers College Press.

Stanton-Salazar, R., & Spina, S. (2003). Informal mentors and role models in the lives of urban Mexican-Oritin adolescents. *Anthropology & Education Quarterly, 34*(3), 231–254.

Stanton-Salazar, R., & Spina, S. (2005, June). Adolescent peer networks as a context for social and emotional support. *Youth and Society, 36*(4), 379–417.

Steele, C. (1997). A threat in the air: How stereotypes shape intellectual identity and performance. *American Psychologist, 52*(6), 613–629.

Steele, P., & Baum, S. (2009). *How much are college students borrowing?* New York: College Board.

Stillwell, R. (2009). *Public school graduates and dropouts from the common core of data: School year 2006–07* (NCES 2010-313). Washington, DC: National Center for Education Statistics, Institute of Education Sciences, U.S. Department of Education. Retrieved October 11, 2009 from http://nces.ed.gov/pubsearch/pubsinfo.asp?pubid = 2010313

St. John, E. P. (2003). *Refinancing the college dream: Access, equal opportunity, and justice for taxpayers.* Baltimore, MD: Johns Hopkins University Press.

St. John, E. P., Cabrera, A., Nora, A., & Asker, E. (2000). Economic influences on persistence reconsidered. In J. Braxton, *Reworking the departure puzzle.* Nashville, TN: Vanderbilt University Press.

St. John, E. P., & Chung, C. (2004). Merit and Equity: Rethinking Award Criteria in the Michigan Merit Scholarship Program. In E. P. St. John & M. Parsons (Eds)., *Public funding of higher education.* Baltimore: The Johns Hopkins University Press.

St. John, E., & Musoba, G. (2007). Academic access. In E. St. John (Ed.), *Education and the public interest: School reform, public finance, and access to higher education.* Springer Netherlands.

Stuart Wells, A., & Serna, I. (2006). The politics of culture: Understanding local political resistance to detracking in racially mixed schools. In A. Halsey, H. Lauder, P. Brown, A. Stuart Wells (Eds.), *Education, culture, economy, and society* (pp. 718–735). New York: Oxford University Press.

Suarez-Orozco, C., Suarez-Orozco, M., & Todorova, I. (2008). *Learning a new land: Immigrant students in American society.* Cambridge, MA: Harvard University Press.

Sum, A., Khatiwada, I., McLaughlin, J., & Palma, S. (2009). *The consequences of dropping out of high school: Joblessness and jailing for high school dropouts and the high cost for taxpayers.* Boston, MA: Center for Labor Market Studies-Northeastern University. Retrieved September 1, 2010, from http://www.clms.neu .edu/publication/

Swail, W., Redd, K., & Perna, L. (2003). Retaining minority students in higher education: A framework for success. ASHE Reader Series, Volume 30, (2).

Swanson, C. (2004a). Projections of 2003–04 high school graduates: Supplemental analyses based on findings from *Who Graduates? Who Doesn't?* Washington, DC: The Urban Institute. Available at http://www.urban.org/url.cfm?ID = 411019

Swanson, C. (2004b). The real truth about low graduation rates, an evidence-based commentary. Washington, DC: The Urban Institute. Retrieved [DATE] from http://www.urban.org/url.cfm?ID = 411050

Swanson, C. (2004c). Sketching a portrait of public high school graduation: Who graduates? who doesn't. In G. Orfield (Ed.), *Dropouts in America.* Cambridge, MA: Harvard Education Press.

Swanson, C., & Chaplin, D. (2003). *Counting high school graduates when graduates count: Measuring graduation rates under the high stakes of NCLB.* Washington, DC: Urban Institute.

Swanson, C., Christopher, B., & Chaplin, D. (2003). *Counting high school graduates when graduates count: Measuring graduation rates under the high stakes of NCLB.* Washington, DC: Urban Institute Education Policy Center.

Telles, E., & Ortiz, V. (2008). *Generations of exclusion: Mexican Americans, assimilation and race.* Russell Sage Foundation.

The American GI Forum v. Texas Education Agency, 87 F. Supp. 2d 667 (W.D. Tex. 2000).

The nation's report card. (2005). National Assessment of Educational Progress. U.S. Department of Education Institute of Education Sciences (NCES 2006–453).

The Next Step: Using Longitudinal Data Systems To Improve Student Success. (2009). Publication of the Data Quality Campaign (DQC). Downloaded, November 20, 2010 at: www.dataqualitycampaign.org/resources/details/38

Thomas, W. P., & Collier, V. (1997). *School effectiveness for language minority students.* Washington, DC: National Clearinghouse for Bilingual Education. The George Washington University. Retrieved April 25, 2011, from http://www.thomasandcollier.com/Downloads/1997_Thomas-Collier97.pdf

Tienda, M., Cortes, K., & Niu, S. (2003, October 3–5). *College attendance and the Texas Top 10 Percent Law: Permanent contagion or transitory promise?* Paper presented at the Conference on Expanding Opportunity in Higher Education sponsored by the Harvard Civil Rights Project, Sacramento, CA.

Tienda, M., Kevin T., Leicht, K., Sullivan, T., Maltese, M., & Kim Lloyd, K. (2003). Closing the gap? Admissions & enrollments at the Texas public flagships before and after affirmative action (Paper produced by the Texas Higher Education Opportunity Project at Princeton University). Available at http://www.texastop10.princeton.edu/reports/wp/closing_the_gap.pdf

Tienda, M., & Mitchell, F. (2006). *Multiple origins, uncertain destinies. Hispanics and the American future.* Washington, DC: National Academies Press.

Trostel, P. (2003). The long-term economic effects of declining state support for higher education: Are states shooting themselves in the foot? (Paper prepared for the Wisconsin Center for the Advancement of Postsecondary Education).

Trostel, P. A., & Ronca, J. M. (2007). *A simple unifying measure of state support for higher education.* Madison, WI: Wisconsin Center for the Advancement of Postsecondary Education, University of Wisconsin-Madison. (Working paper 0007)

Trumbull, E., Rothstein-Fisch, C., Greenfield, P. M., & Quiroz, B. (2001). *Bridging cultures between home and school: A guide for teachers.* Mahwah, NJ: Lawrence Erlbaum Associates.

U.S. Census Bureau. (2004). American Community Survey. U.S. Census Bureau Reports.

U.S. Census Bureau. (2008). Current population reports: Voting and registration in the election of November 1992, 1994, 1996, 1998, 2000, 2002, 2004, 2006, and 2008.

U.S. Census Bureau. (2009). Latino population growth. Retrieved February 22, 2011, from http://www.census.gov/compendia/statab/2011/tables/ 11s0010.pdf

U.S. Department of Education. National Center for Education Statistics. (1998). *First-generation students: Undergraduates whose parents never enrolled in postsecondary ducation* (NCES 98-082), by Anne-Marie Nunez and Stephanie Cuccaro-Alamin.

U.S. Department of Education, Institute of Education Sciences, National Center for Education Statistics. (2005). *High school transcript study (HSTS).*

U.S. Department of Education, Office of Planning, Evaluation and Policy Development. (2010). *ESEA blueprint for reform.* Washington, DC: Author

U.S. Department of Veteran Affairs. (2010). Post 9/11 GI Bill facts. Retrieved November 6, 2010, from http://www.gibill.va.gov/

Usher, A., & Cervenan, A. (2005). *Global higher education rankings 2005.* Toronto, Ontario, Canada: Educational Policy Institute.

Valdés, G. (1996). *Con respeto.* New York: Teachers College Press.

Valdés, G. (1997). Dual-language immersion programs: A cautionary note concerning the education of language-minority students. *Harvard Educational Review, 67*(3) 391–429.

Valdés, G. (2001). *Learning and not learning English: Latino students in American schools.* New York: Teachers College Press.

Valencia, R. (2000). Inequalities and the schooling of minority students in Texas: Historical and contemporary conditions. *Hispanic Journal of Behavioral Sciences, 22*(4), 445–459. Thousand Oakes, CA: Sage.

Valencia, R. (2002). *Chicano school failure and success* (2nd ed.). London: Routledge/Falmer.

Valencia, R. (2008). *Chicano students and the courts.* New York: New York University Press.

Valencia, R. R., & Villarreal, B. J. (2003). Improving students' reading performance via standards-based school reform: A critique. *The Reading Teacher, 56*(7).

Valencia, R., Villarreal, B., & Salinas, M. (2002). Educational testing and Chicano students: Issues, consequences, and prospects for reform. In R. Valencia (Ed.), *Chicano school failure and success.* New York: Routledge/Falmer Press.

Valenzuela v. O'Connell (2007). No. CPF-06-506050 (San Francisco County Ct. Mar. 23, 2006). Retrieved March 16, 2011, from http://www.cde.ca.gov/nr/ne/yr07/yr-07rel100.asp

Valenzuela, A. (1999). *Substractive schooling.* Albany: State University of New York Press.

Valenzuela, A. (2004). *Leaving children behind: How "Texas-style" accountability fails Latino youth.* Albany: State University of New York Press.

Wang, X. (2008). Baccalaureate attainment and college persistence of community college transfer students at four-year institutions. *Research in Higher Education, 50*(6), 570–588.

Warren, J., Jenkins, K., & Kulick, R. (2006). High school exit examinations and state-level completion and GED rates, 1975 through 2002. *Educational Evaluation and Policy Analysis, 28*(2), 131–152.

Williams et al. vs. State of California et al. (2004) Settlement Implement Agreement. CN 312236 in the Superior Ct. in and for the City and County of San Francisco. Retrieved March 16, 2011, from http://www.cde.ca.gov/eo/ce/wc/wmslawsuit.aspCalifornia,+et+al.+%282004%29+&pbx=1&bav=on.2,or.r_gc.r_pw.&fp=c58e84f80faa2c58

Wilson, W. J. (1990). *The truly disadvantaged. The inner city, the underclass, and public policy.* University of Chicago Press.

Wong, S. W., & Hughes, J. N. (2006). Ethnicity and language contributions to dimensions of parent involvement. *School Psychology Review, 35*(4), 645–662.

Yosso, T. (2006). *Critical race counterstories along the Chicana/Chicano educational pipeline.* New York: Routledge.

Young, J., & Fisler, J. (2000). Sex differences on the SAT: An analysis of demographic and educational variables. *Research in Higher Education, 41*(3). Pp. 410-416.

Young, J., & Johnson, P. (2004). The Impact of an SES-based model on a college's undergraduate admissions outcomes. *Research in Higher Education, 45*(7), 777–797.

Zarate, M. E., & Fabienke, D. (2007). Financial aid as a perceived barrier to college. *American Academic, 3*(1). American Federation of Teachers. Washington, D. C.

Zarate, M. E., & Pachon, H. P. (2006). *Perceptions of college financial aid among California Latino youth.* Los Angeles: Tomas Rivera Policy Institute.

Zwick, R. (2004). *Rethinking the SAT: The future of standardized testing in university admissions.* New York: Routledge.

Index

NAMES

SUBJECTS

About the Author

Frances Contreras is an associate professor of Higher Education in the area of Education Leadership and Policy Studies at the University of Washington. She also serves as the Director for the Higher Education Program. Her research focuses on educational equity for Latino students, the transition to college for underrepresented students, the role of Hispanic serving institutions in expanding higher education persistence and success, and public policies that influence educational access across a P-20 continuum. Her previous works include a book with Pátricia Gándara, *The Latino Education Crisis* (Harvard University Press, 2009), as well as articles in the *Harvard Educational Review, Educational Policy, Journal of Hispanics in Higher Education, Journal of Advanced Academics*, the Handbook on Latinos and Education and a number of book chapters in edited volumes.